Belkıs Balpınar

*Through Woven Times –
Works from Four Decades*

edited by Necmi Sönmez

SKIRA   ANNA LAUDEL

Cover
DNA-3, 2023, 226 x 136 cm,
Anna Laudel Gallery

Art Director
Luigi Fiore

Design and Layout
Francesca Zucchi

Editorial Coordination
Vincenza Russo

Editing
Anna Albano

Translation from Turkish to English:
Nazım Hikmet, Richard Dikbaş
Translation from German to English:
Oona Smyth for Scriptum, Rome

First published in Italy in 2025
by Skira editore S.p.A.
via Agnello 18
20123 Milano, Italy
skira-arte.com

Printed and bound in Italy First edition

ISBN: 978-88-572-5380-0

Distributed in USA, Canada,
Central & South America by
ARTBOOK | D.A.P.
75 Broad Street Suite 630, New York,
NY 10004, USA.
Distributed elsewhere in the world
by Thames and Hudson Ltd.,
181A High Holborn, London WC1V 7QX,
United Kingdom.

The publisher is at the disposal of the
entitled parties as regards all unidentified
iconographic.

Photo on pages 4–5
Belkıs Balpınar in her studio in Demirciköy,
Istanbul, 2001. Photo Laila Pozzo

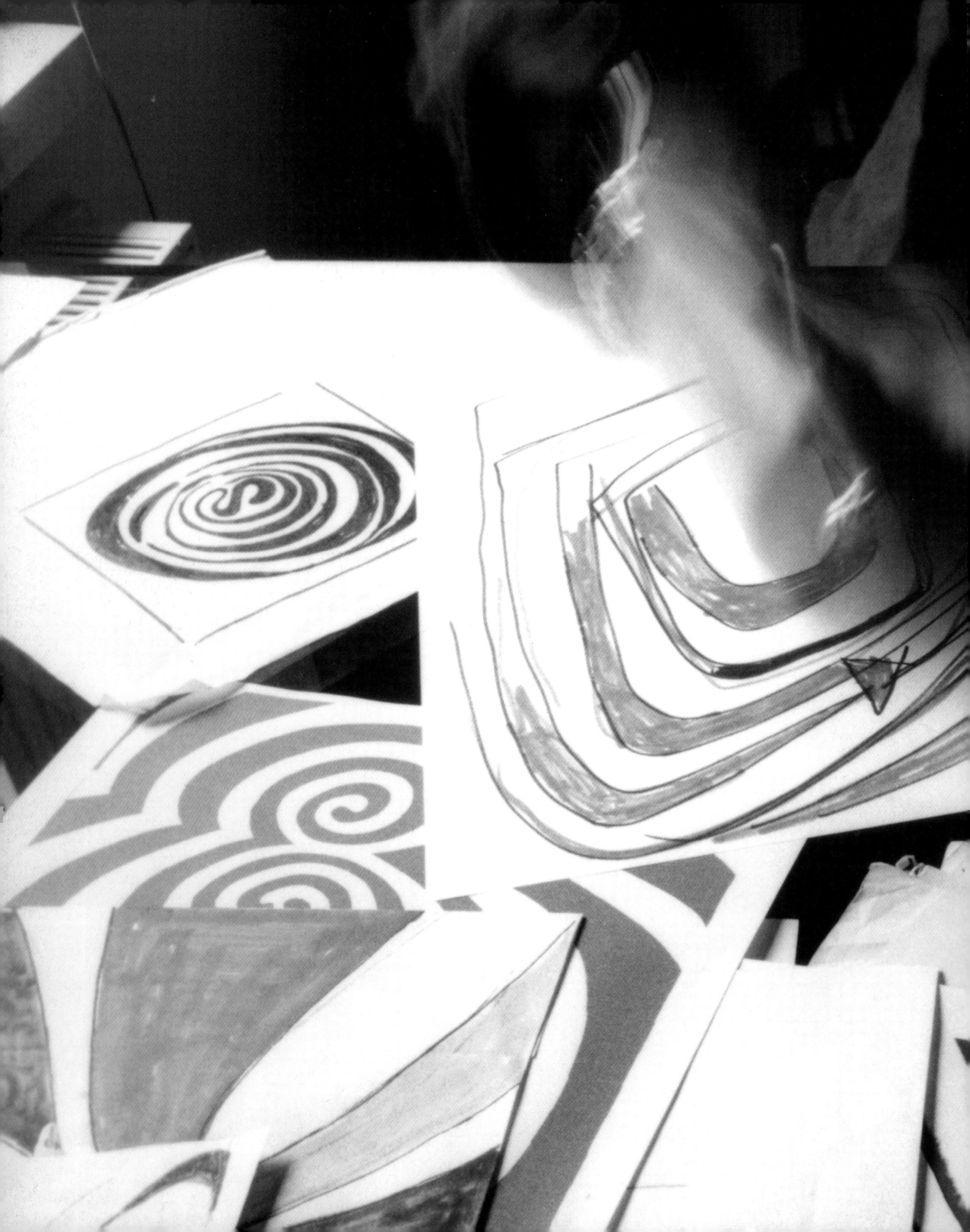

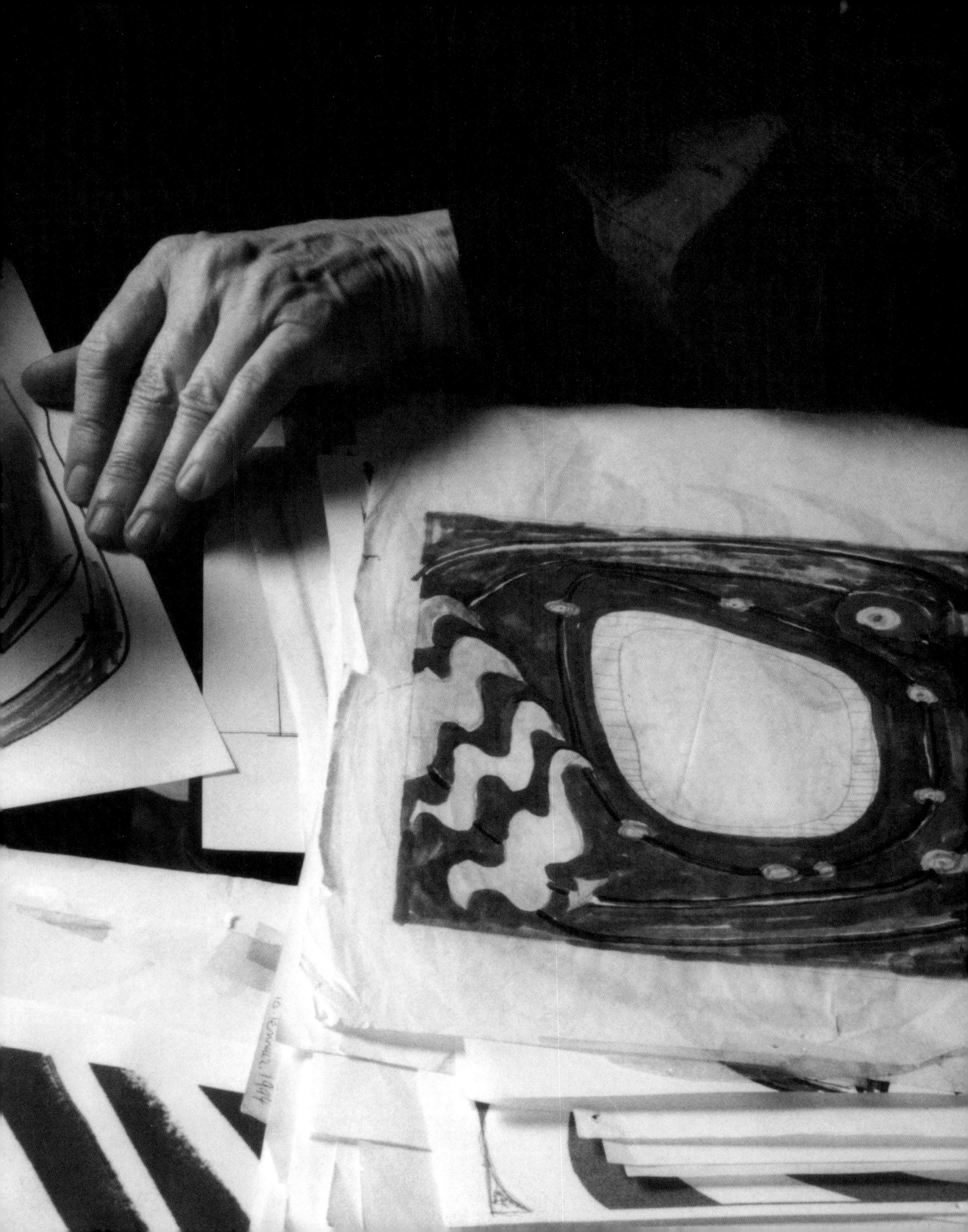

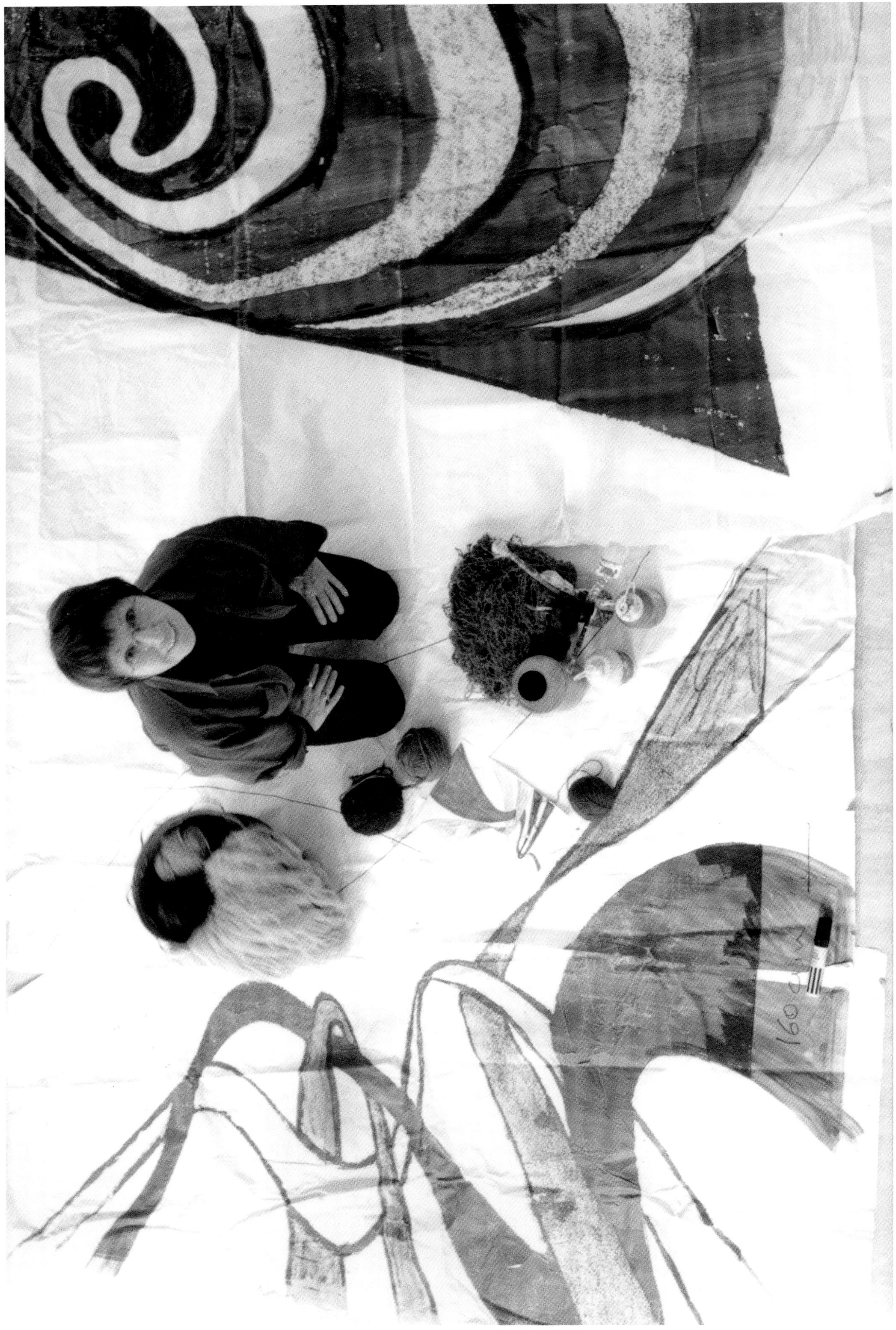

Belkıs Balpınar in her studio in Demirciköy,
Istanbul, 2001. Photo Laila Pozzo

The Imaginative Transformation of Form About the Works of Belkıs Balpınar
Necmi Sönmez

In 1986, while I was a university student, I first knocked on the door of Belkıs Balpınar's studio in the Salacak neighborhood of Üsküdar. At the time, I was trying to get my work published in newspapers and magazines. Out of the blue, I received an offer to interview her. Her house, complete with a garden and a stunning view of old Istanbul, set the scene for an experience unlike any other. The works I encountered in her studio were remarkably distinctive.

I recall staying for quite some time after our conversation had concluded, meticulously taking notes on various flat-weaves and rugs. Now, 38 years later, as I revisit those notes, I see not only the sincerity of Belkıs's personality but also the "processes of creation and sharing" she undertook — largely unnoticed by those around her or the Istanbul art circles of the time. Her artistic journey involves extraordinary periods of development and is reminiscent of an archipelago. A geographical term, the word archipelago describes a chain of scattered islands, large and small. Describing the works of a visual artist as an archipelago aims to define the unique regions their works have formed around themselves. Belkıs's life, marked by her unique synthesis of museology, art history, and interdisciplinary experimentation, displays a wholeness aptly described as an archipelago.

This book progresses via a selection from works Balpınar has produced from 1986 to the present day, and references not the standard periodization in mainstream artistic terminology, but rather seeks to define the different islands she has formed. Like the captain of a ship sailing forth across her own archipelago, Belkıs determines her ports of call and then sets out towards unknown horizons, only to return to her safe harbours to map out the directions of her future journeys. In my opinion, it would be an oversimplification to define as *rugs* the pieces she has created using different flat-weaving techniques. Neither do I accept it as an accurate viewpoint to opt for the term *textile art*, in the manner conventionally understood. I can hear those of you who ask, "So how should we define her oeuvre?" I believe that Belkıs's powerful designs possess a character that is open-ended and does not require definition. These works which, when hung on the wall, with their shades, curves, and refractions reveal their forms by shedding the weight of the materials certainly are deeply rooted in ancient Anatolian weaving traditions. However, they break free from the uniformity of tradition based on repetition and develop a different interpretation that belongs to the present time.

Belkıs's artistic evolution is related to processes that progress via her different identities in her life. She won a grant during her artistic training at the Istanbul State Fine Arts Academy Department of Textiles, which enabled her to work as a designer at Sümerbank, reinforcing her independent character, and helping her to stand on her own feet from an early age. In addition to her artist-designer identity, her pioneering work for the preservation of wildlife in Turkey is testament to Belkıs's holistic view of the world. In the early 1970s, she was in charge of the Turkish-Islamic Arts Museum Department of Textiles where she specialized on woven textiles, and it was here that her researcher-museologist identity flourished. Her expertise, which gained international attention with books she published on rugs and flat weaving, was crowned with the founding of two important museums in a period when the country faced tough conditions: in 1979, the Istanbul Vakıflar Carpet Museum and in 1981, the Vakıflar Kilim and Flat Weaves Museum. She persevered under challenging conditions, and as a result, was internationally accepted as an authority in the field. The researcher-museologist identity Belkıs developed revealed Anatolia's ancient history of weaving. The interesting aspect regarding Belkıs

Balpınar's artistic trajectory is that, precisely at a period when she could have collected the fruit of her research, she chose to step into an even more challenging field and began to create her own designs and pursue artistic quests.

1986-1990 Tabula rasa / New beginnings

Belkıs left her institutional career as a researcher-museologist, curator and antique rug researcher by her own decision in 1983. That same year, she founded the Carpet and Rug Restoration Workshop in Üsküdar, Istanbul. However, it would not be long before she herself faced a testing period. Where could she have her designs woven, and who would undertake this task? Following a long period of investigation, she found skilled women weavers adept in the traditional weaving techniques that would shape her designs. Although other designers persistently refuse to discuss the issue, when talking about her works, Belkıs always indicates the contribution of weavers, each the contemporary bearer of an ancient Anatolian weaving tradition. She provides detailed information about all the stages of the dialogue she established with them.[1] It is understandable that she departed from abstract motifs in her first works. She made this important statement about those years:

"In 1982, on the Anatolian side of Istanbul, I met women weavers who had migrated from Malatya. I began providing them with looms and commissioning them to weave rugs. I'd like to tell an interesting story here. I had visited the studio of Atilla Galatalı, a renowned ceramics artist of the time. I had some photographs of the rugs I had ordered woven with me. I had my hair straight, long and auburn, and I was wearing a very modern mini dress with a belt. He looked at the photographs of the rugs, and then looked at me and said, 'Make them like yourself'. That was all. I only realized much later that, from that evening on, I began to design far more modern patterns. It was a turning point for me. I can say that I began to produce my first modern designs, as very large triptychs in 1986. Since then, I have worked with the same weaver — she has almost become like my own hand. I could say that we have trained each other."[2]

Her works evolved towards forms beyond classical kilim weave from the 1990s onwards, both heralding a new process and triggering three-dimensional exploration.

1
Balpınar discusses this topic in many of her interviews, and provides a particularly detailed account of her relationship with her weavers in the interview she gave to Selçuk Erez, published in *Cumhuriyet Dergi* on 22 May 1995.

2
https://www.unlimitedrag.com/post/boyutlararasi-dokuma, An interview with Belkıs Balpınar by Necmi Sönmez, accessed on 1.1.2025

1990 – 1996: interdimensional weaving

Having focused on the history of Anatolian kilim weaving for over three decades, Belkıs possesses an intimate knowledge of the evolution of looms and patterns, spanning from the Neolithic era to modern times. This background drove her towards interdimensional pursuits. This stage, which could be summarized as a struggle to go beyond weaving, suggests, in my view, two critical points of inspiration that deserve closer examination.

The first was her perception of architects like Mario Botta and Peter Zumthor, who displayed minimalist tendencies. The second was her orientation towards the "spiral" form, to discover fields that are not often interpreted in rugs and weaves due to technical difficulties. Thus, she focused on a visuality that can be included within international textile art.[3] This was the first time that Belkıs entered into a radical struggle against the shapes imposed by the loom. This lead to her first comprehensive solo exhibition in 1995, an event that marks an important point in her artistic journey:

"It was 1993, and I had hung my own rugs, which I had woven, on the walls of my flat in Doğan Apartmanı [a luxurious apartment block built in 1894 in the Pera district of Istanbul]. One day, Amélie Edgü, the director of Millî Reasürans Galerisi, visited my home after a gathering of friends. She perceived my rugs on the wall as *artwork* and invited me to exhibit at her gallery in two months. This was in 1995. With the excitement and tension brought on by this unexpected invitation, I created a massive black-and-white spiral, a triptych and several other works. That's how I found myself holding an exhibition at Millî Reasürans Galerisi, one of Istanbul's most prominent galleries at the time. it was another turning point in my life. Looking back, you see certain events that changed the course of your life. At the time, we don't fully realize their significance. Atilla Galatalı and Amélie Edgü are individuals who brought on changes that re-oriented my life."[4]

1996 – 2024: new ideas, new forms

The year 1996 stands as a turning point for Belkıs that would always accompany her in her future research, marking the beginning of experiments "with no before or after" that she conducted on the wefts, the very backbone of the art of weaving. Her initial partial, and then complete elimination of wefts

3
Sabine Maria Schmidt, *Musterung. Pop und Politik in der zeitgenössischen Textilkunst*, exhibition catalogue, Ravensburg: Kunstsammlungen Chemnitz und Kunstmuseum, 2022.

4
https://www.unlimitedrag.com/post/boyutlar-arasi-dokuma, accessed on 1.1.2025.

from her work liberated her from all restrictions and granted her newfound freedom. It would be no mistake to describe this as her most impressive visual weapon. This is what the artist has to say about the process:

"Over the years, I realized that, in order to shed the restrictions of kilim weaving, if I were to leave the background empty without weaving, I could apply any type of pattern I liked. So I began to leave sections that were not woven, and then, to make framed pieces, imagining that a third dimension would be added to the two-dimensional plane since between the patterns, shadows would be cast behind the loose threads. In this way, I transformed my work into canvasses — canvasses where shadows were cast on the patterns formed. I don't remember whether I first read publications on modern physics and astronomy. The two must have begun around the same time, I guess. I think this interest of mine is also reflected in the work I do. I try to express the different planes that escape our gaze at first sight by using the means provided by weaving."[5]

This abstraction of the wefts, which bear and shape the weave, led Belkıs to explore "space" as an integral element of her creations from the 2000s onward. This heralded a new phase where she would conduct three-dimensional experiments. One could, in fact, see this in line with the attempt to form a different perspective, the first examples of which she produced in the 1990s (*Toprak ve Güneş* [*Earth and Sun*], 1998). Works like *Patlama* [*Explosion*] (1990), *İkili Spiral* [*Double Spiral*] (1997), *Asimetrik Spiral / Gözler* [*Asymmetrical Spiral/Eyes*] (1999) and *Another Perspective / Wing* (1999) surprise and absorb the viewer at first sight, clearly revealing she is chasing after different perspectives: Belkıs seeks to capture a visuality that will change the perception of the eye. With persistent research into perception, the artist discovered different dimensions in weaving.

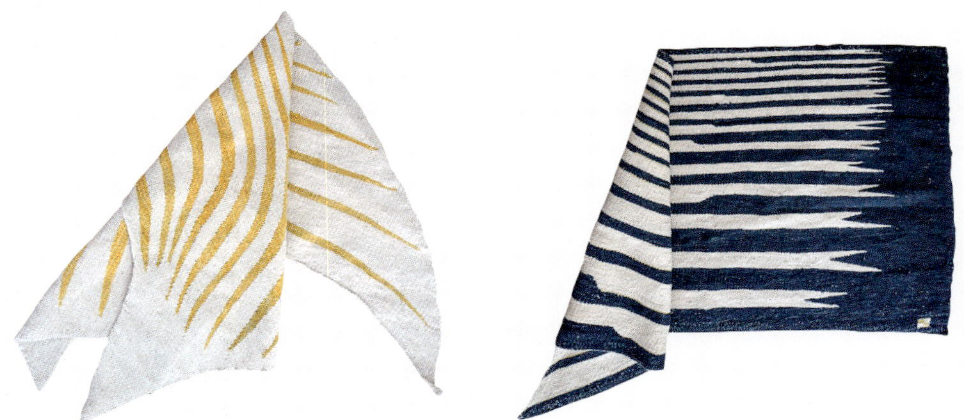

Another Perspective II, 1999, 50 x 70 cm, private collection. Photo Murat Germen

Spatial Fabric III, 2000, 50 x 75 cm, private collection. Photo Murat Germen

By the 2000s, she increasingly focused on releasing wefts, and as seen in her works titled *Olasılıklar* [*Possibilities*] (2013), *Nöronlar* [*Neurons*] (2015), *Akış* [*Flow*] (2015) and *Küresel Isınma-ma* [Global *Non-Warming*] (2017), she began to pursue a sculpture-like aesthetics. This new opening resulted in the placing of "deconstructive perception" in the focal point of her works, the examples of which we see in the 2020s. What I mean by "deconstructive" is that Belkıs dared to upend almost half a century's worth of weaving-related visuality in her memory, and decided to implement processes, all of which were not expected from weaving. In this way, "the memory of the woman's hand" that invented the ancient tradition of Anatolian weaving and for centuries carried it from one generation to the next, enters Belkıs's work in erotic integrity, bestowing the iconography of her work with unforgettable emphasis. In this context, the work titled *Dişi* [*Feminine*] (2002) is a harbinger. Belkıs courageously progressed along the path paved by this work, and as she clearly exhibits in her works titled *Sperm I and II* (2020) and *Nipple Eyes* (2024), she completes a circle she began tracing with her unique efforts. She treated weaving with erotic tension that places it in the focal point of "the human being's moment of existence".

To clarify, when we look at the first image in this book, the work titled *Koza I* [*Cocoon I*] (1989) we see that Belkıs is using self-inseminating forms. This is a work that can be interpreted as the beginning of Belkıs's own circle. The "fertile forms" she meticulously developed culminated in 2024 into a cosmic explosion that is the symbol of our coming into the world. Here, the trajectory that began with *Koza 1* [*Cocoon*] came full circle. In this way, the borders not only of space and perspective but also those of weaving are lifted, and an imaginative transformation becomes the focal centre of the artist's unique creation.   Toronto, January 2025

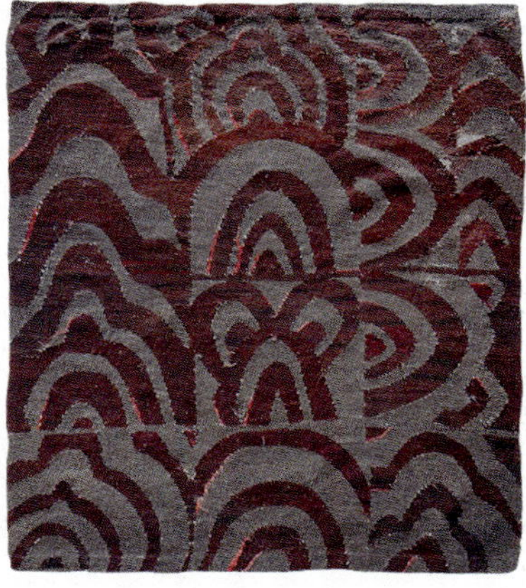

Neolithic Dreams II, 2004, 45 x 45 cm,
private collection. Photo Murat Germen

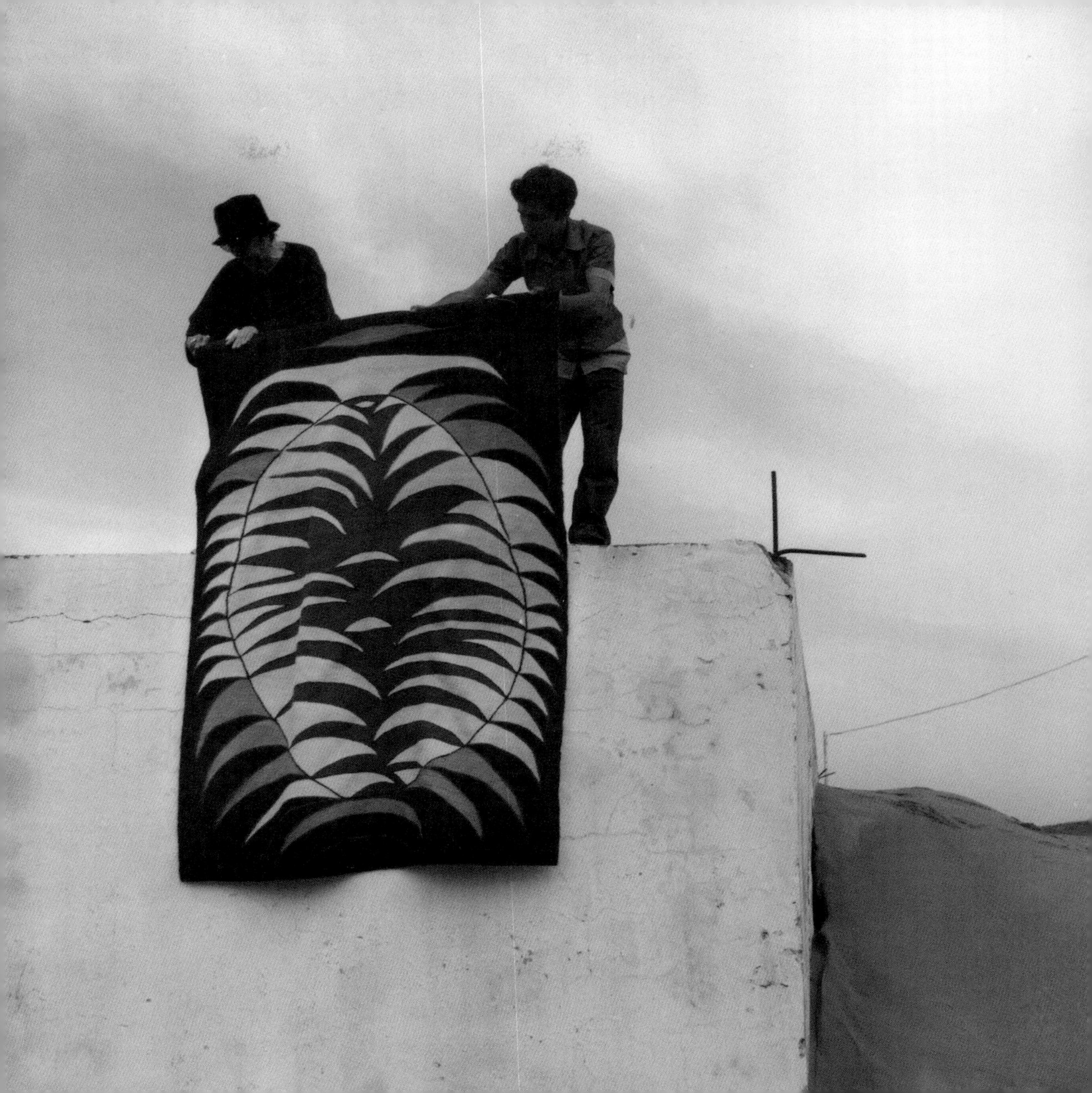

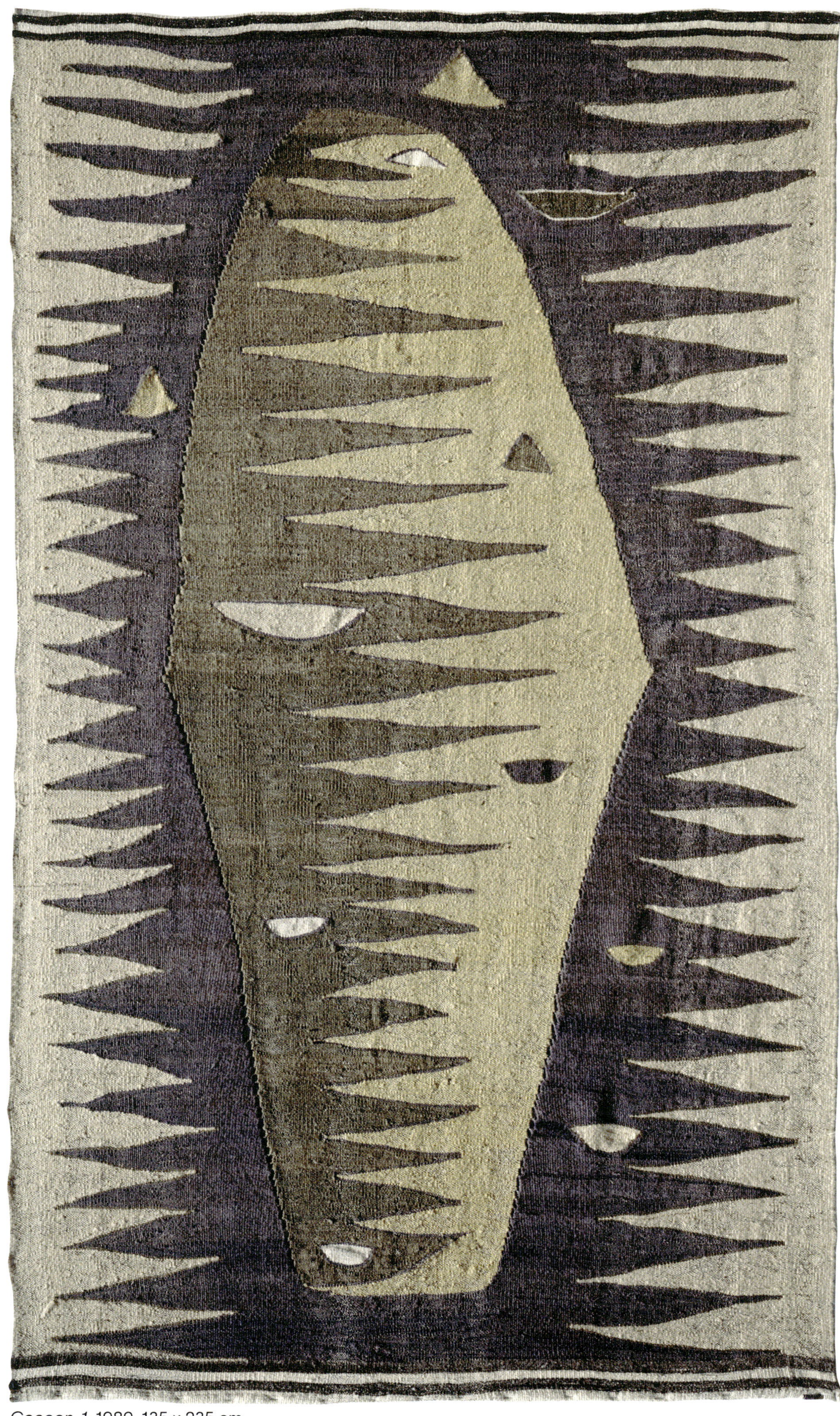

Cocoon-1, 1989, 135 x 235 cm,
artist's collection

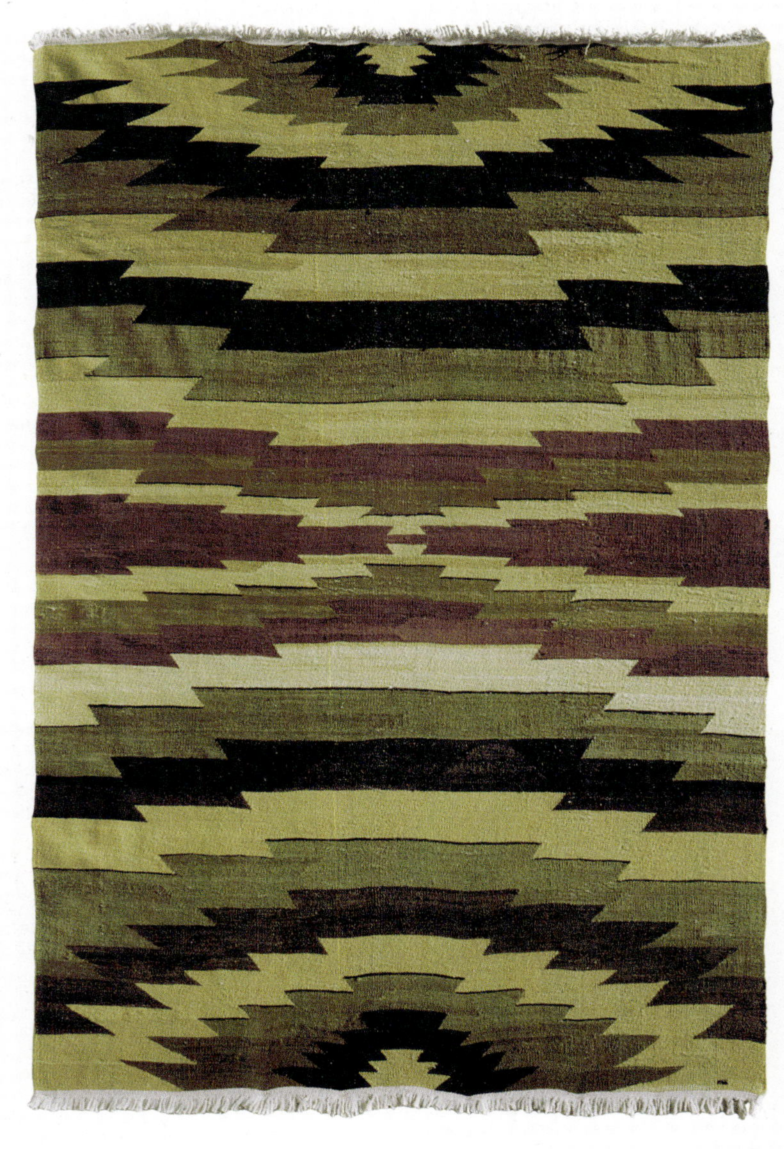

Rainbow, 1989, 175 x 270 cm,
artist's collection

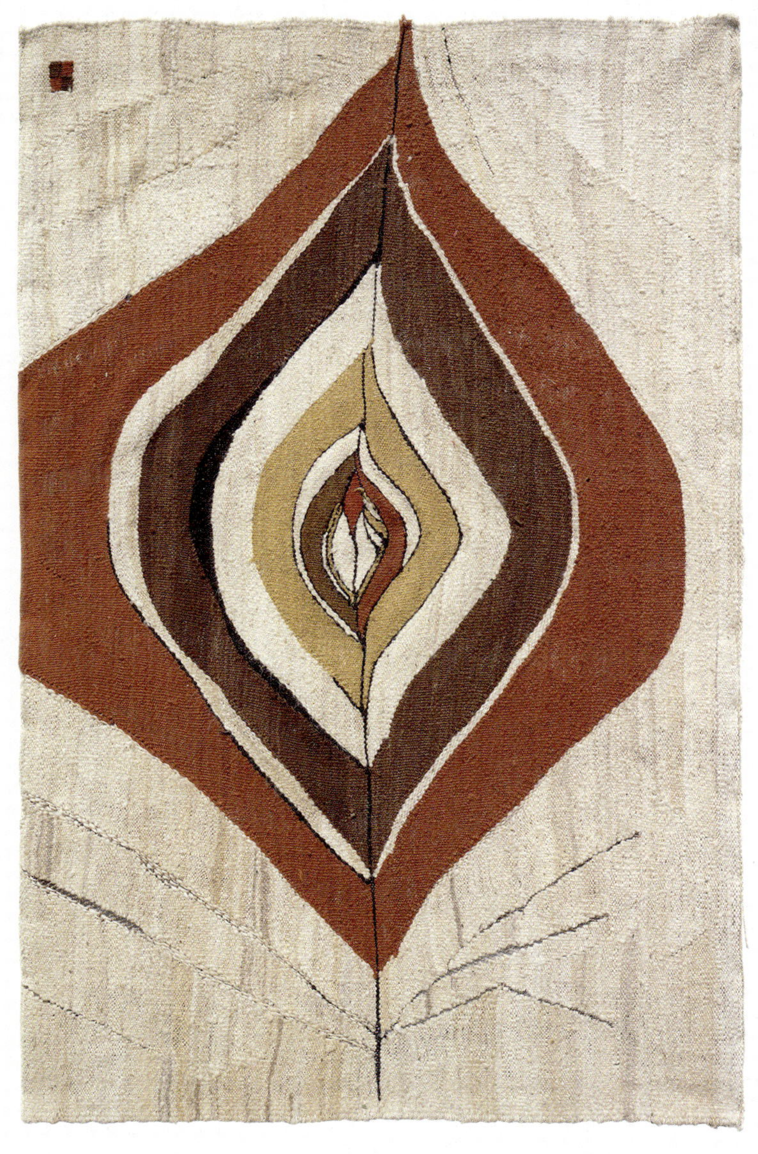

A Seed-2, 1990, 114 x 161 cm,
private collection

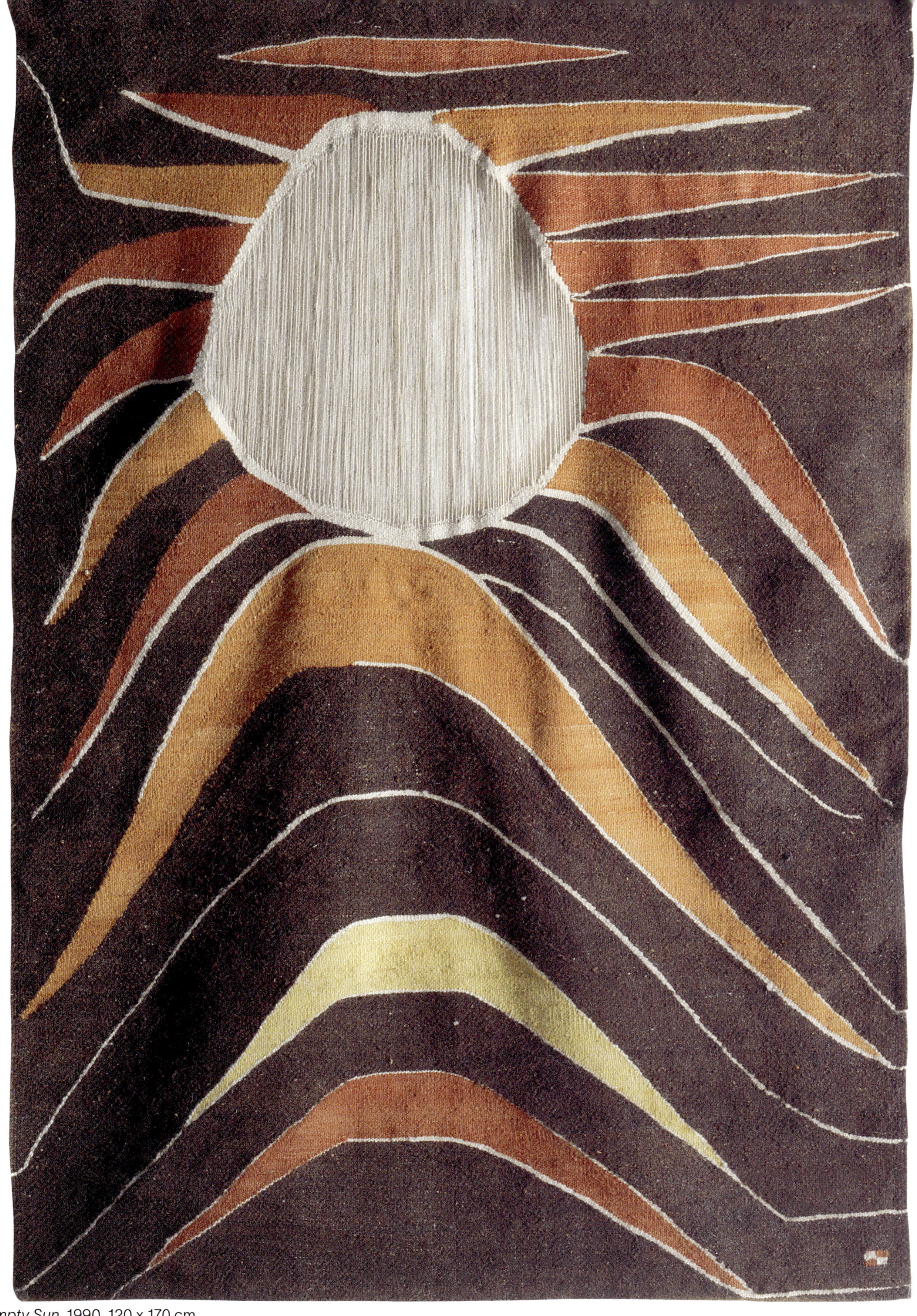

Empty Sun, 1990, 120 x 170 cm,
private collection

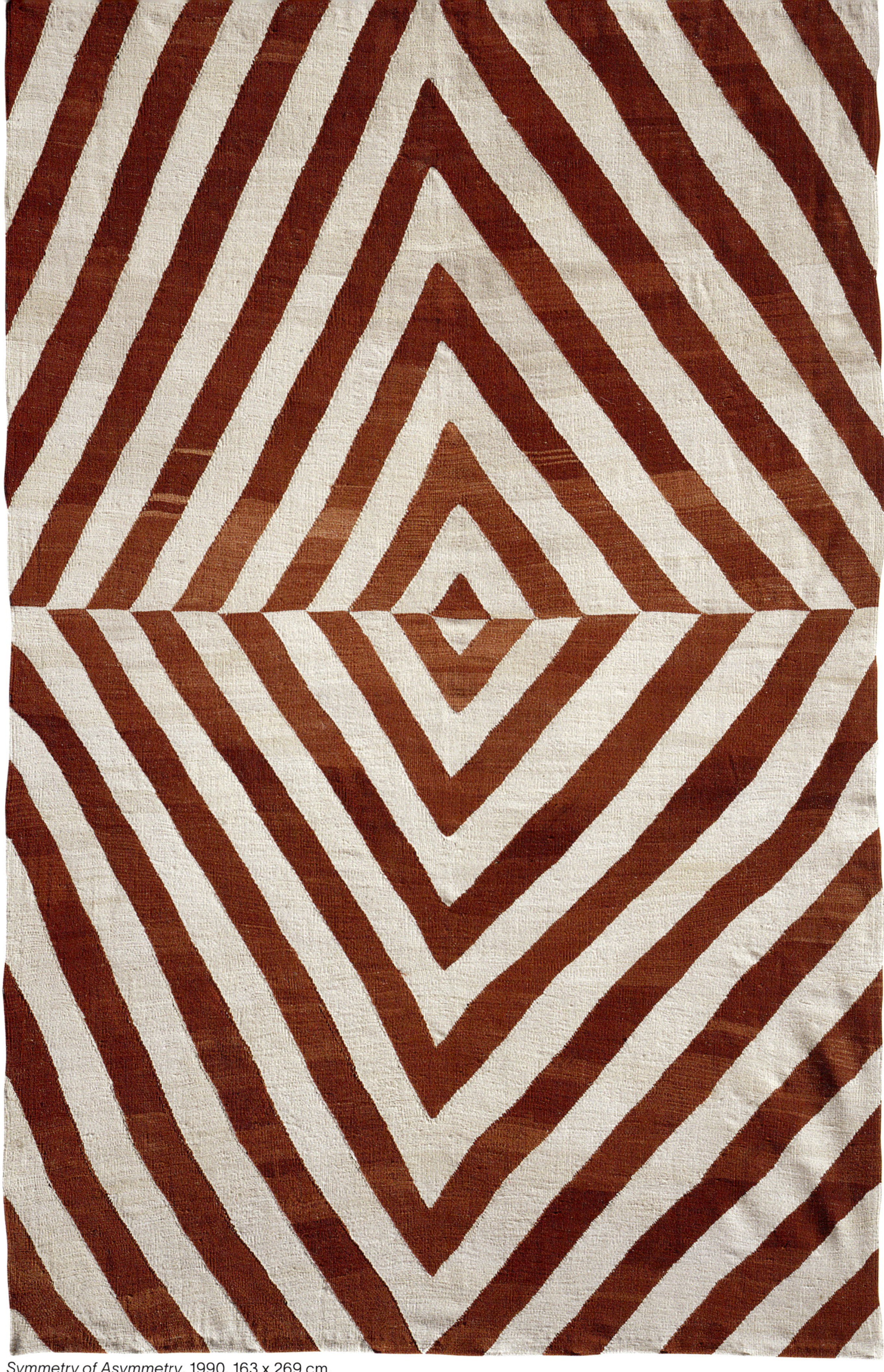

Symmetry of Asymmetry, 1990, 163 x 269 cm,
private collection

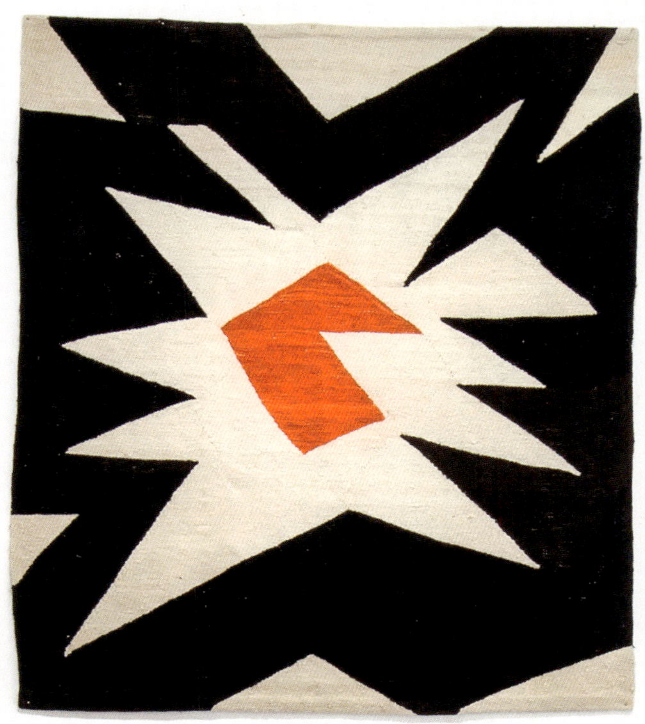

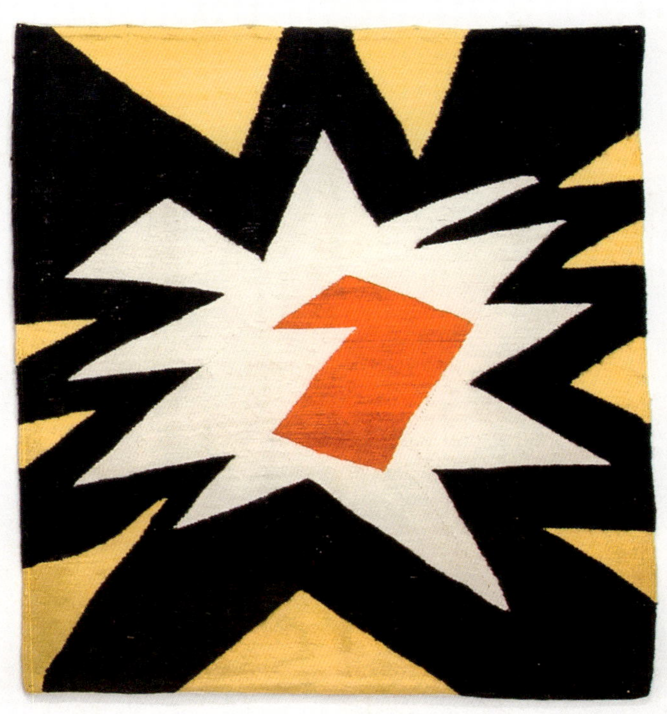

Mini Bangs, 1991, 105 x 105 cm,
private collection

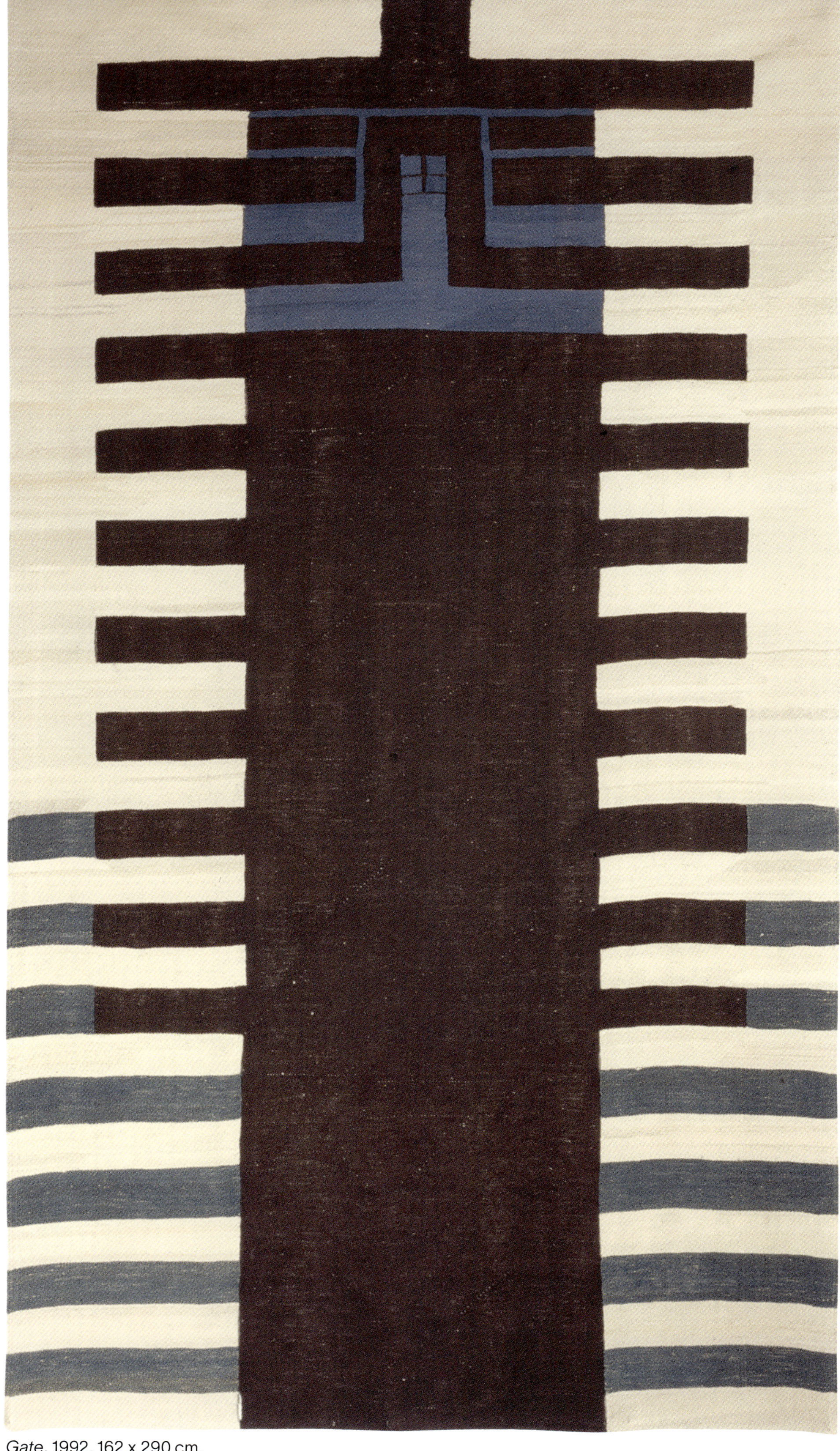

Gate, 1992, 162 x 290 cm,
private collection

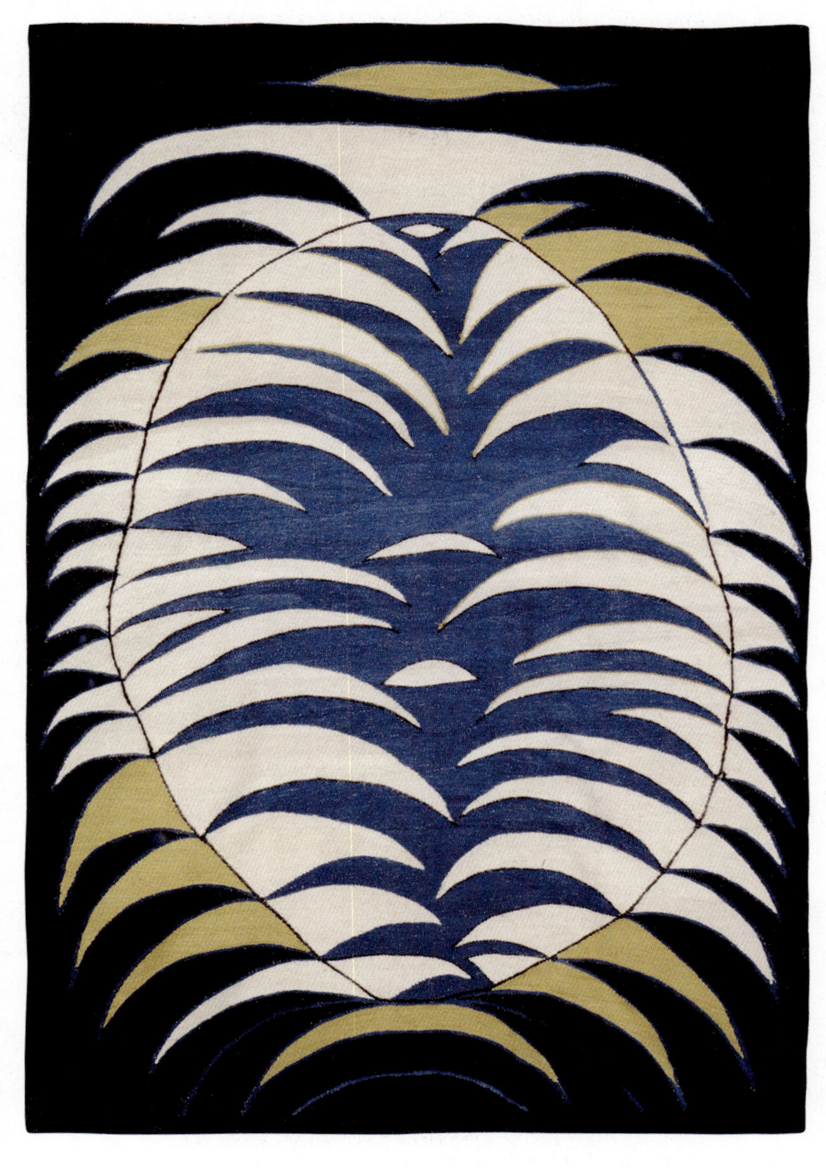

Centric Excentric, 1993, 134 x 170 cm,
private collection

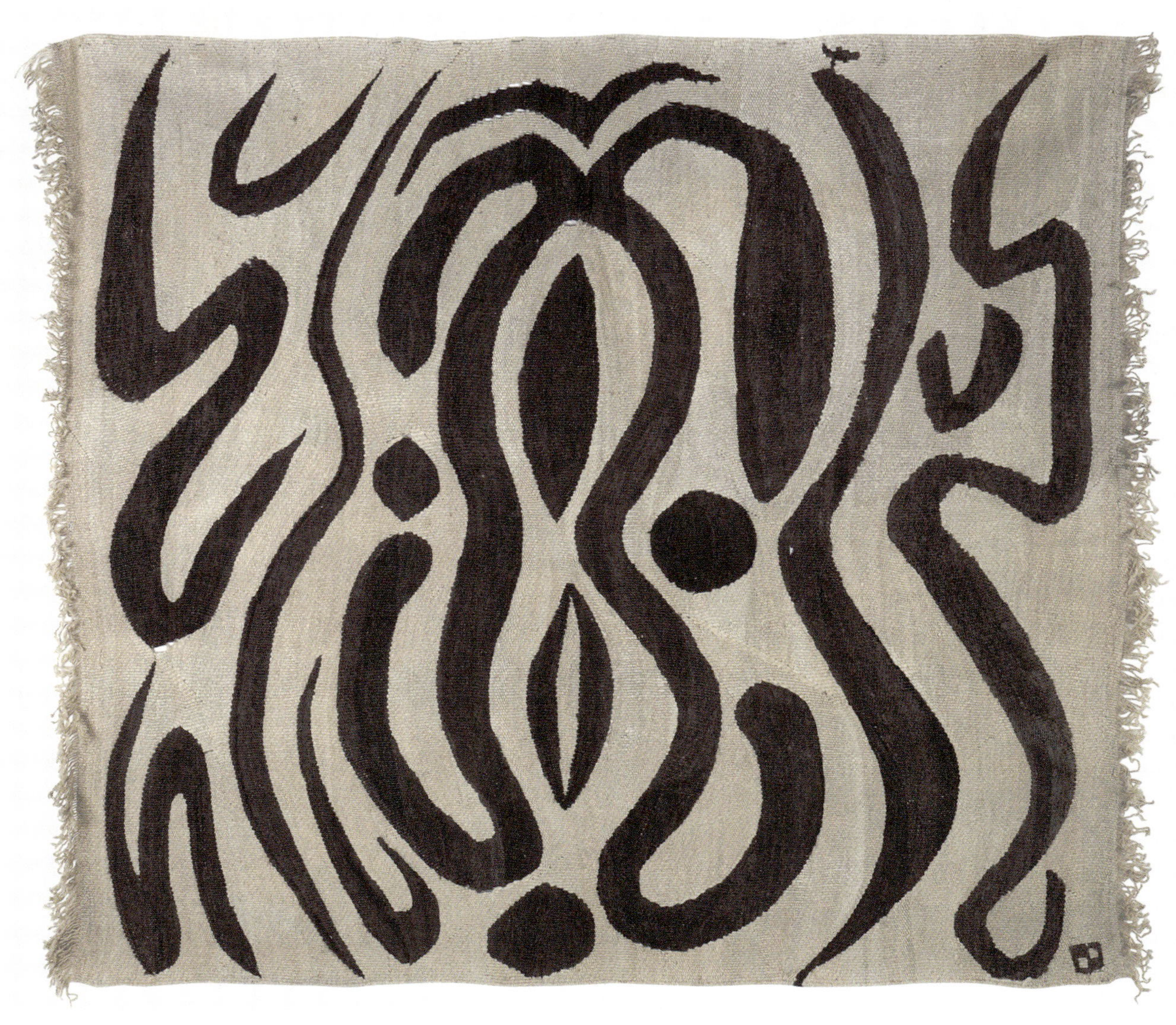

Birth-1, 1994, 127 x 115 cm,
Anna Laudel Gallery

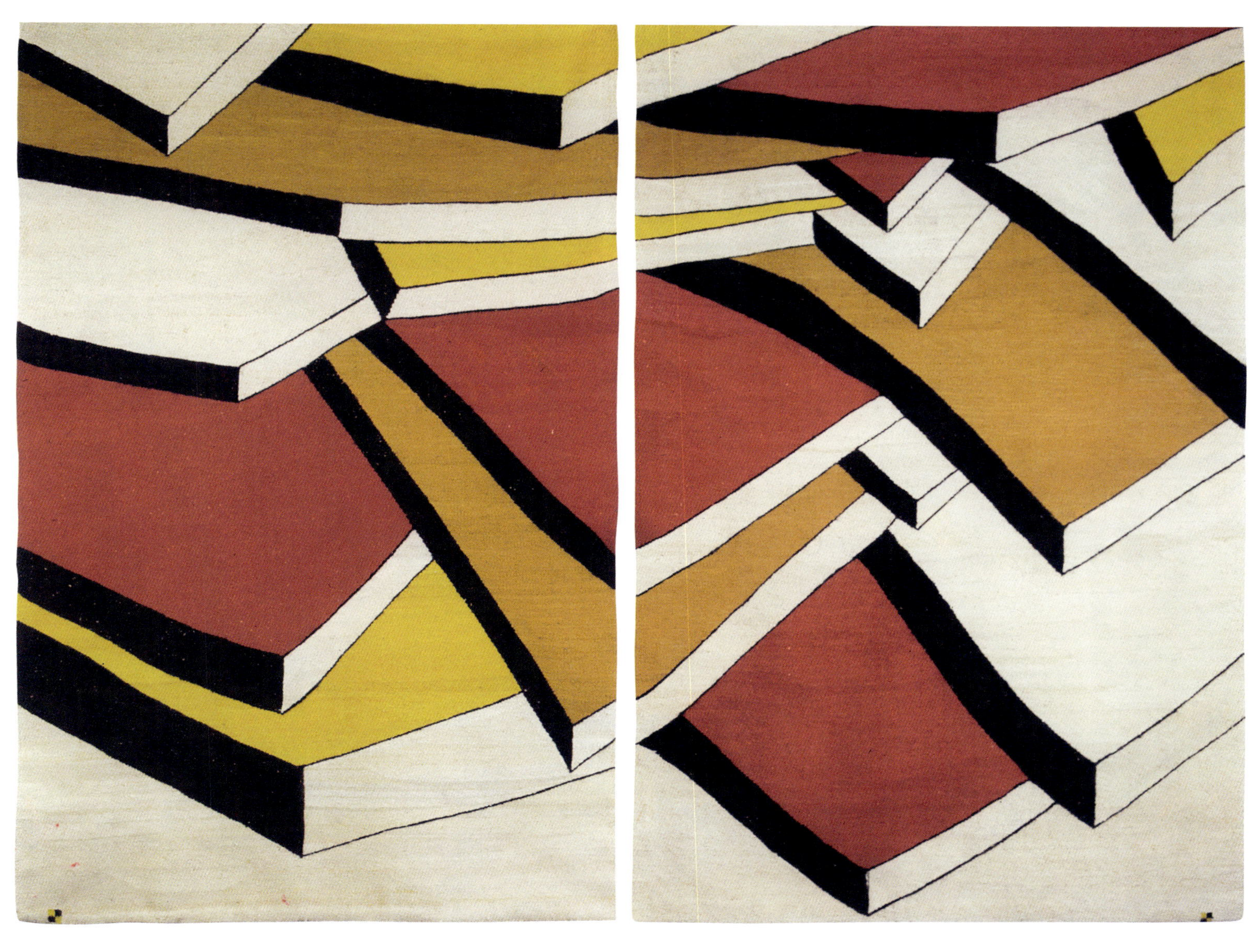

Layers – Diptych, 1995, 178 x (120 x 2) cm,
private collection

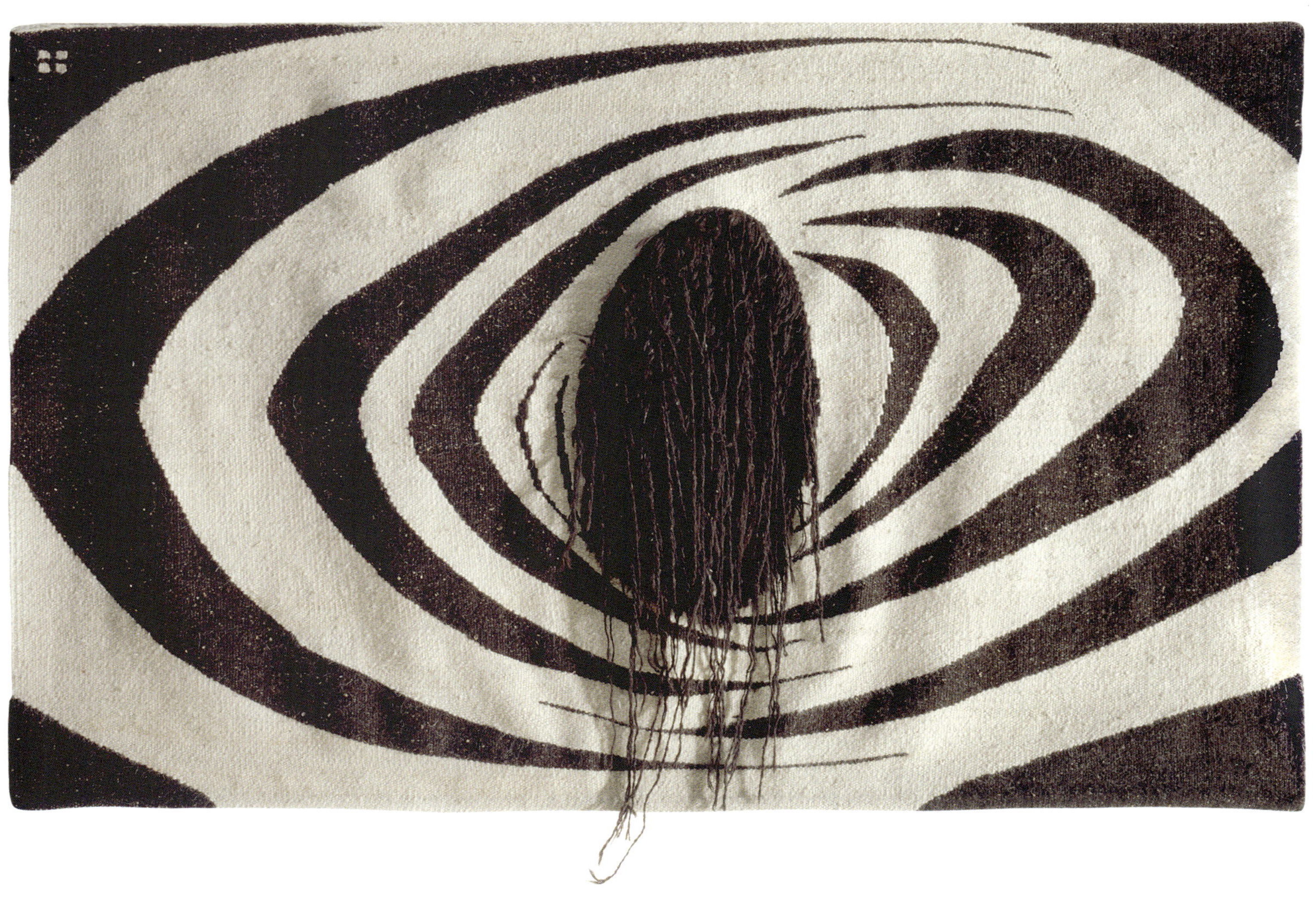

Wild Thing, 1996, 102 x 164 cm,
private collection

Flying Stars, 1999, 150 x 270 cm,
Anna Laudel Gallery

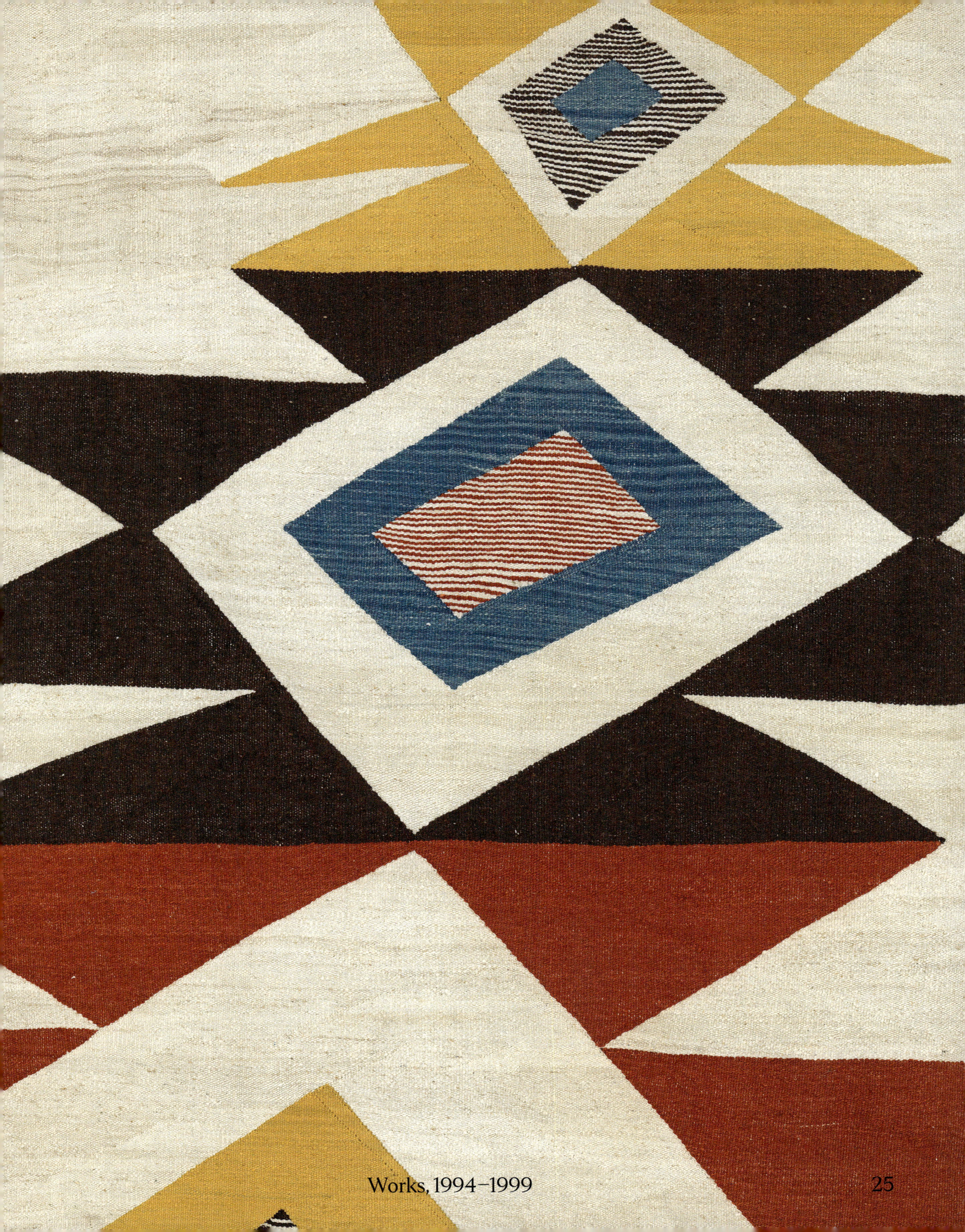

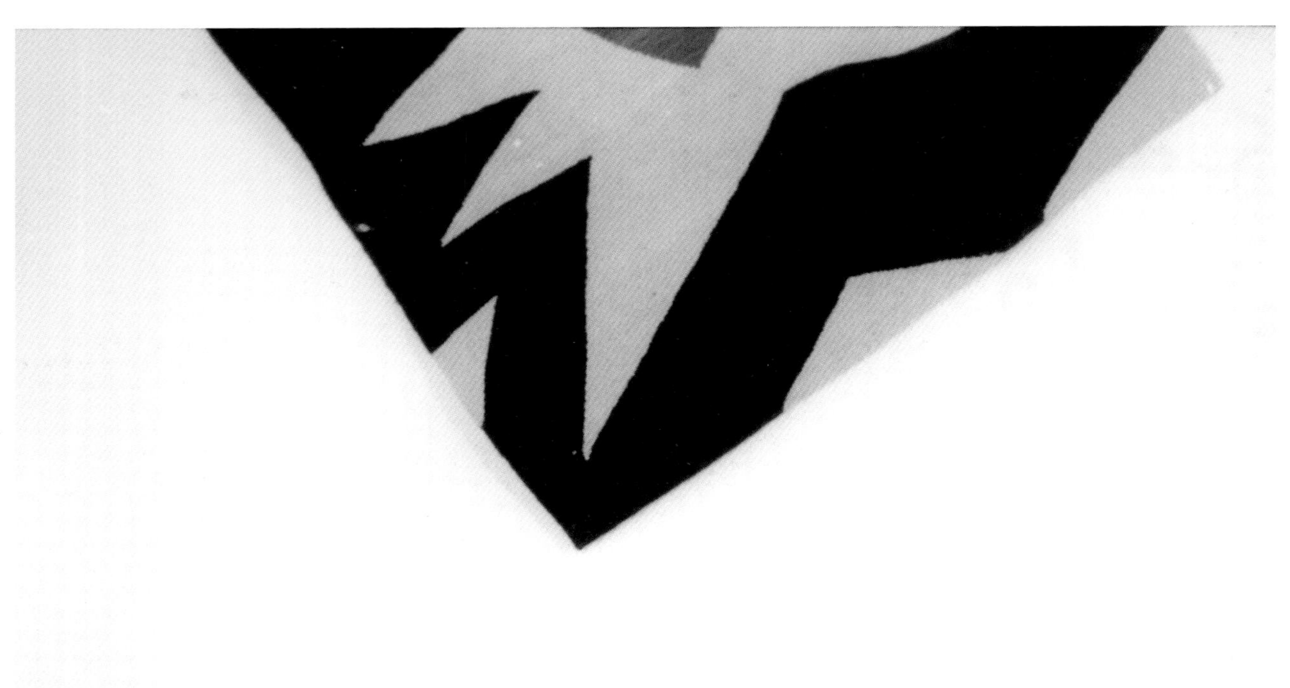

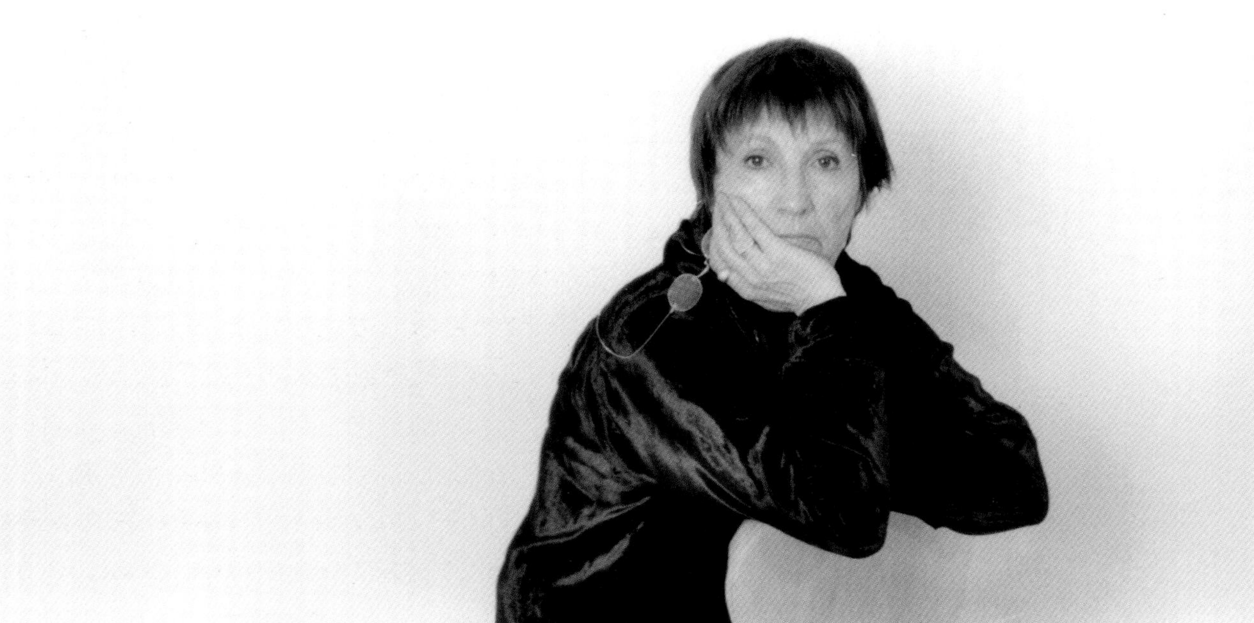

Belkıs Balpınar in her studio in Demirciköy,
Istanbul, 2001. Photo Laila Pozzo

Sabine Maria Schmidt

Farewell to the Grip or Pull of the Abstract
On Belkıs Balpınar's Contemporary Interpretations of Flatweaves

Sabine Maria Schmidt

Sometimes it is just a brief moment — a fleeting glance, a small piece of work or image — that captivates you, sparking a search and questions. *Doğan Güneş* [*Sunrise*] (2022) is an astonishing wall-hung woven piece with a large pom-pom spilling out of it. The sunny yellow bundle of yarn perches on top of a violet-black spiral shape that could be interpreted as a hat left behind on a carpet. The woven textile image is simply witty, fresh, and sensual, without seeking to please.

Doğan Güneş [*Sunrise*] was my first encounter with the work of Belkıs Balpınar. It came about in the context of my research into a thematic issue on textile revivals for the German art magazine *Kunstforum International.*[1] But is this work being interpreted correctly? Does it have anything to do with Pop Art? Who is this artist who so effortlessly awakens figurative associations with her cheeky mix of materials (in this case, flatweave, pile, and wool yarn)? And then there are other works that open up different contexts, like *Yukarıya Doğru* [*Towards the Sky*] from 2022. It evokes Bauhaus forms as well as motifs from naïve folk art, executed with artisan sophistication combined with a spontaneous sketch-like quality: a piece where everything seems to literally overlap. Other works seem more psychedelic and have a slightly 1970s palette. *Dişi I* [*Nipple Eyes*] (2024), which has more feminist undertones, features a delicate open vulva shape flanked by sinuous black lines, two of which have cowboy hats on top.

[1]
Sabine Maria Schmidt, ed., *Textile Revivals,* thematic issue, vol. 297, Cologne: Kunstforum International, 2024.

Underneath things are spiced up by a pubic-like pom-pom. Two small black squares in the bottom corner form a symbolic signature. The weaving mark of the designer? These squares crop up everywhere, albeit in different colours. Other woven pieces with spiral or fan-like forms, such as *Time Plane II*, 2022, appear positively deconstructed. The flat warp threads stretched out on the loom remain open, producing a spatial effect on the surface and giving these works an object-like quality. The colours are bold and clearly defined, creating abstract compositions. The pieces are skilfully developed thanks to the artist's grasp of kinetic and optical effects (*Yukarıya Doğru* [*Towards the Top*], 2023). Occasionally, these flat-weave compositions will take on the character of utility objects. *Eriyen Parmak İzi* [*Finger Print Melting*] (2023) could serve either as a wall hanging or as a floor covering: a decorative kilim, a buyer might think, observing the melting whorl of a fingerprint. Belkıs Balpınar is an artist who has passionately dedicated herself to a particular type of textile: a modern interpretation of a wall-hung Turkish kilim, a flat-woven textile traditionally used as a rug.

Textile art is very in vogue. And has been for at least almost two decades. A surprising number of artists have been discovering fabric-based materialities for themselves, revital-

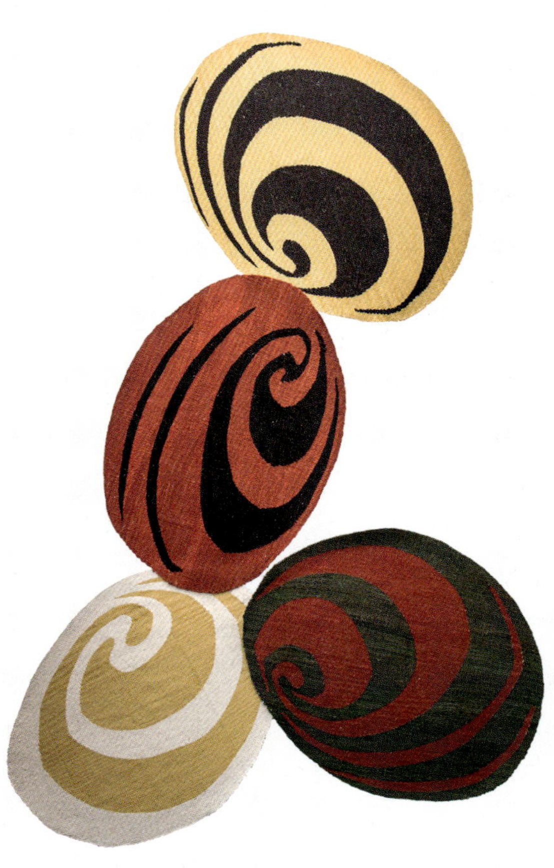

Probabilities, 2013, 170 x 280 cm,
Private Collection

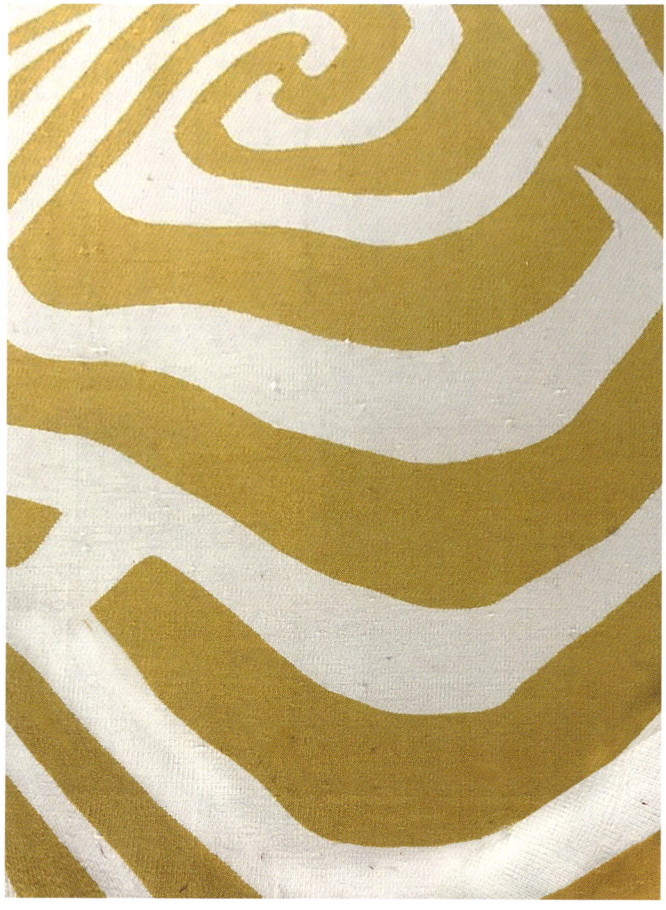

Finger Print Melting, 2023, 225 x 128 cm,
Anna Laudel Gallery

izing old techniques or bringing about significant developments in traditional craft approaches like embroidery, weaving, knotting, and sewing. As a universal cultural practice, both traditional textile art and contemporary art using textiles promote global connections as well as reflecting regional identities. This interest in textiles also emerges in a striking number of thematic and monographic exhibitions on this theme, initially at major exhibitions and art fairs like ARCO Madrid or the Venice Biennale, and increasingly also in institutions, museums, and galleries. Practically every gallery has at least one artist working with textiles on their roster. With chosen approaches that are endlessly diverse. Younger female artists, in particular, are consciously turning to this "slow medium" in response to the digital aesthetic and connected production processes. Others — artists like Goshka Macuga, Pae White, Sarah Morris, Shannon Bool, Laure Prouvost, Margit Eicher and many more — use digital technologies, such as digitally controlled Jacquard looms to create unprecedented fine-detail image compositions on a monumental scale that are often based on photographic templates or digital collages.

It is all the more surprising then to discover that the youthful creator of the above pieces was already considered one of the established figures in contemporary textile art in Turkey. For the past forty years, she has constantly renewed her artistic practice. Like many of her generation — female artists born in the 1930s like Magdalena Abakanowicz (Poland), Sheila Hicks (USA), and Marion Baruch (Italy) — the quality of Belkıs Balpınar's work is now receiving recognition and has undergone an art-historical re-evaluation, as well as attracting growing market interest after decades of relatively modest attention. This type of reappraisal may also spur an exuberant and joyful late production by these artists. I am thinking, for example, of the extensive body of late works by Sheila Hicks, which are currently in high demand internationally. In a conversation with me, Balpınar confided, "I never felt disadvantaged as a woman in Turkey. I was also fortunate enough to work with internationally connected institutions very early on."

For a long time, textile art was relegated to the realm of applied arts and the craft-oriented offshoots of fine arts rather than being aligned with the clear, radical concepts of academic art movements like Minimalism, Concept Art, Arte Povera, sculpture and abstract-expressionist painting, not to mention the many facets of film, video and media art. Moreover, textile art was seen in a negative light because it was considered a handicraft practiced by women. This bias has a long tradition, extending to the legendary and ostensibly progressive Bauhaus school. Women students were simply shunted off to the weaving workshop, which later produced many famous textile artists and designers like Gunta Stölzl, Lilly Reich, Ida Kerkovius, and Marianne Brand. Several Bauhaus instructors made it quite clear that female students were unwelcome in their workshops, whether pottery, printing, metalworking, or wall painting. Oskar Schlemmer, who joined the Bauhaus in 1921, famously claimed, "Where there is wool, there is also a woman who weaves, even if only for her own amusement."[2]

For many female artists, working with textiles was a gateway into the world of the established art schools and academies, which were mostly dominated by men. This was also true for many female artists in Turkey. They often used their textile practice to diffuse their own avant-garde influence throughout the country.

Belkıs Balpınar wanted to study art, choosing to do so in Istanbul. She was supported by her artistically inclined family but needed a scholarship. An opportunity arose in 1963 thanks to Sümerbank. Because the bank only funded textile design studies, she decided to seize this chance to enrol in the academy. Ultimately, this detour ended up becoming her calling and life's work. She made her debut in 1964, exhibiting textile pieces designed during her studies and created with the help of a professional weaver.

Before deciding to pursue an independent career as an artist, Balpınar worked for many years as a textile historian, and, later, as the curator of the carpet collection at the Istanbul Vakiflar Museum. In 1968, she completely shifted roles, transitioning from producer to researcher and collector. Initially, she conducted research for the museum on antique carpets and flatweaves from mosques, building up a unique collection that led to the establishment of a dedicated department. Her work helped to heighten interest in her country's cultural legacy. From the mid-1970s onwards, she travelled through Anatolia on behalf of the Vakiflar Foundation to source antique carpets and kilims from mosques, Qur'ānic schools, and other religious institutions for the museum's collection. These journeys also presented her with the

2
"Wo Wolle ist, ist auch ein Weib, das webt, und sei es nur zum Zeitvertreib." Ursula Muscheler, *Mutter, Muse und Frau Bauhaus. Die Frauen um Walter Gropius*, Berlin: Berenberg Verlag, 2018, p. 97.

3
Belkıs Balpınar and Udo Hirsch: Flatweaves of the Vakiflar Museum Istanbul = Flachgewebe des Vakiflar-Museums Istanbul / Türkiye Cumhuriyeti Vakiflar Genel Müdürlügü, Wesel: Uta Hülsey, 1982 (English), followed a year later by Belkıs Balpınar, Udo Hirsch, *KILIM-CICIM-ZILI-SUMAK. Türkische Flachgewebe*, Muhittin Salih Eren, ed., EREN Yayinlari: Istanbul, 1983 (German).

4
On 2 March 1972, an international report commissioned by the Club of Rome was published under the title *The Limits to Growth. A Report for the Club of Rome on the Predicament of Mankind*. It examined timeless, fundamental systemic behaviours like the dynamics of exponential growth, the risks arising from delays, and the opacity of complex systems.

opportunity to explore the wealth of cultures present in Anatolia, with their eventful histories and contributions from so many different ethnic groups. Together with photographer Udo Hirsch, she produced significant publications that were translated into German as well as English.[3] Belkıs Balpınar became actively involved in nature conservation, establishing a private environmental protection association and running its secretariat for a lengthy period. The 1970s and 1980s saw a growing international awareness of our role in the destruction of nature and extinction of many species.[4] Balpınar built enduring relationships with NGOs like the World Wildlife Fund. Al Gore, former vice president of the United States turned environmentalist, was presented with an important piece personally designed by Balpınar. Titled *Green Sun*, it was a gift from WWF Turkey with the support of Garanti Bank. This series of works later included *Red Sun*, which featured a glowing, bleeding planet in danger of being swallowed up by a black hole. A further variation on this theme showed the planet surrounded by spirals (*The World in Danger*).

The carpets discovered and collected by Balpınar are still conserved in the Vakiflar Museum in Istanbul. In 1979, she helped establish a new carpet museum in the Hünkar

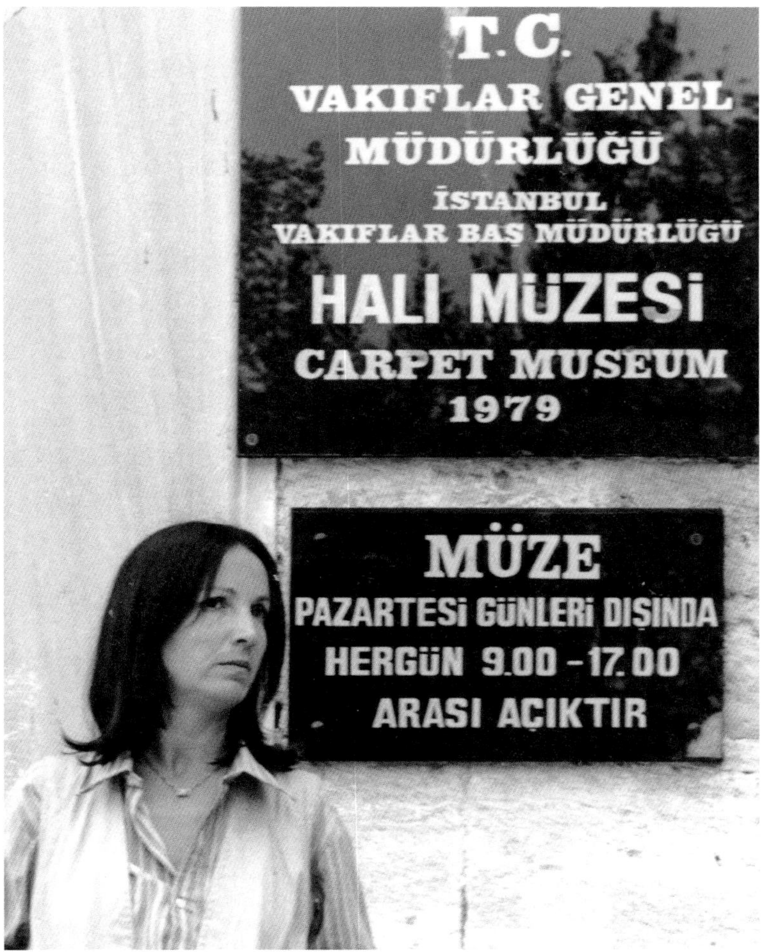

Balpınar at the Istanbul Vakiflar Carpet Museum.
Photo Cengiz Cıva

Pavilion at the Sultan Ahmet Mosque. At the age of 32, she became founding director of the museum and curator of the exhibitions of its collections. In 2006, the museum was relocated to the former Almhouse of Hagia Sophia.

Nothing is as inspiring as absorbing the rich, layered traditions of historical carpet culture — the kaleidoscopic appearance of the geometric motifs of Mamluk carpets, the grid-like arrangements distinguishing Seljuk carpets, the vibrant colours and meandering vine patterns decorating carpets in the Majid style, an endless variety of borders featuring scrolls, rosettes, or small medallions as filling elements. Figurative representations like the Persian dragon-phoenix carpets also developed abstract concepts that were passed down for many centuries. Since the Renaissance, these cultural artefacts were also much appreciated in the West and were included in important pictures of the time. Artists like Hans Holbein skilfully incorporated the striking patterns of "Turkey carpets" — usually knotted, pile-woven Anatolian rugs — into their paintings. At that time, very little was known about the significance and origins of these carpets. Yet they have lost none of their capacity to inspire.

However, nothing is more hidebound and outdated than a centuries-old carpet-making art that continues to replicate long-gone cultures and lifestyles in a self-referential manner. Many of the artisan carpet productions closely associated with nomadism were threatened with extinction, just like the nature reserves where their crafters formerly lived. However, people are also very proud of their roots, although today this is often intertwined with nationalistic praise for the glorious achievements of a now politicized Ottoman Empire. Today, younger artists in particular are turning to traditional forms in order to reinterpret their iconographies and meanings. Artists like Ramazan Can are emblematic of this tendency. German-based artist Nevin Aladağ uses "oriental" rugs of different origins and qualities as well as industrial products made from synthetic fabrics for abstract collages depicting anything from playing fields to abstract compositions. She calls her pieces *Social Fabric*, highlighting the global interconnectedness of carpet production and trade. Both the traditional patterns of these representations and life-styles co-exist peacefully. In this way, a carpet becomes an allegory of a societal, intercultural utopia.

After twenty years in the sector, Balpınar decided to move on from museum work. She opened a carpet restoration workshop in Üsküdar and began to develop her own carpet designs. Her designs followed their own distinct path and style, breaking away completely from the traditions of Anatolian carpets. To this day, she remains faithful to important work principles. Everything is produced in an analogue way. She sketches her designs herself and scales them up to the desired size. All her pieces are handmade, albeit not by her. The designs, at a 1:1 scale, are placed behind the warp threads set up on the loom, serving as a map for the labyrinthine paths of the infinite possibilities of the threads.

Contemporary art generally lacks the conceptual terminology and artisan background knowledge necessary to describe the current production of textile artworks. Even the author of this text does not consider herself entirely exempt from such criticisms. How are the warp and weft constructed? What material is the pile made from? Which knotting technique was used (symmetrical or asymmetrical)? How has the fringe been created? What patterns predominate and which motifs determine the overall effect of a composition? These technical questions are often overlooked in order to focus on the creativity or development of a work. Yet they are even more important when observing the originals.

It is possible to identify a series of milestones in Belkıs Balpınar's work that have contributed to the development of her practice. She set out by questioning the classic format of the carpet by creating specific "shaped pieces" comparable to the famous "shaped canvases" that allowed Frank Stella to develop a new type of relational painting. In order to create these shapes, the woven piece had to be partially detached from the weaving frame and its edges secured with threads. In another series of designs, she began to leave the warp open, choosing not to add in any weft threads with the aim of introducing shade and spatial depth into her compositions. Between 1989 and 1992, Balpinar rented an apartment in Soho, New York, where she spent three months every year. We can reasonably assume that this allowed her to engage with some of the important art trends on the New York scene.

Balpınar has often stressed the important role played in her work by scientific publications and phenomena, in particular, by quantum physics, chaos or string theory. She blends the centuries-old tradition of symmetrical kilim patterns with the orderly chaos or chaotic order of scientific phenomena: planets, spiral systems, black holes, and lightning. This frame of reference is vital for Balpınar's practice: "The world created by humans is very complicated. On the other hand, in the billions of galaxies and billions of stars within them, we see a regularity and order regarding our perception of time. Many artists are trying to grasp and reflect on something from the chaos throughout the world. Yet, I try to capture images that imply spaces created by the movements of galaxies and planets in the macro state or particles in the micro-space that seem more ordinate in regard to our understanding of time."[5]

Belkıs Balpınar developed a remarkable variety of interrelated diptychs (*Explosive Layers*), framed or frame-detached planetary forms that are almost entirely composed of warp threads. The frame of the loom becomes the frame of the image. Other pieces turn the decorative elements into explosions reminiscent of illustrations found in comics or in Roy Lichtenstein's Pop Art. Yet her wall hangings consistently break away from the aspiration to be a "picture". They strive to be the "specific objects" referenced by the legendary art critic and artist Donald Judd. This is particularly true of the visually striking works like *Folded Times* or *Time Plane*. While in other works, objecthood is merely an illusion (*Folded In*). What is flat? What qualifies as flat? Her many variations of cylinders also play with the concept of "dis-illusion", clearly referencing scientific theories. In the theory of relativity,

5
Belkıs Balpınar, *Dokuma-ma / Un-weave*, exhibition catalogue, Istanbul: Anna Laudel Gallery, 2018, p. 27.

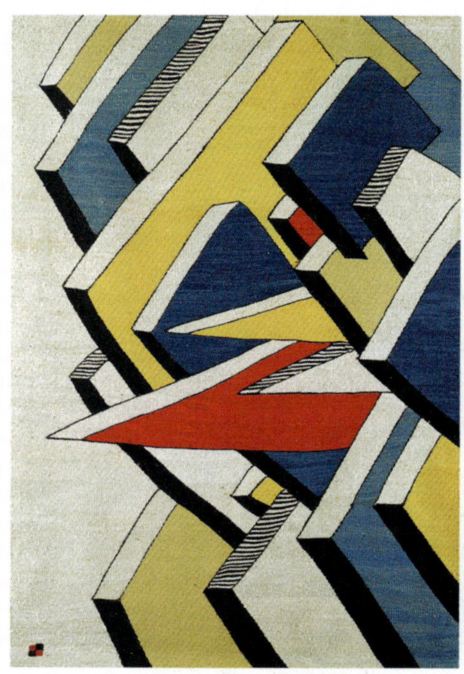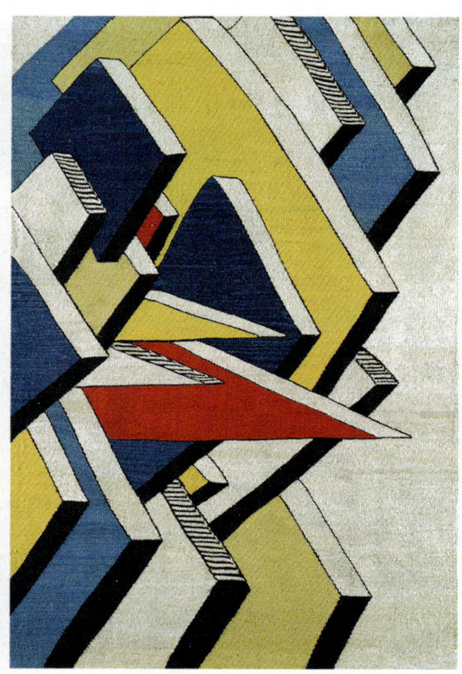

Explosive Layers, 1998, 178 x 132 cm, private collection

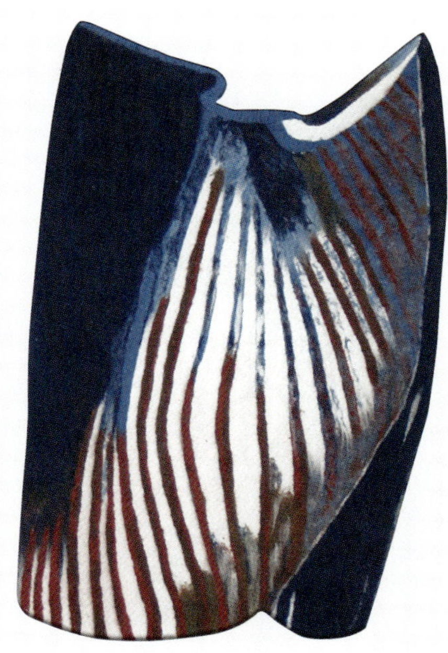

Folded Drape, 2004, 115 x 153 cm, artist's collection

Sabine Maria Schmidt

spatial and temporal coordinates are not universally valid structures of order. Rather, the spatial and temporal distance between two events, or even their simultaneity, is assessed differently by observers in different states of motion. Yet her spirals continue to orbit within the realms of textile design or art. Interestingly, she uses a highly archaic material for these works: goat hair or hand-combed wool, which is some pieces are "stone-washed" after being woven before use. In one of these works, she introduces a cocoon-like form that looks a little like a mummy in a painted coffin. The threads are dyed in stunning colours, including violet, olive green, and a particular type of yellow.

Unlike artists like the Nigerian-born Otobong Nkanga, whose work explicitly focuses on repair and care, Belkıs Balpınar does not charge her work with topical issues or take a direct stance with regard to the current discourse. While the concerns of the two artists may be fundamentally comparable, as both engage with ecological and scientific themes, Balpınar is driven by the desire to attain her own distinct abstract effectiveness through her hanging compositions, which also have the potential to achieve groundedness.

Sometimes, though, her pieces will reveal some connection to the centuries-old tradition of the kilim. The wonderful patterns and ornament distinguishing works like *Flying Stars* or *Lightning* ultimately create a kind of ornamental iconography bridging time and space in an asynchronous and yet deeply intimate manner.

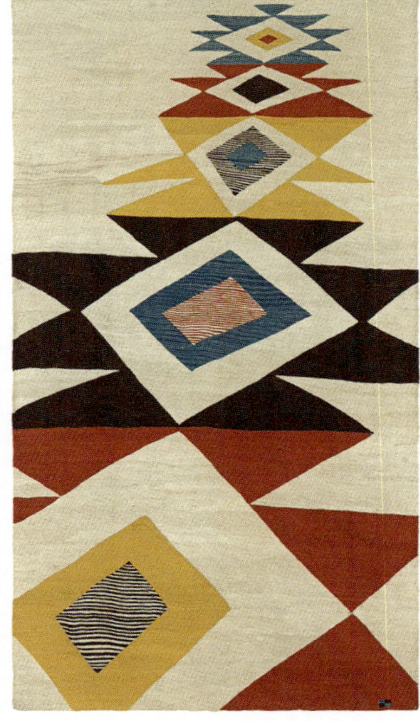

Flying Stars, 1994, 150 x 270 cm,
Anna Laudel Gallery

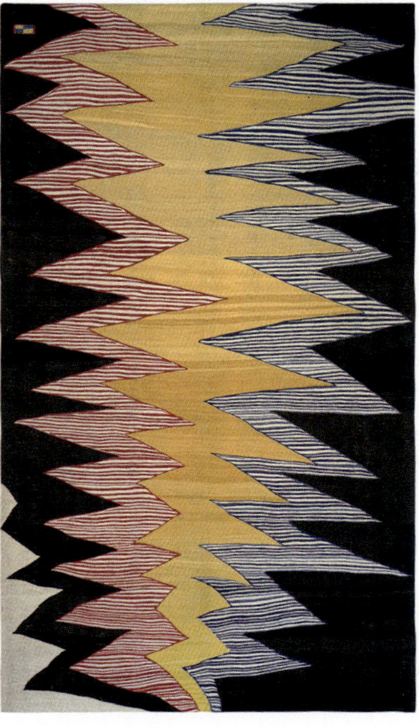

Lightning, 1990, 163 x 260 cm

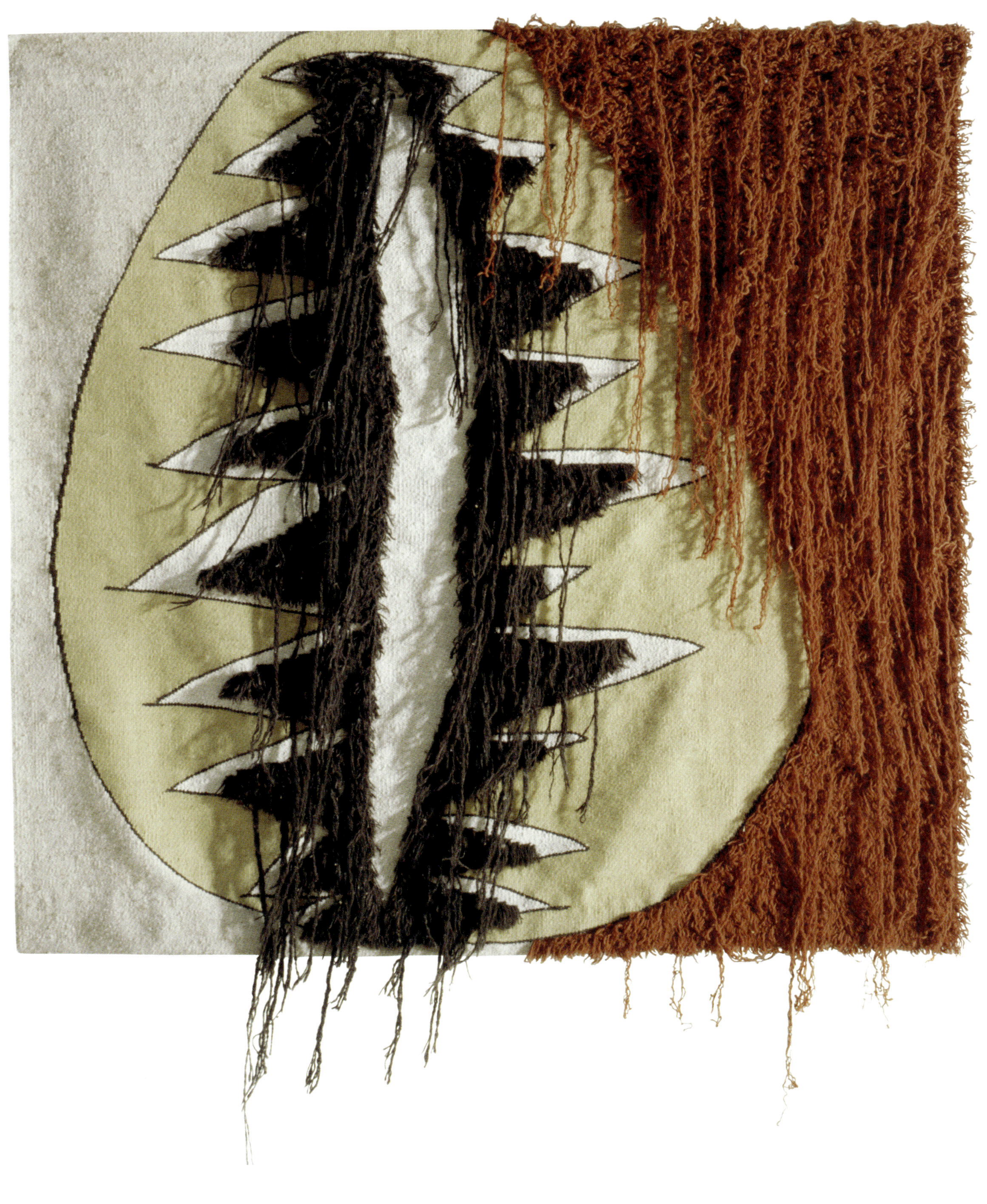

13. *Cowry Shell*, 1998, 155 x 175 cm,
private collection

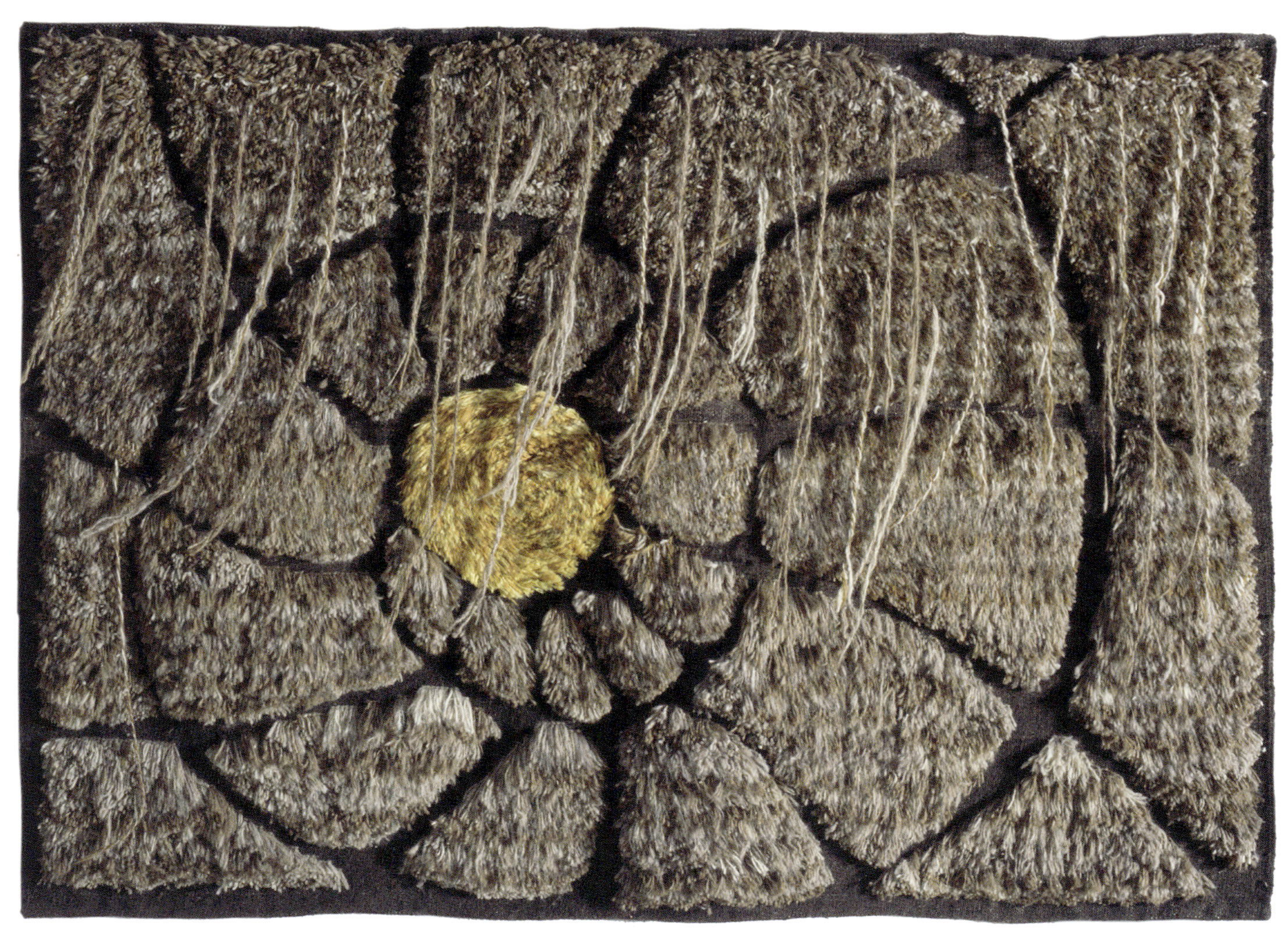

14. *Soil and Sun*, 1998, 116 x 162 cm,
private collection

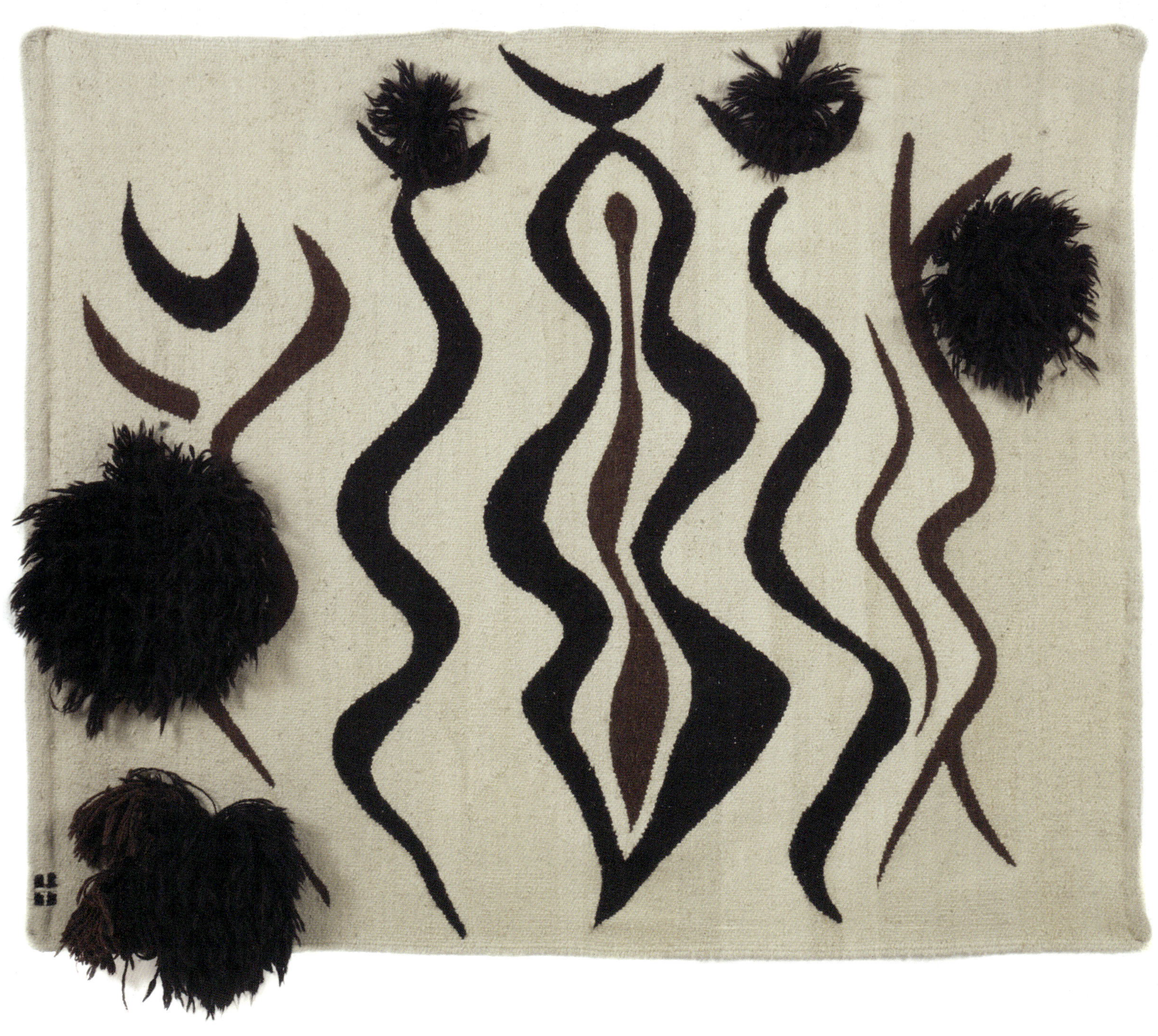

Bushmen and Woman, 1999, 135 x 185 cm,
private collection

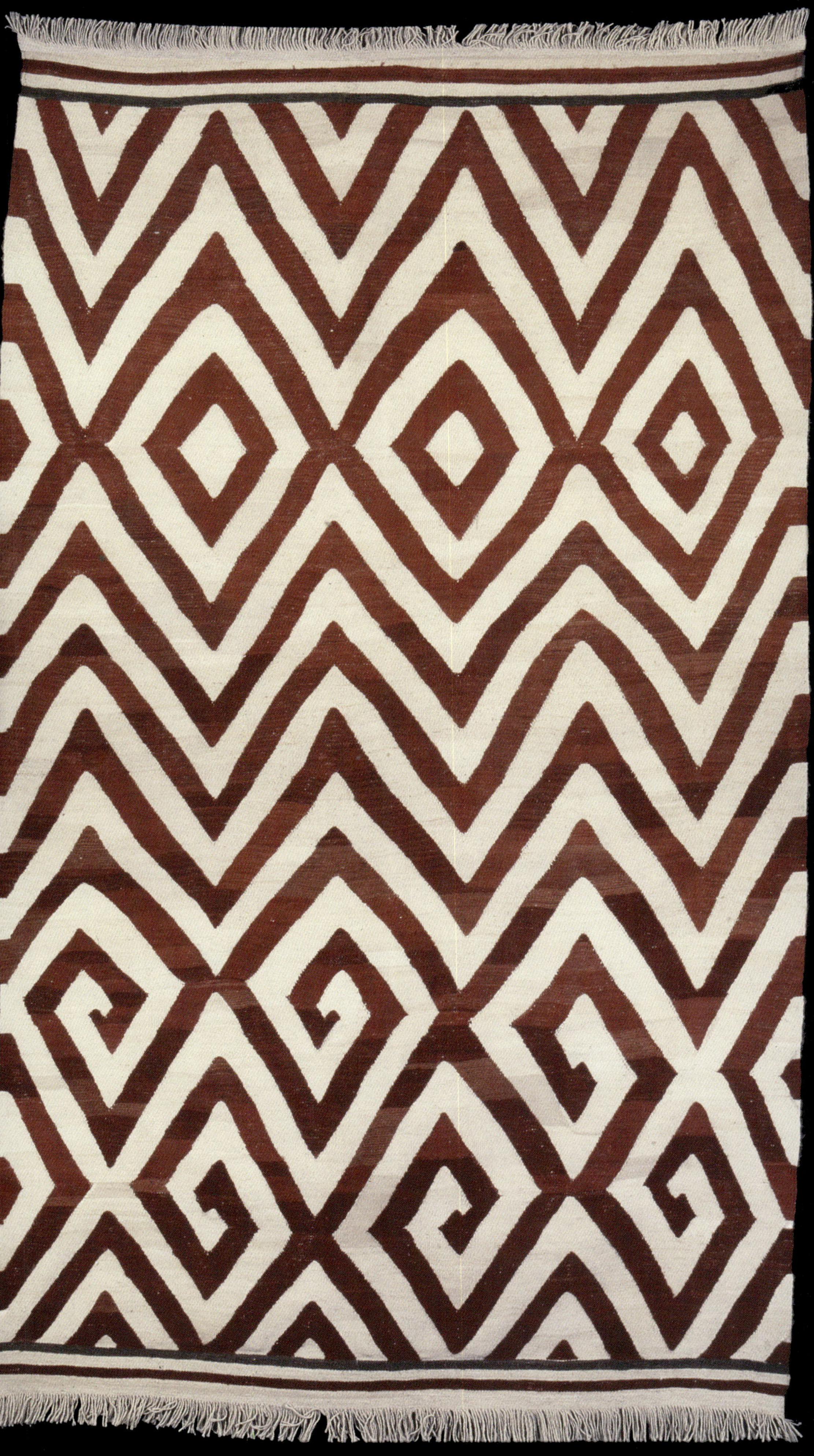

, 150 x 270 cm,

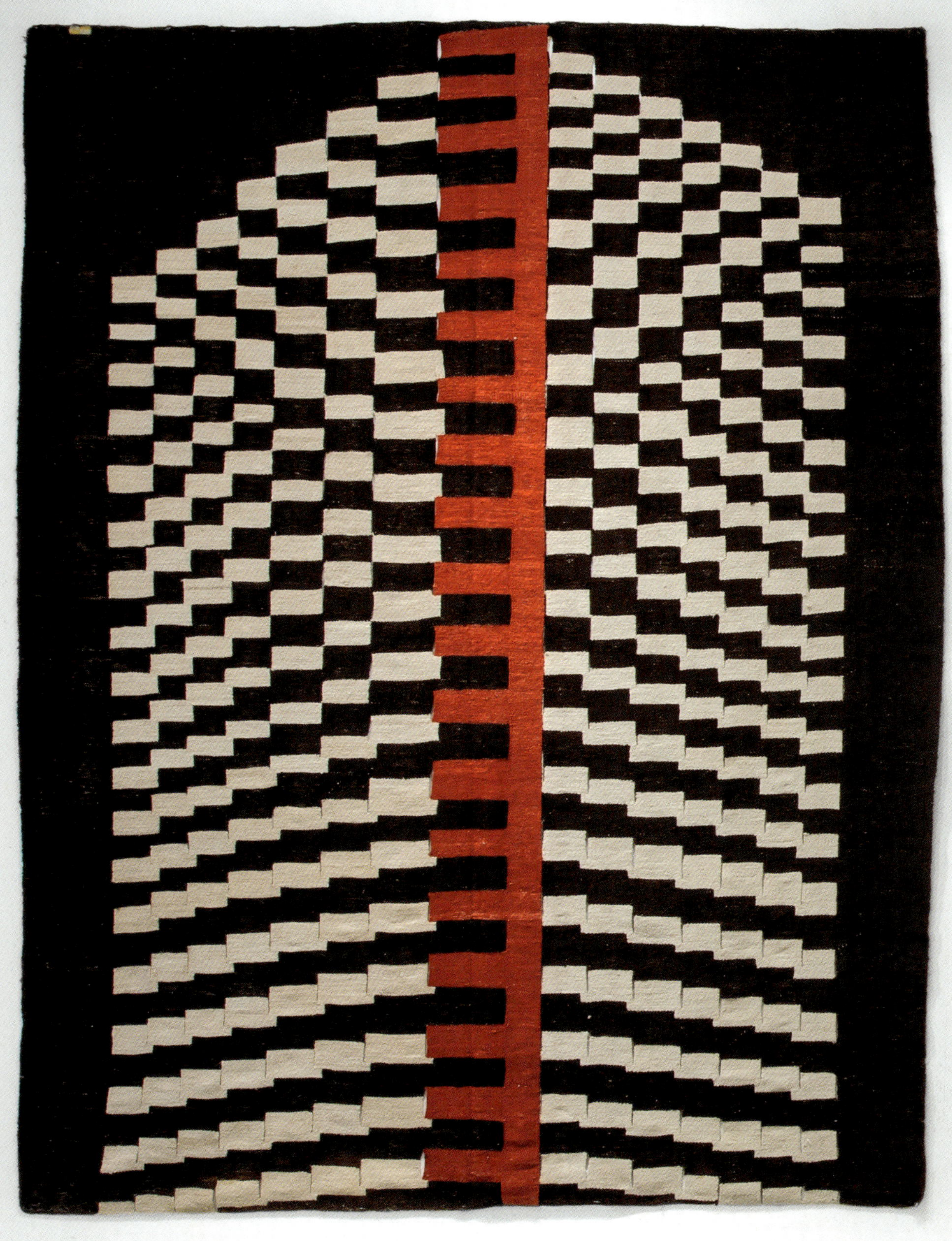

Tower Building, 2000, 200 x 280 cm,
private collection

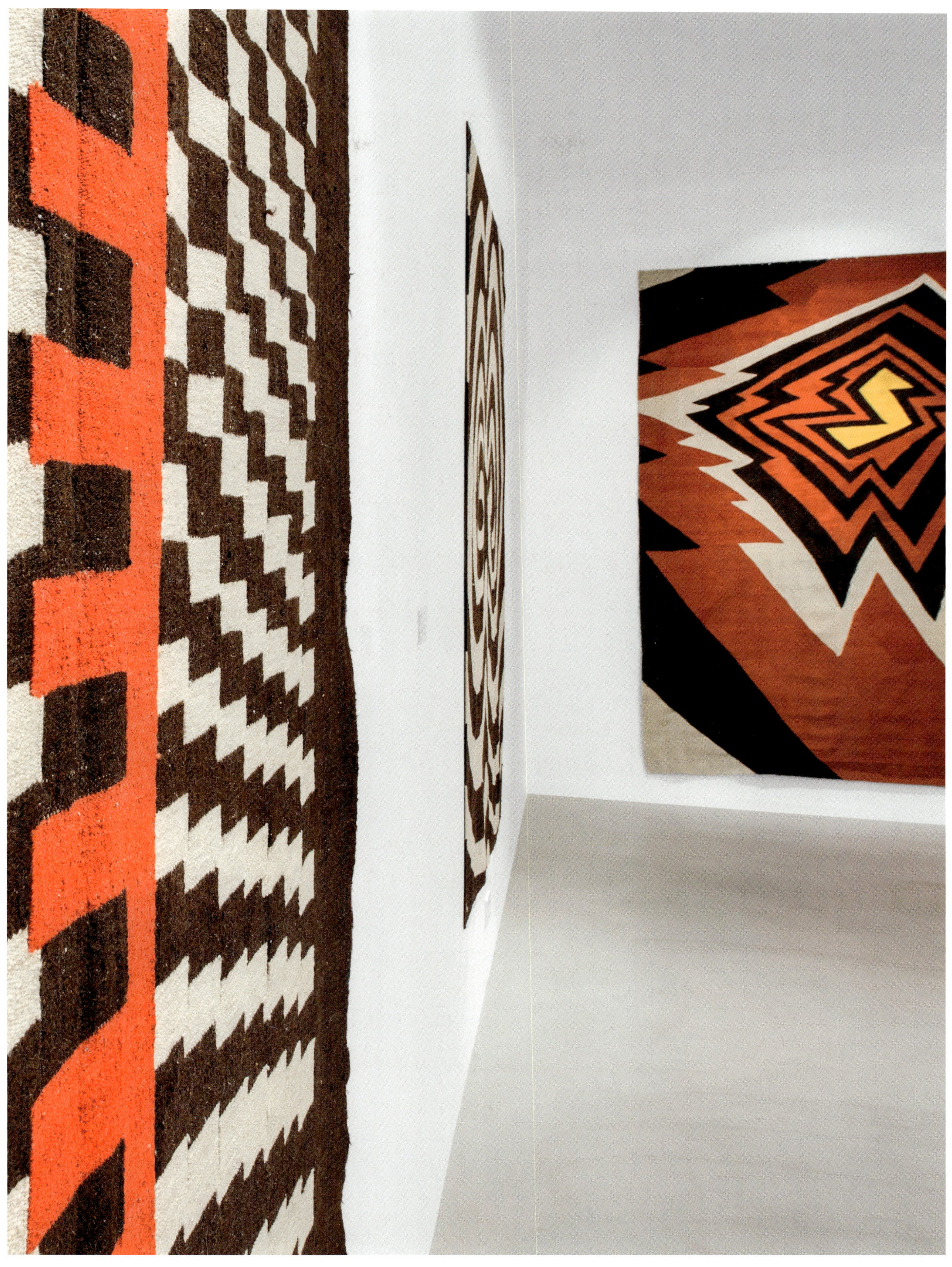

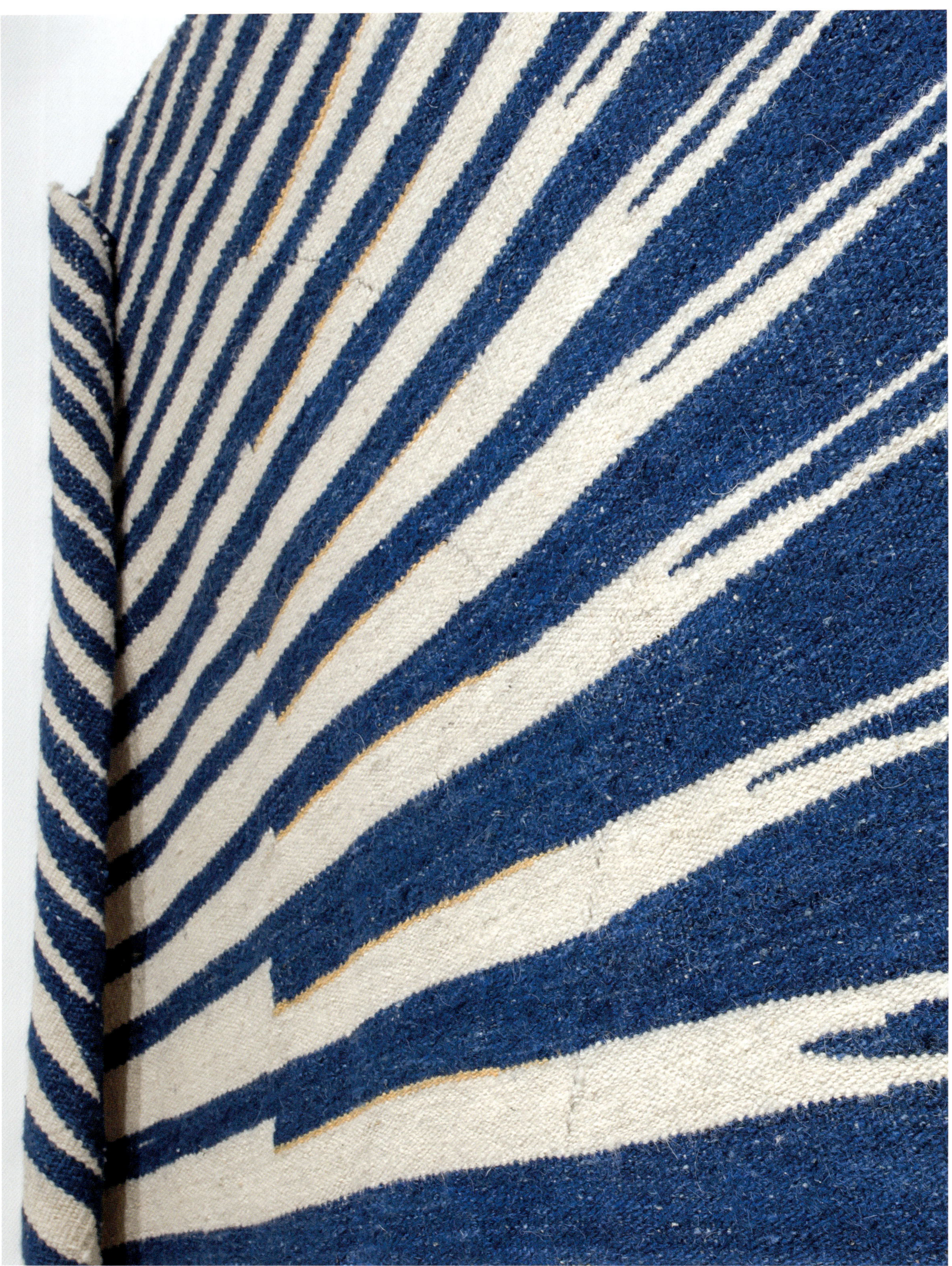

Time Plane, 2001, 160 x 175 cm,
private collection

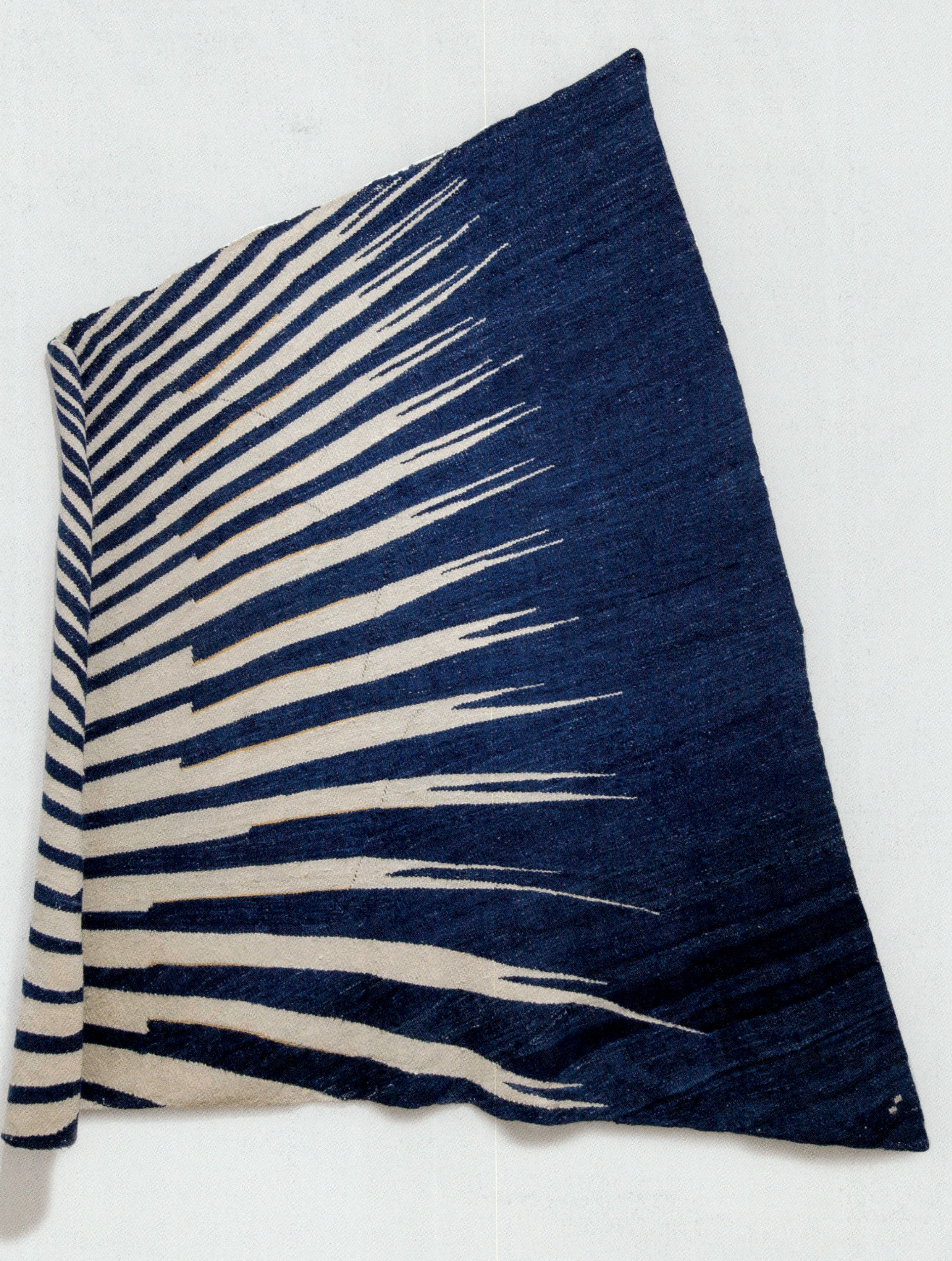

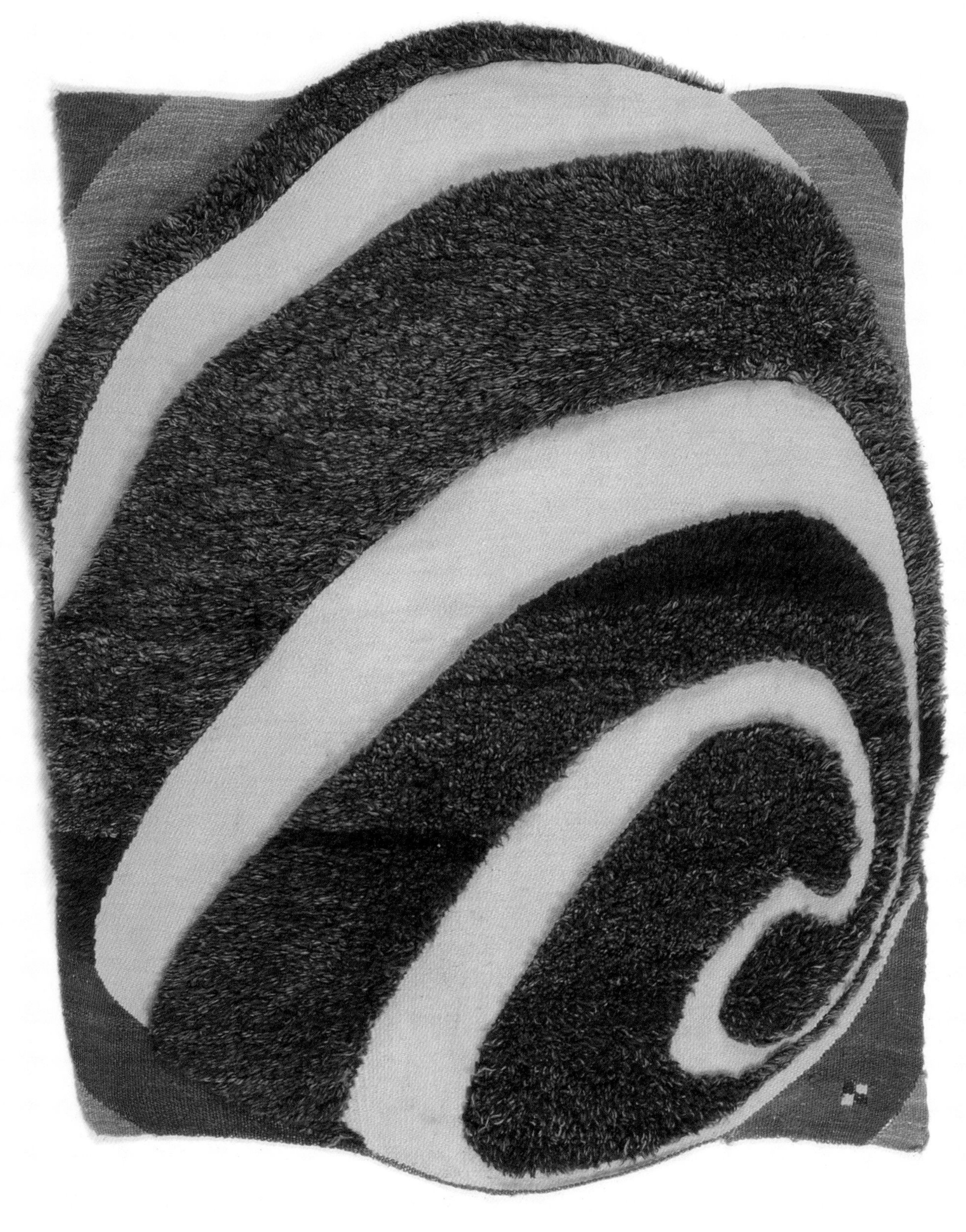

Archipelago

Nebula Spin, 2002, 115 x 145 cm,
private collection

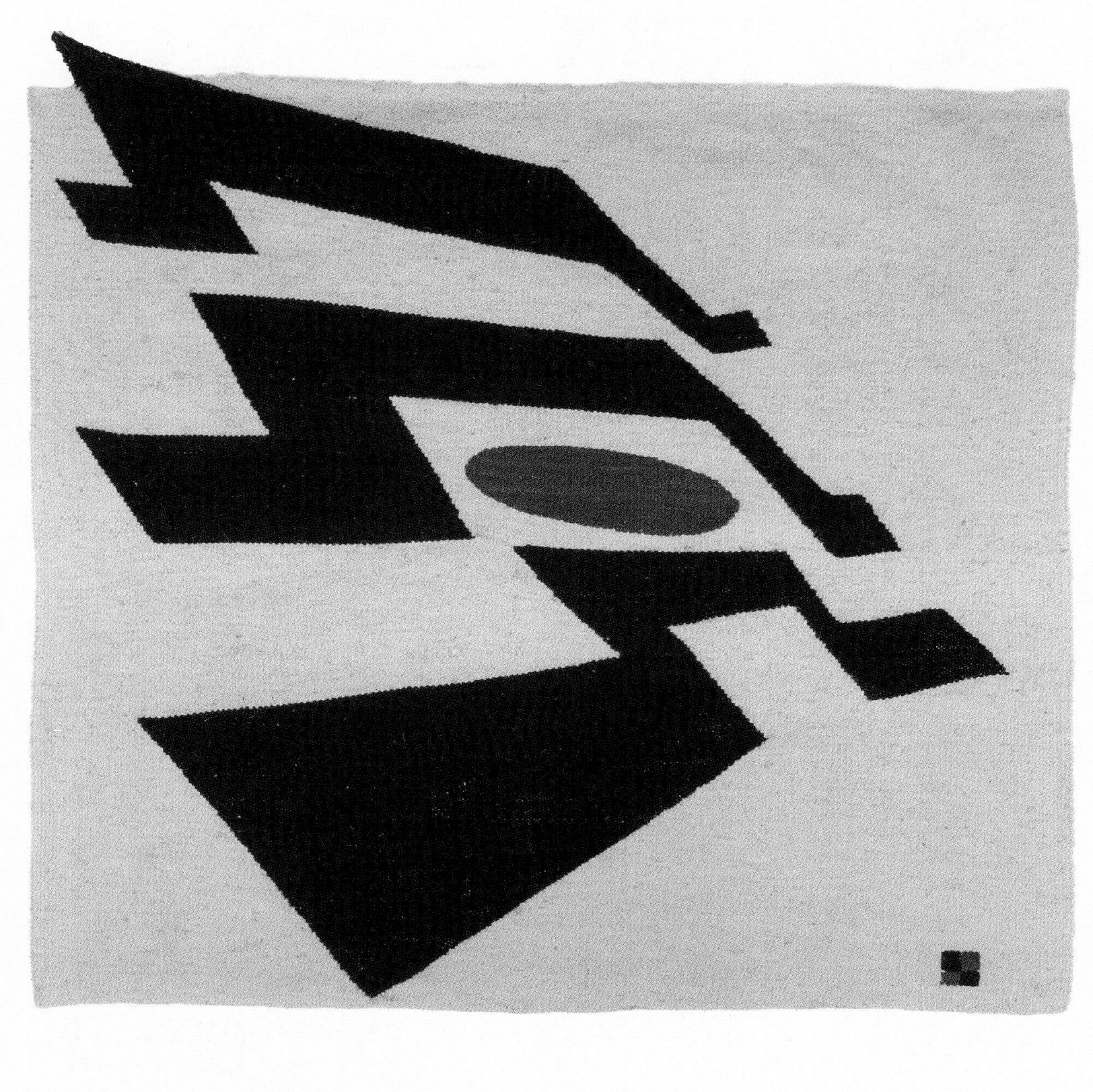

Flying Temple, 2002, 95 x 125 cm,
private collection

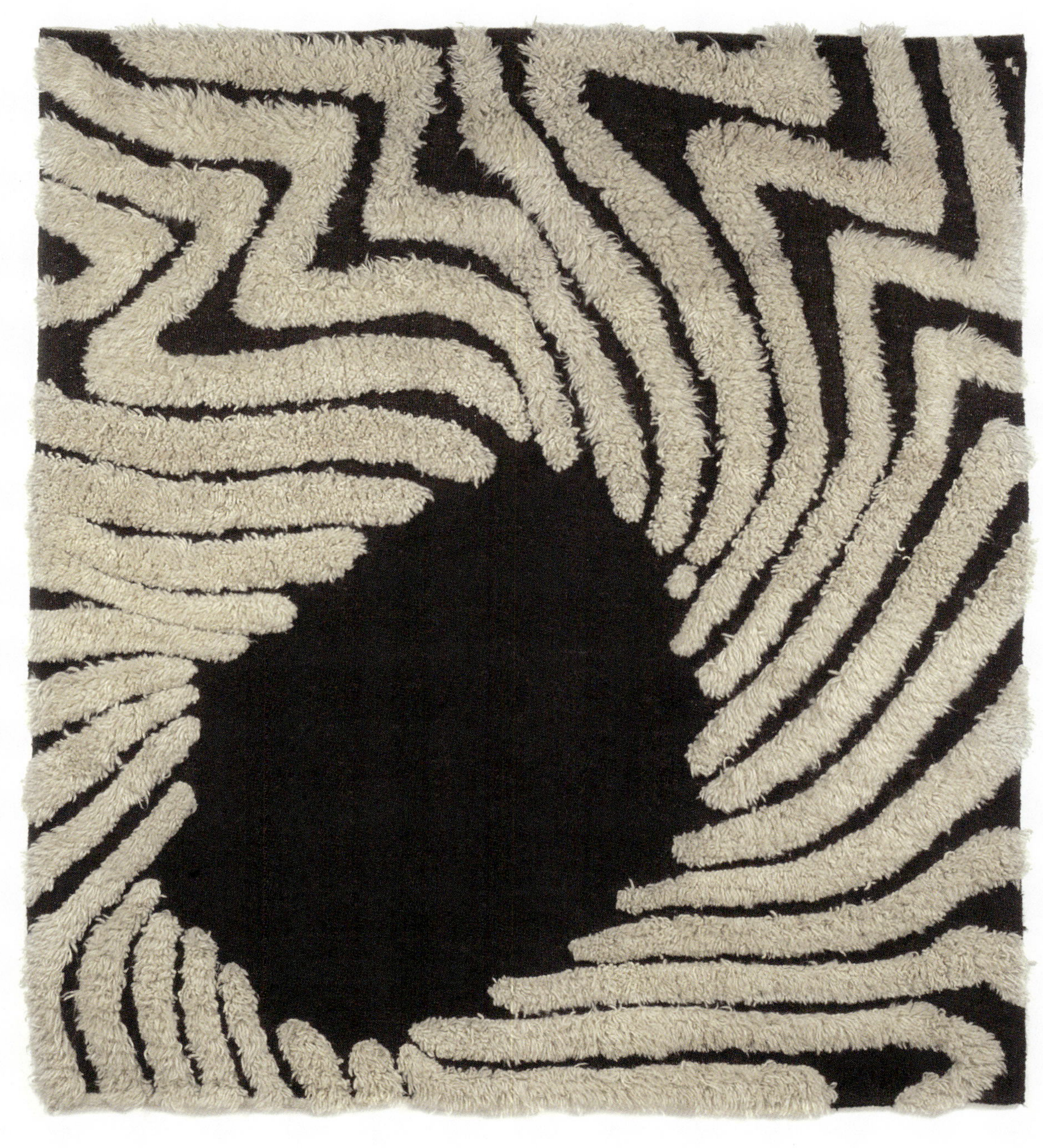

Deep Black Hole-2, 2001, 160 x 190 cm,
private collection

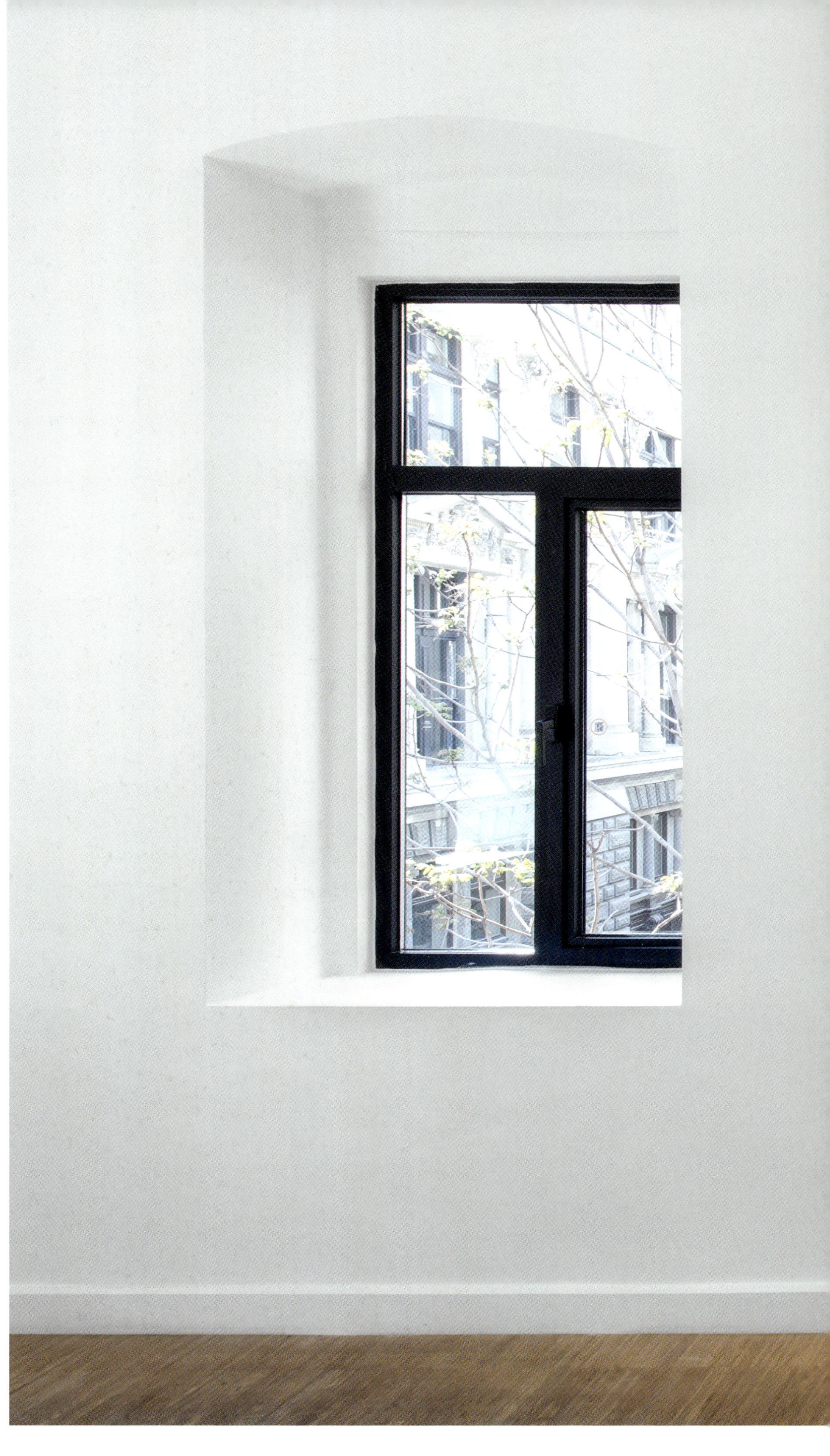

Female, 2002, 240 x 145 cm,
private collection

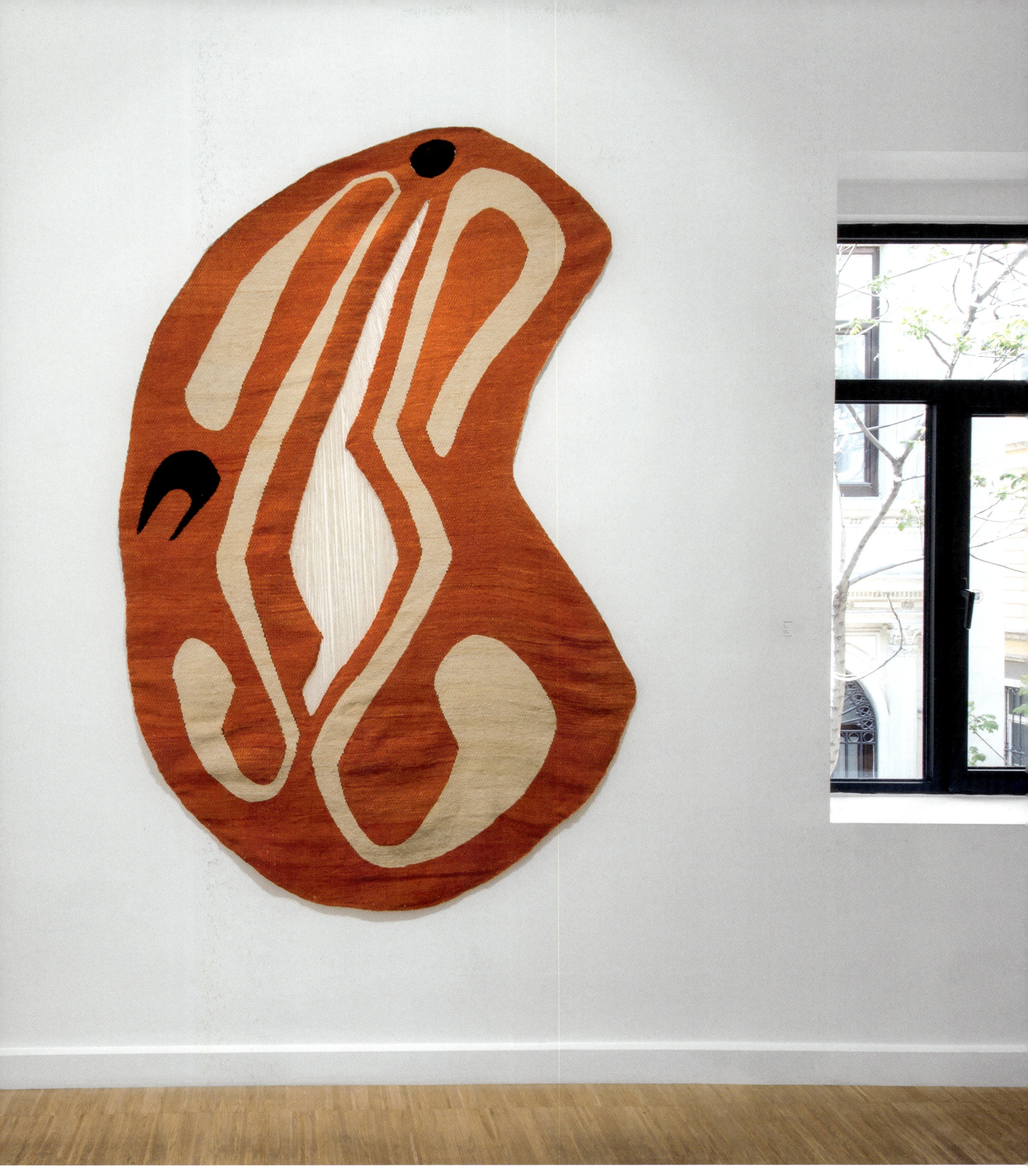

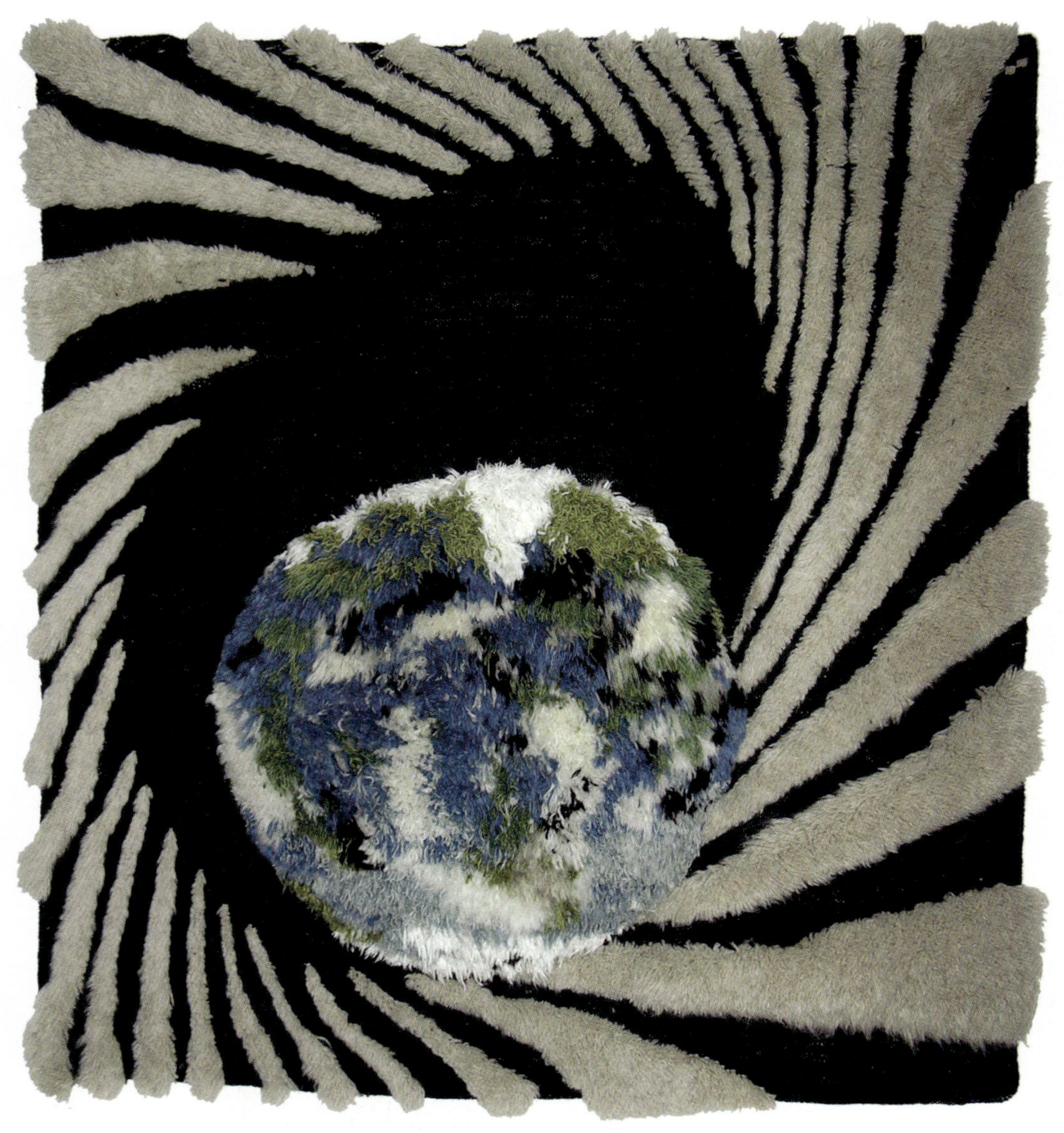

World in Danger, 2008, 120 x 135 cm,
private collection

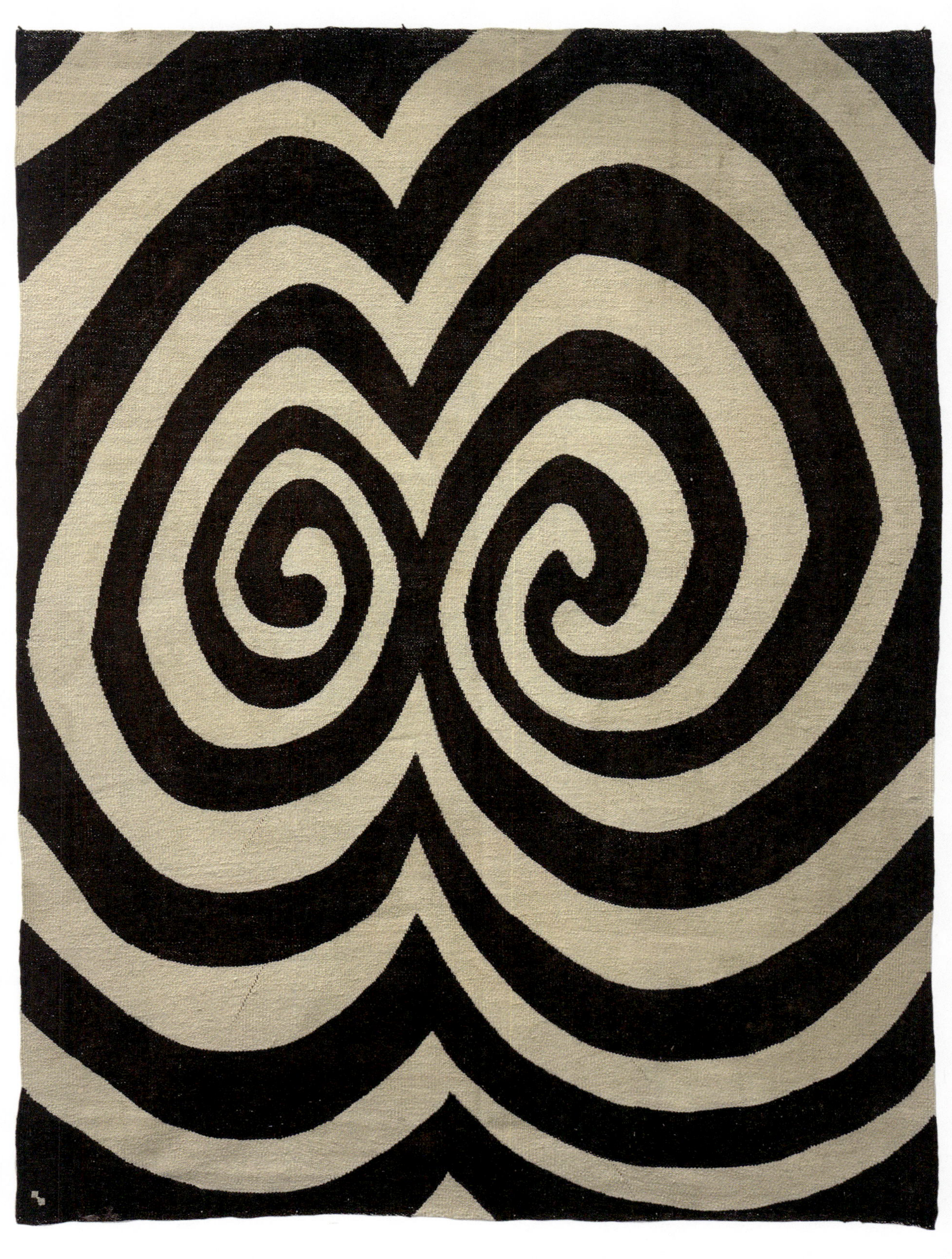

Asymmetry (*Spiral Eyes*), 2005, 175 x 236 cm,
Anna Laudel Gallery

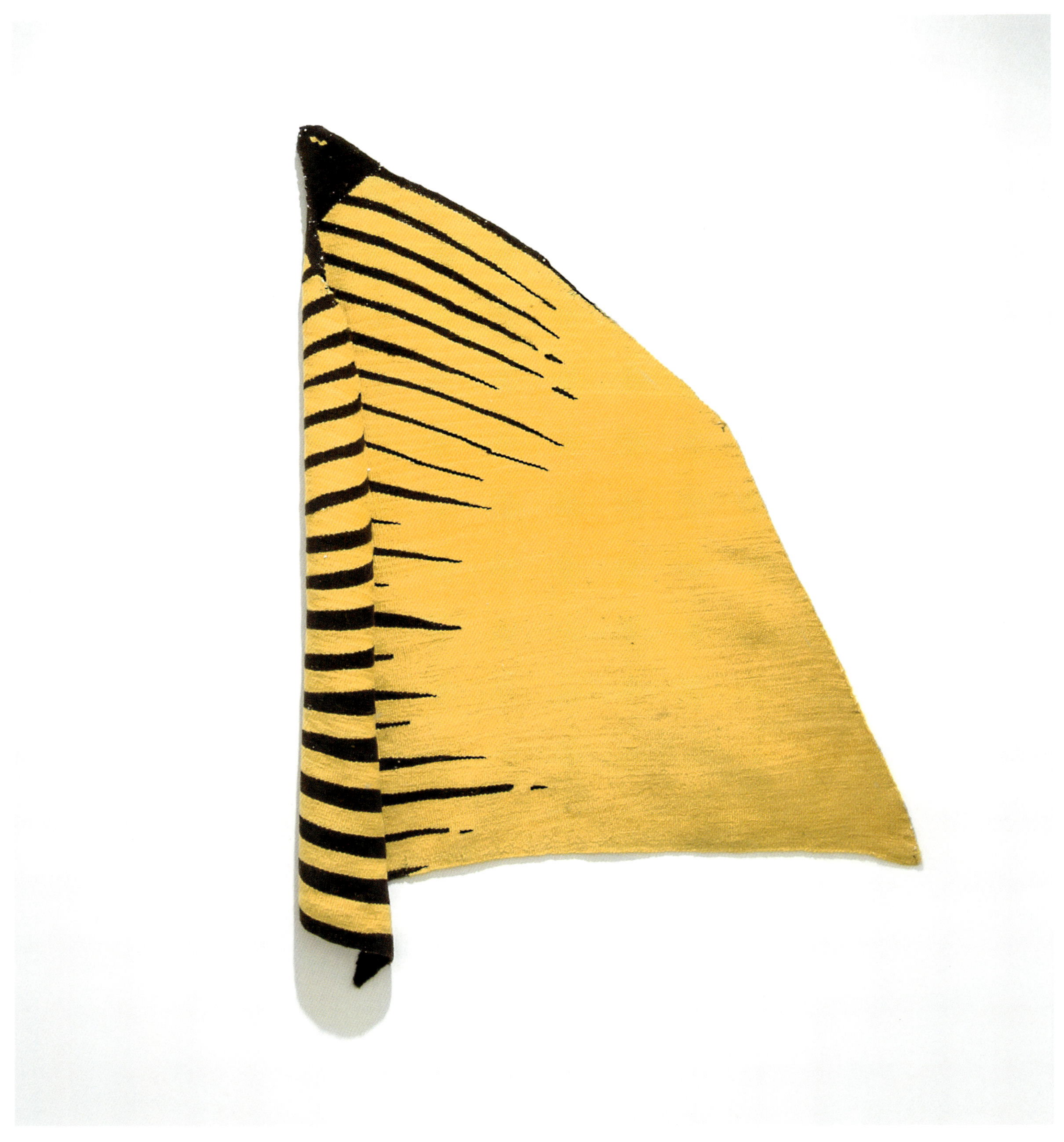

Expansion / Wing, 2013, 140 x 145 cm,
private collection

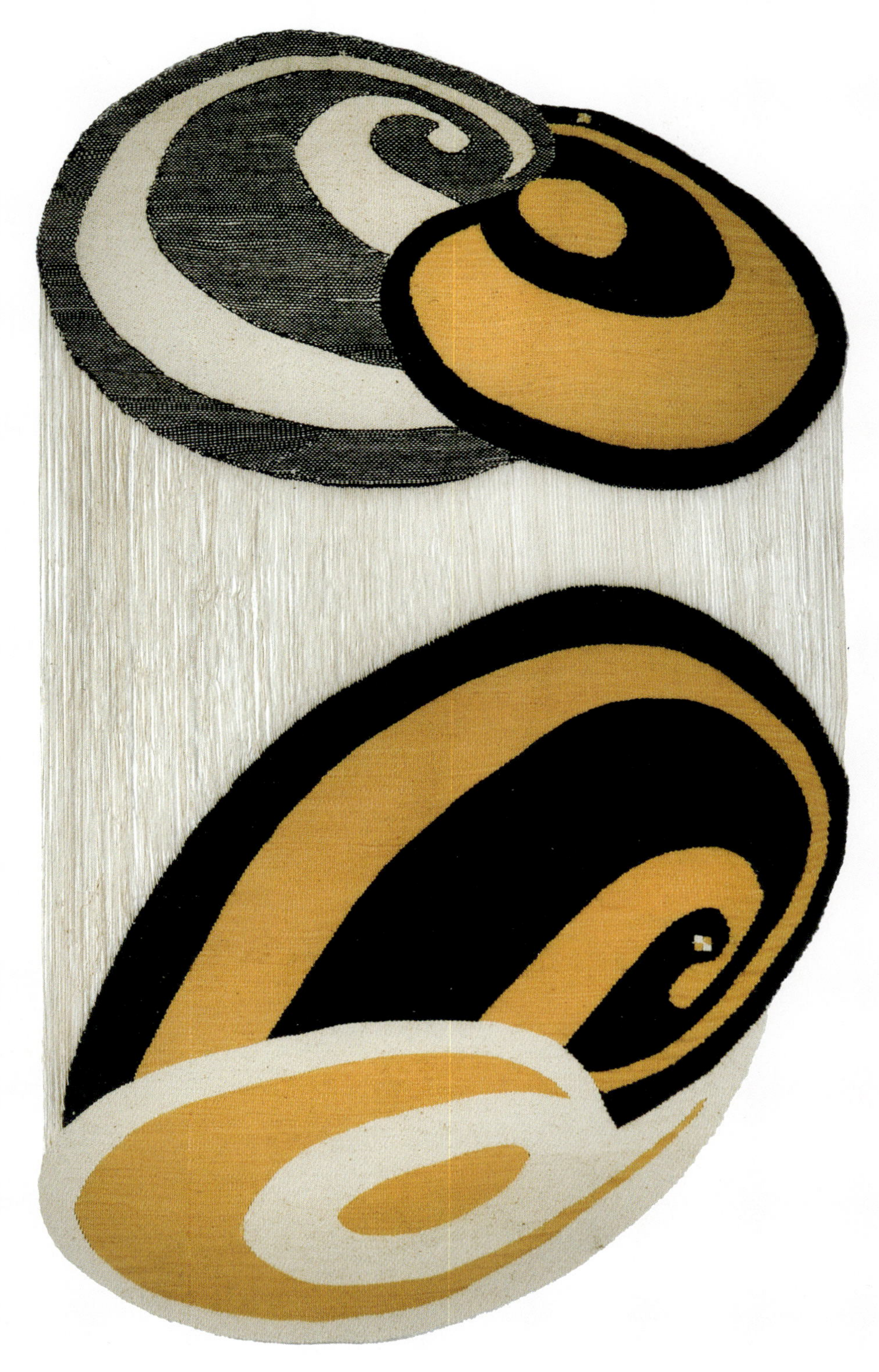

Embryo, 2014, 120 x 190 cm,
private collection

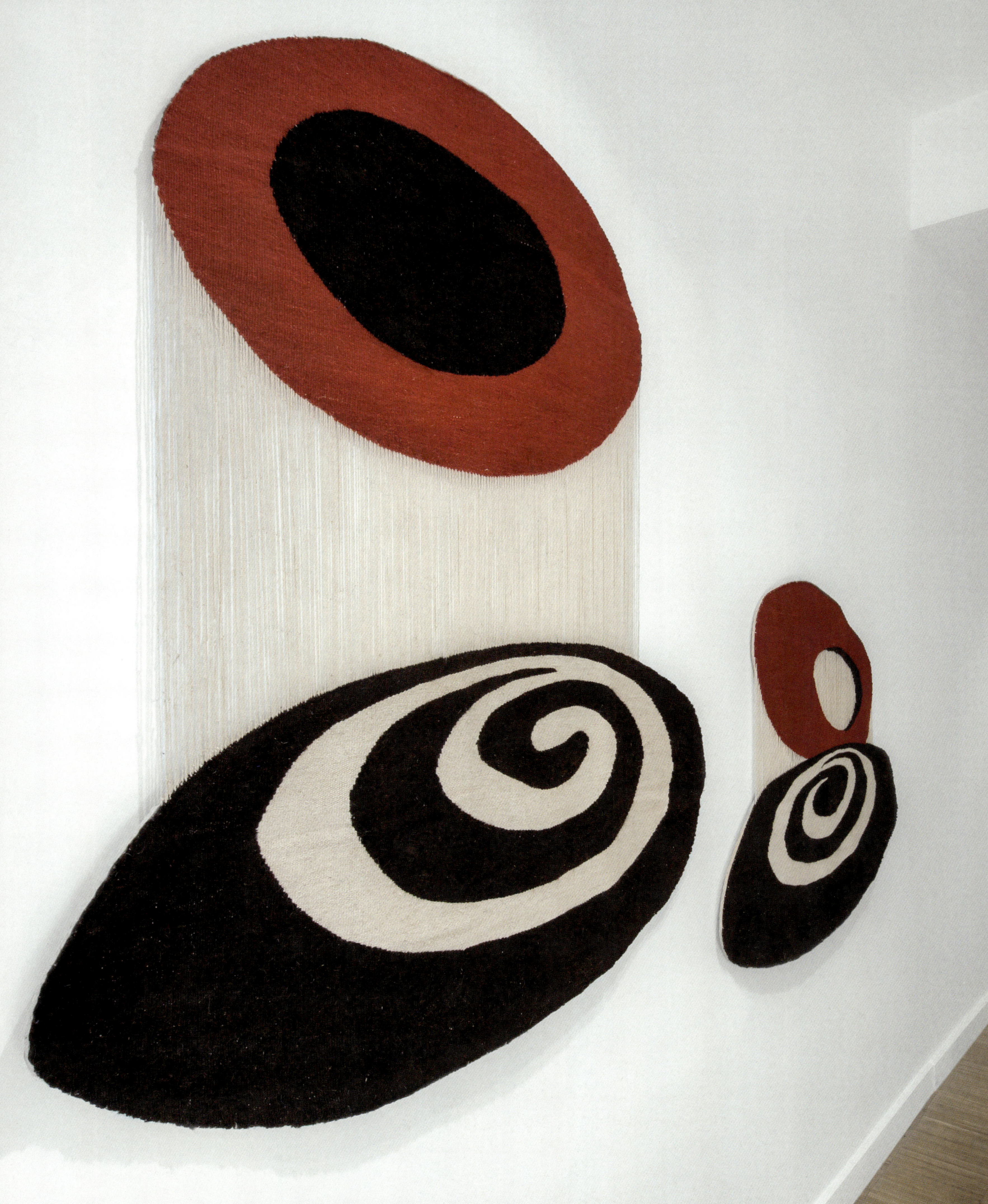

Archipelago

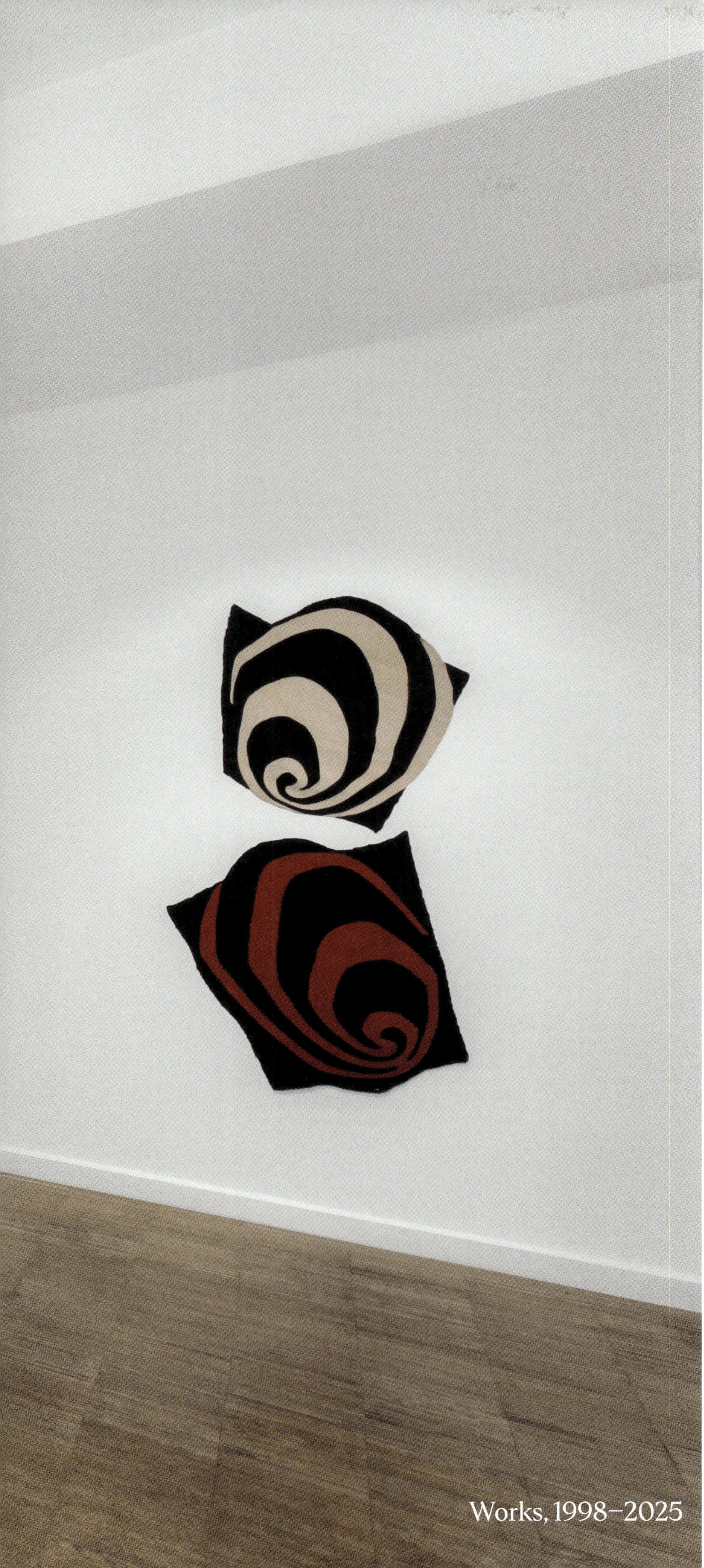

Descending, 2014, 135 x 160 cm,
private collection

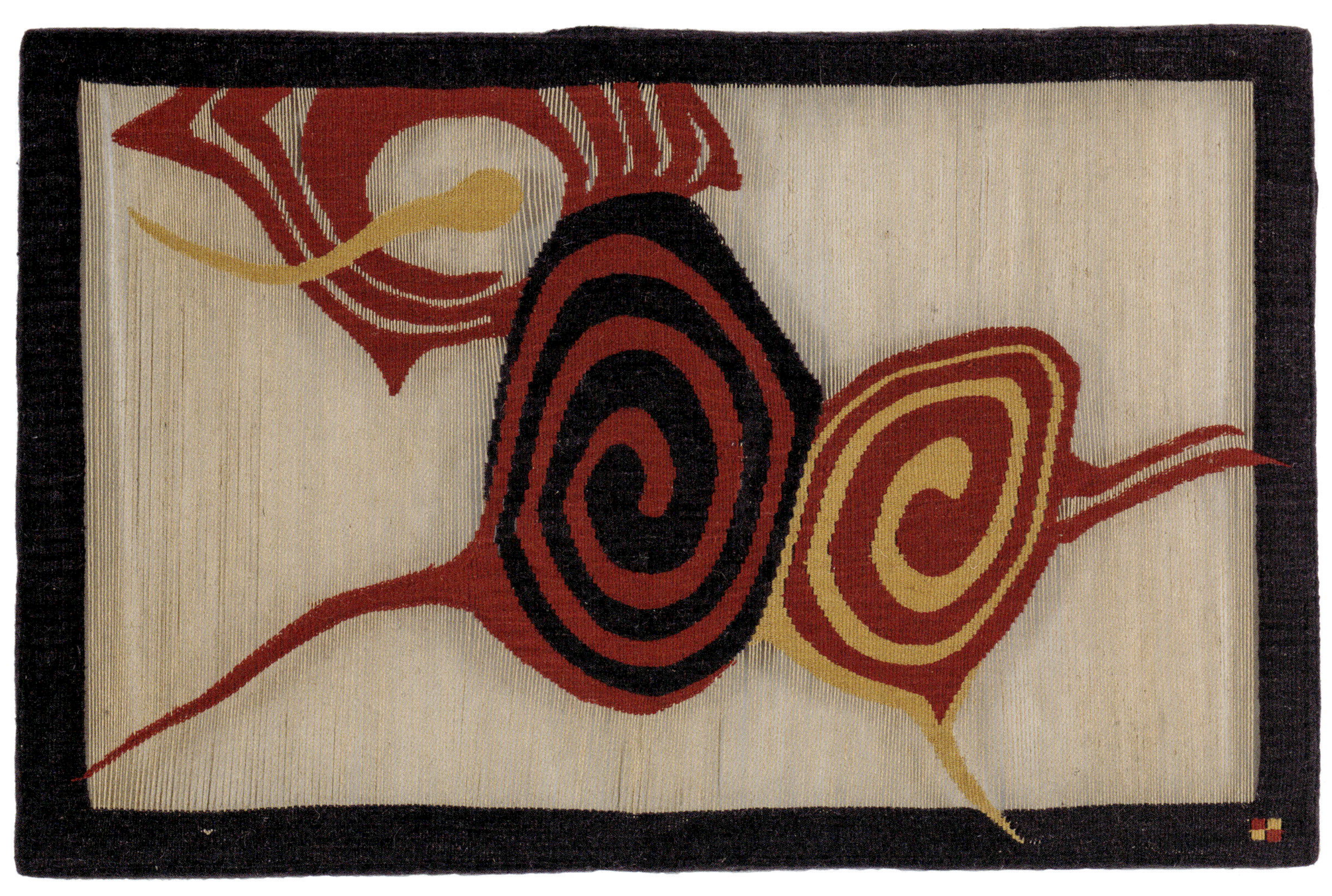

Propagation, 2015, 93 x 147 cm,
private collection

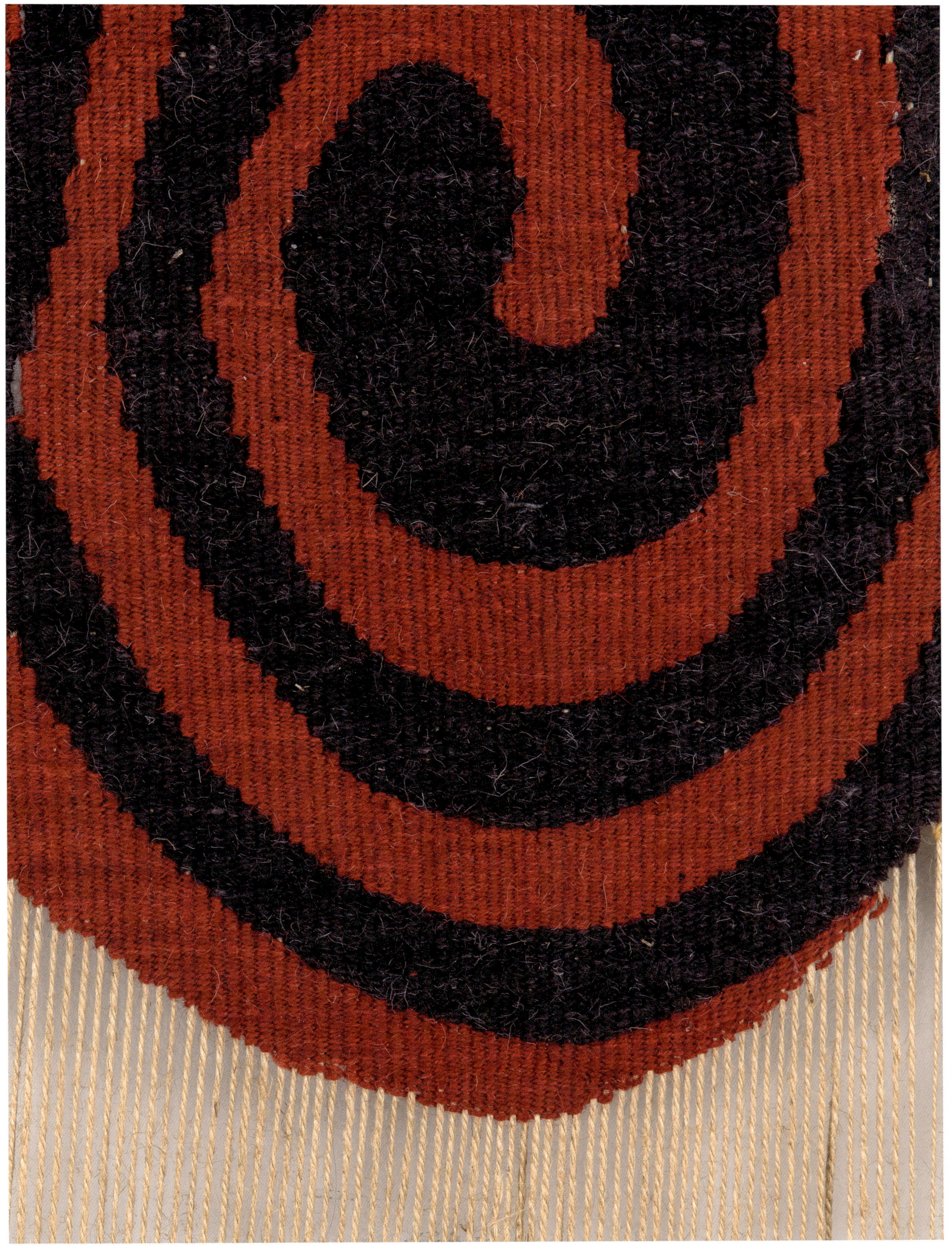

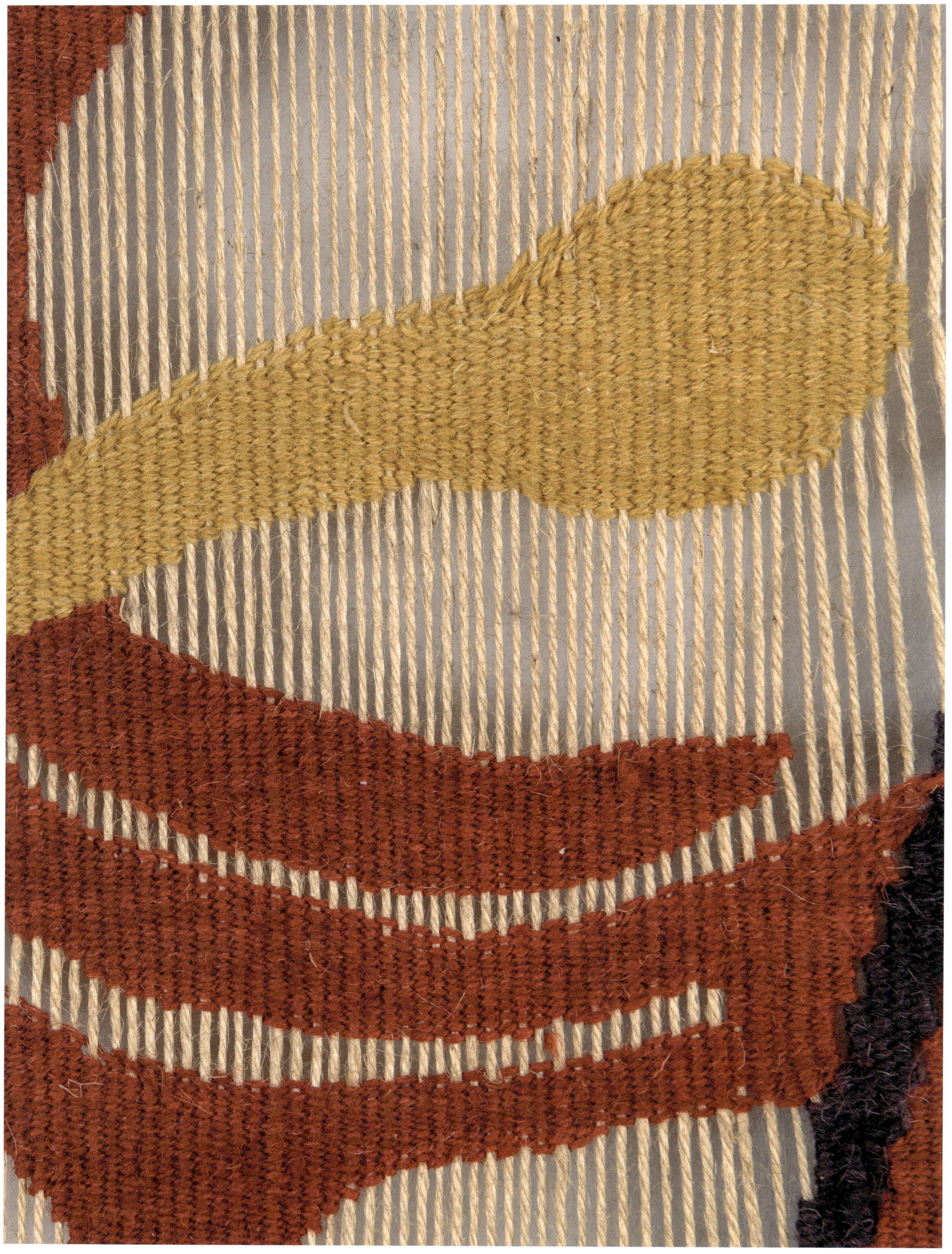

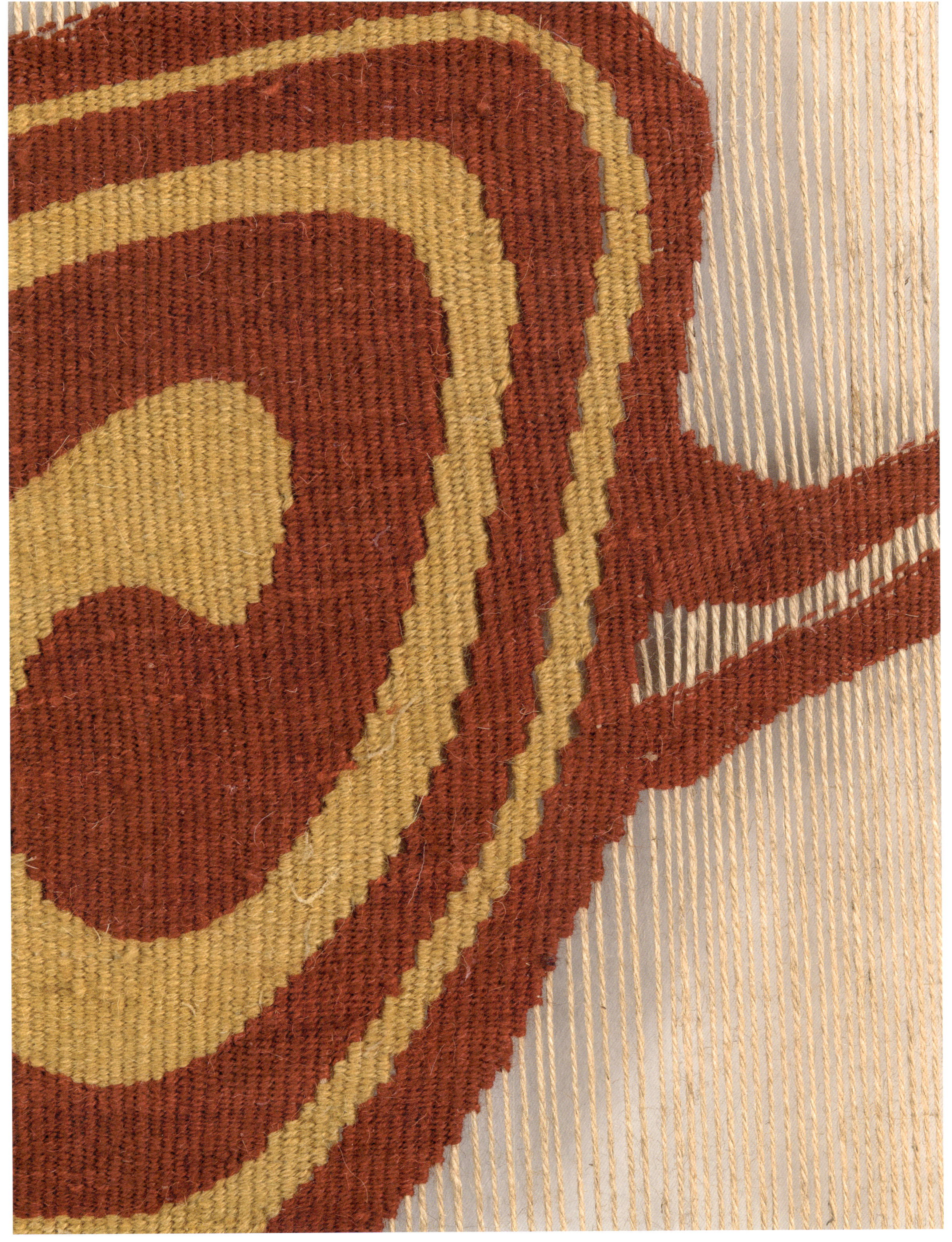

Balloon, 2014, 170 x 140 cm,
private collection

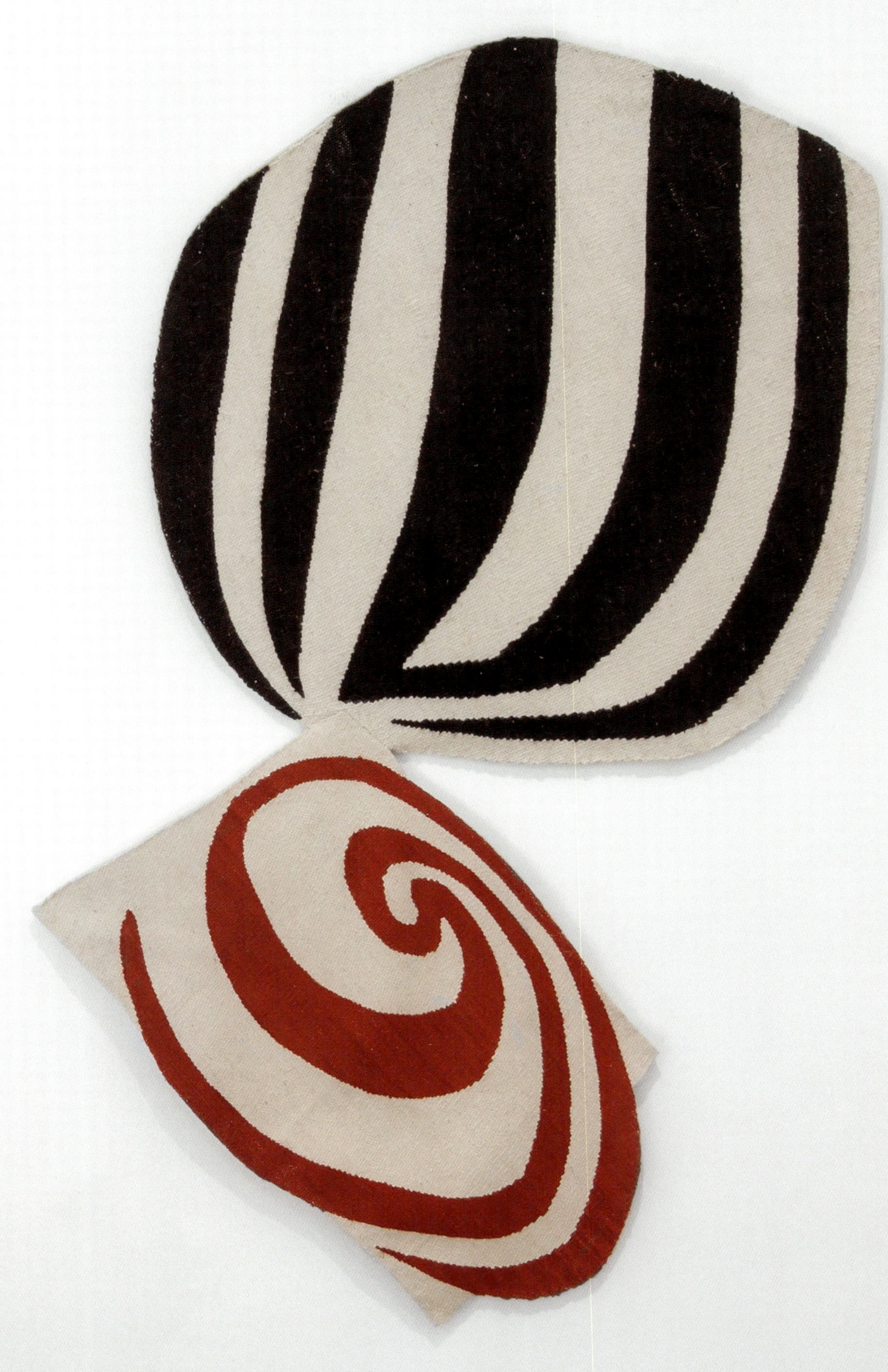

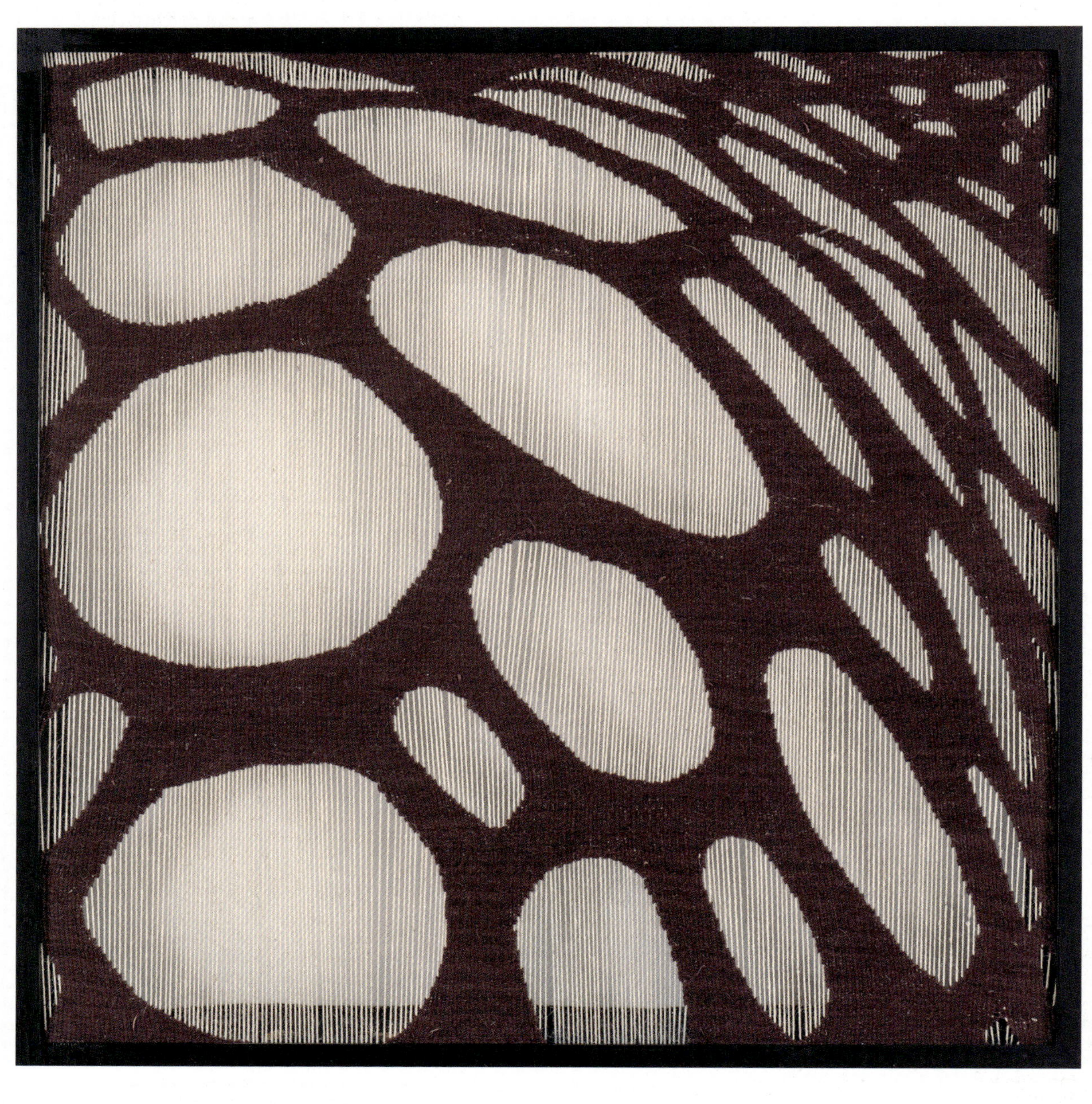

Expansion, 2014, 110 x 124 cm,
private collection

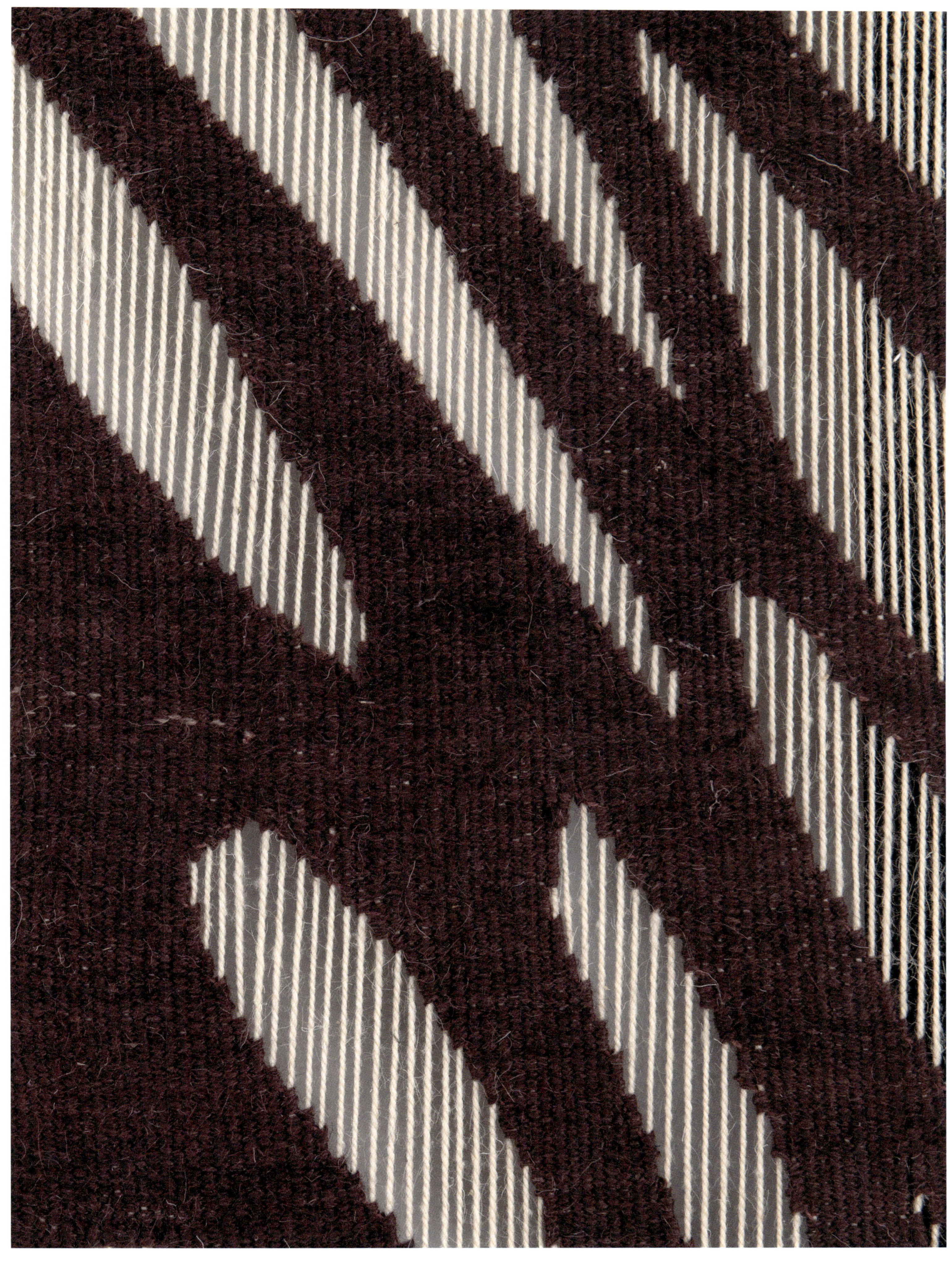

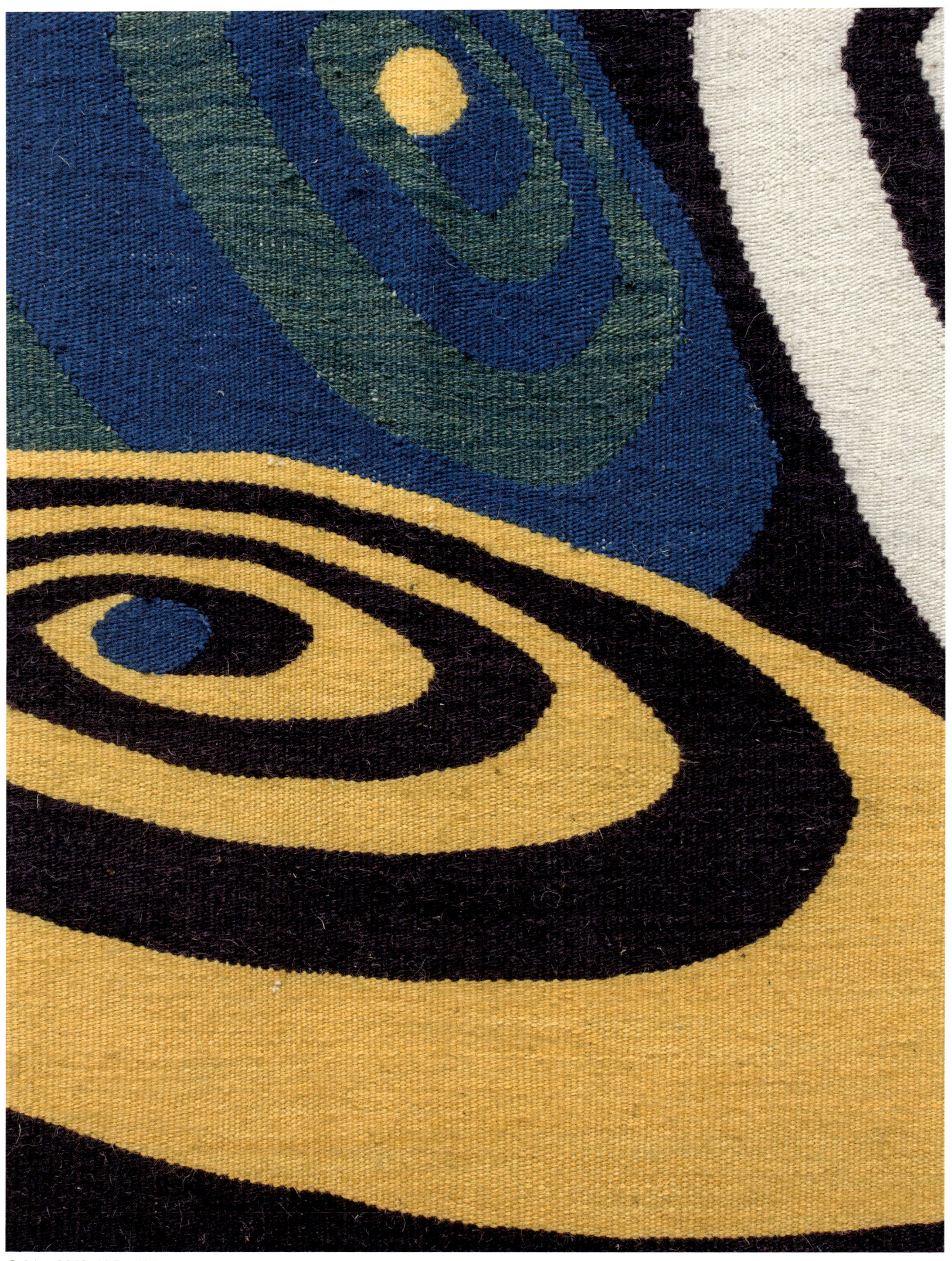

Orbits, 2016, 135 x 124 cm,
private collection

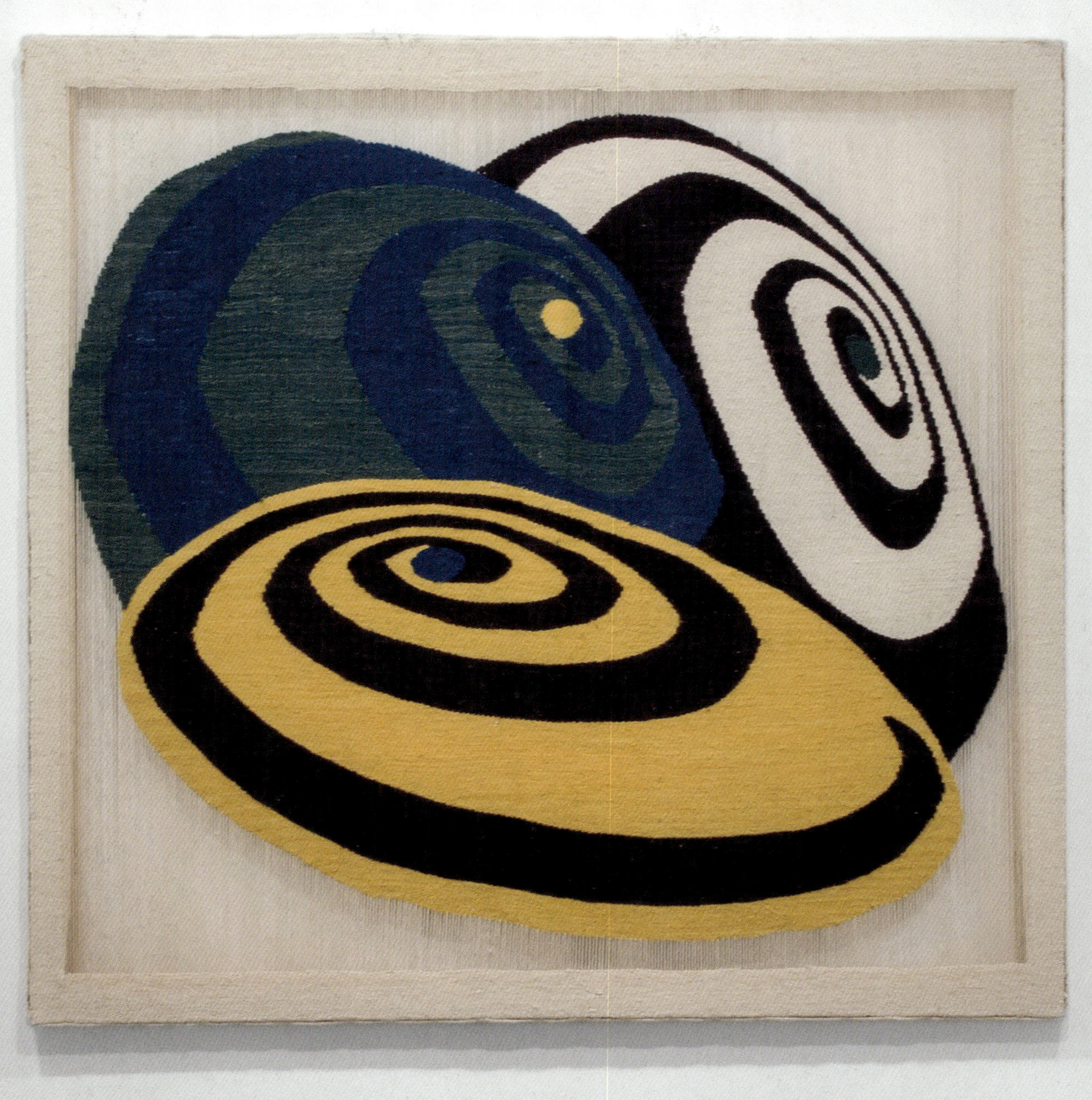

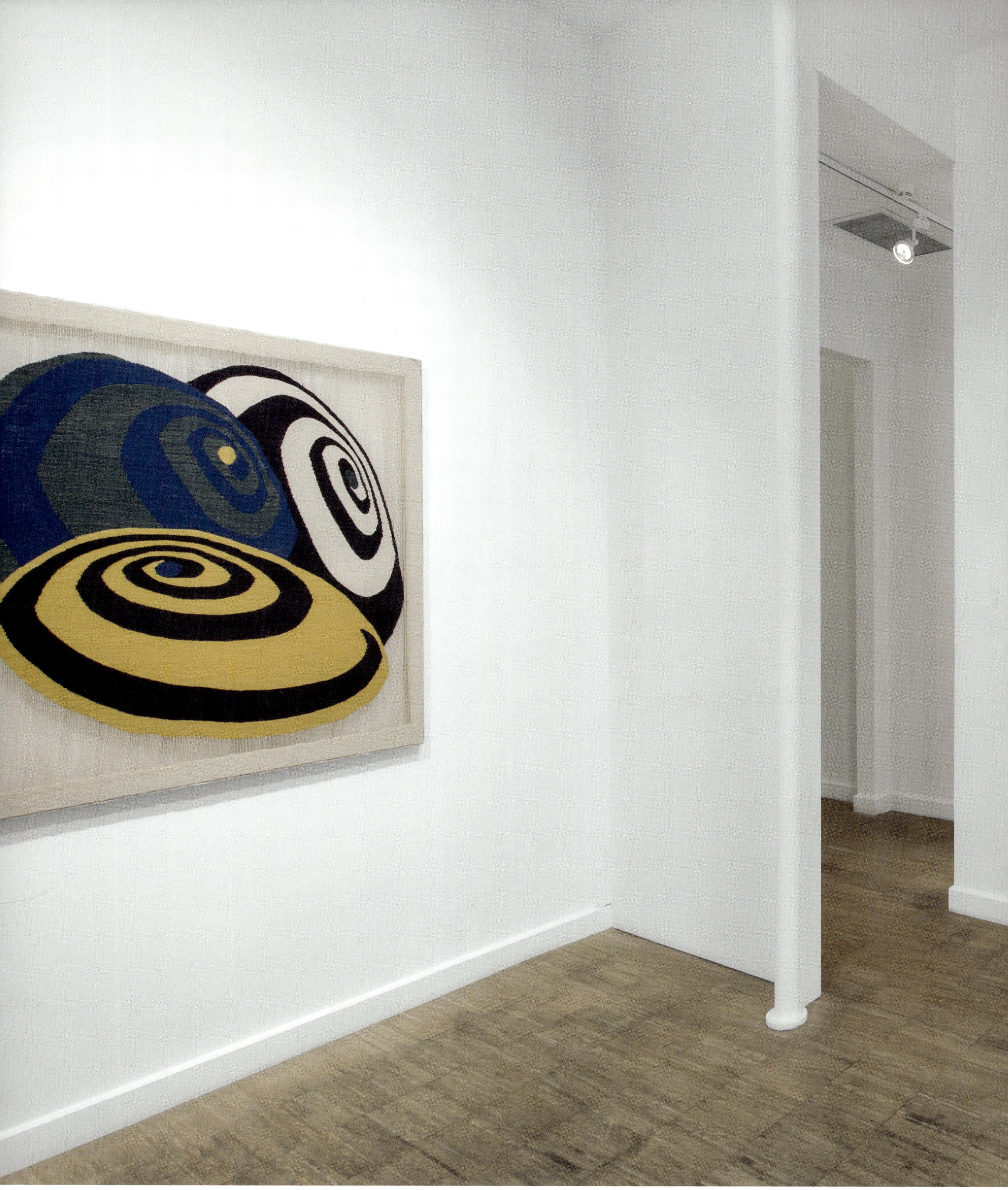

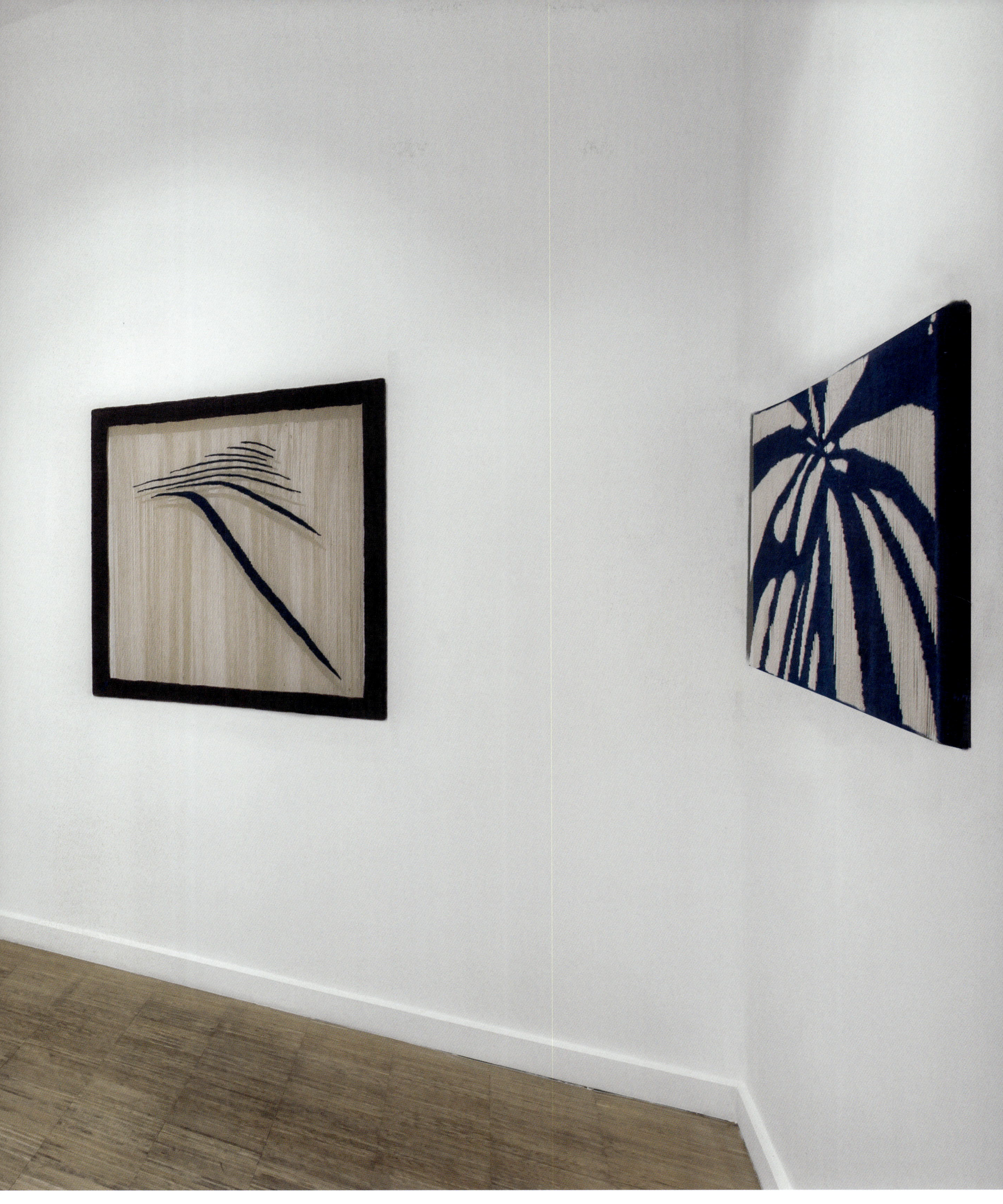

Neurons-2, 2016, 97 x 116 cm,
Anna Laudel Gallery

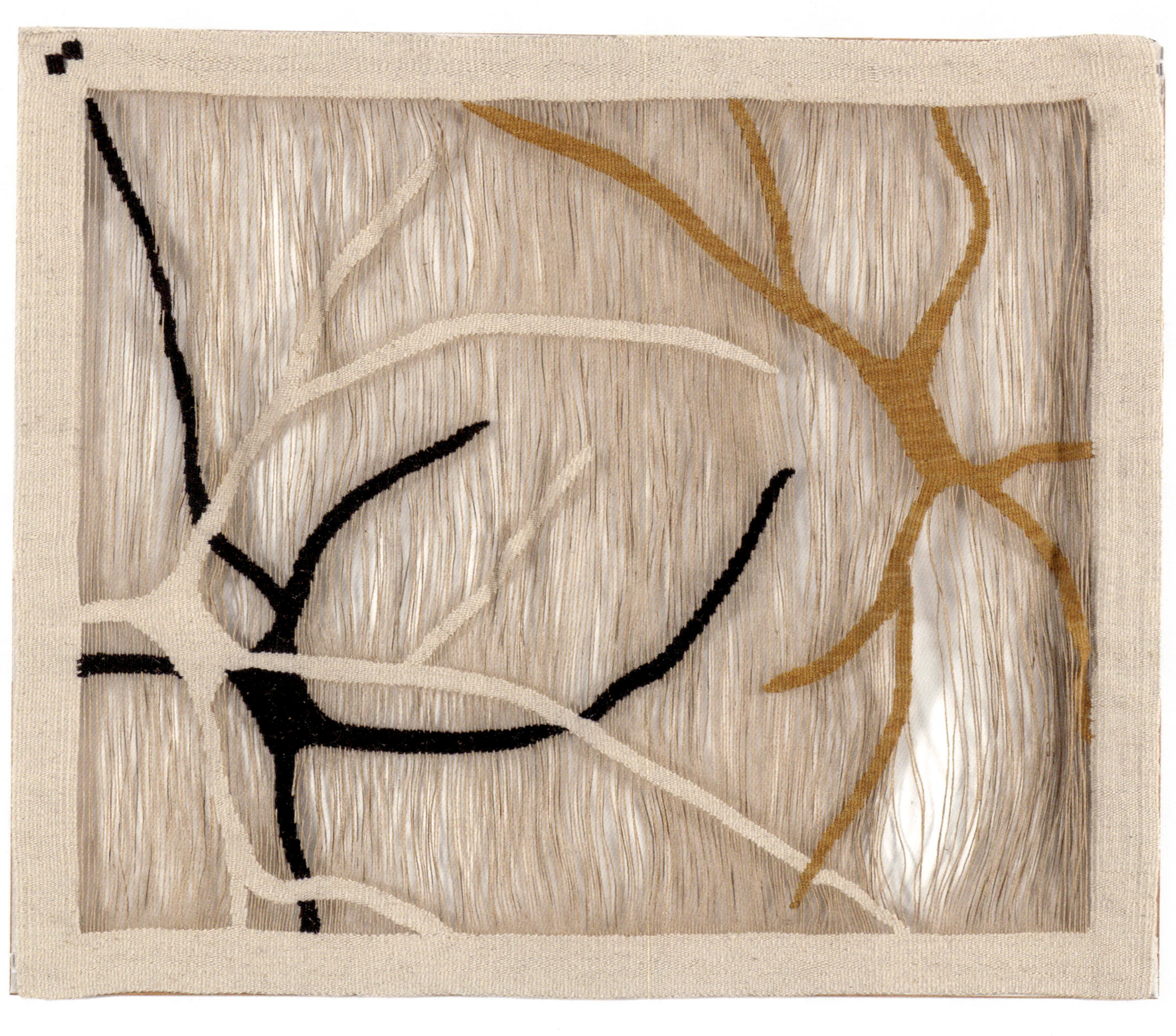

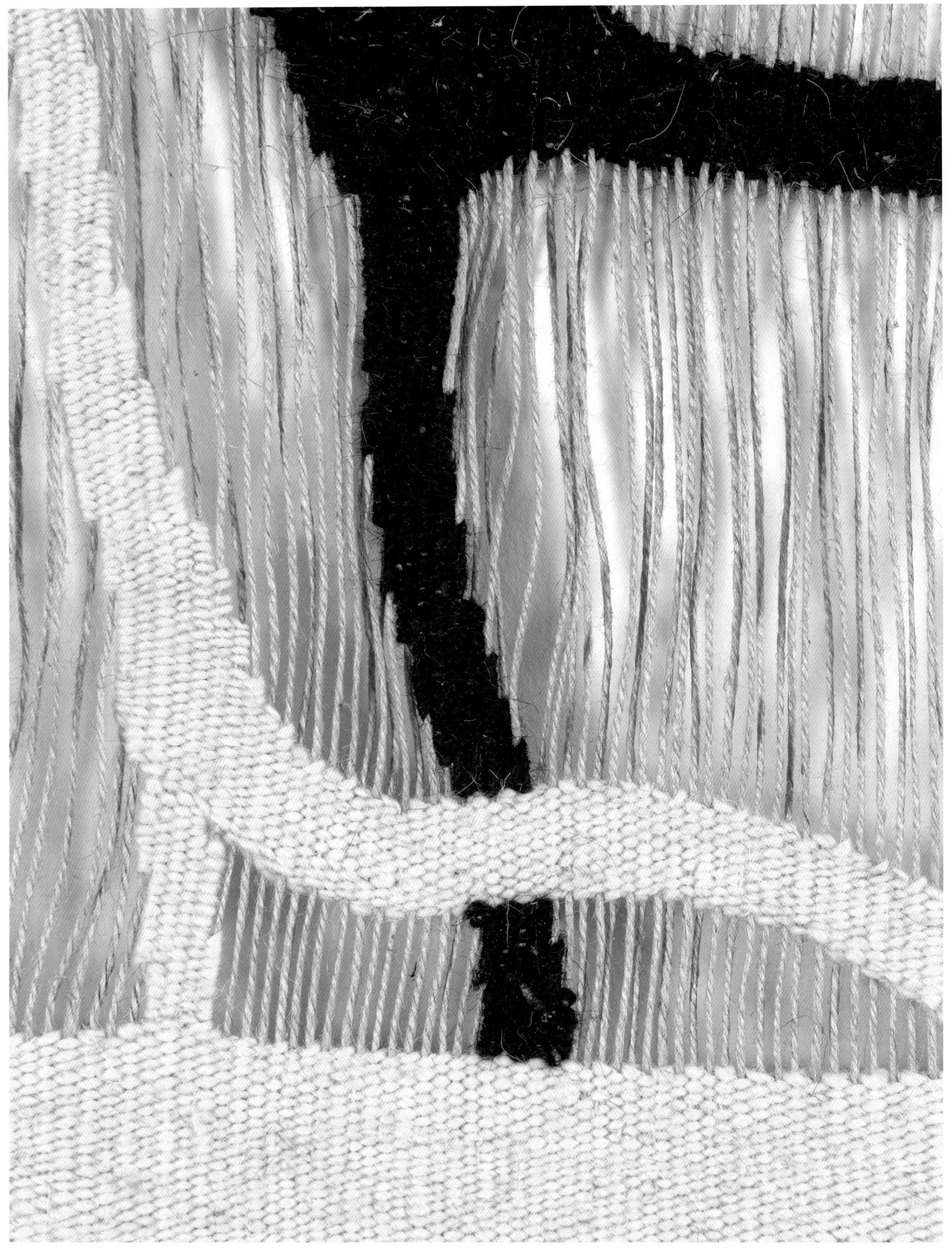

Archipelago

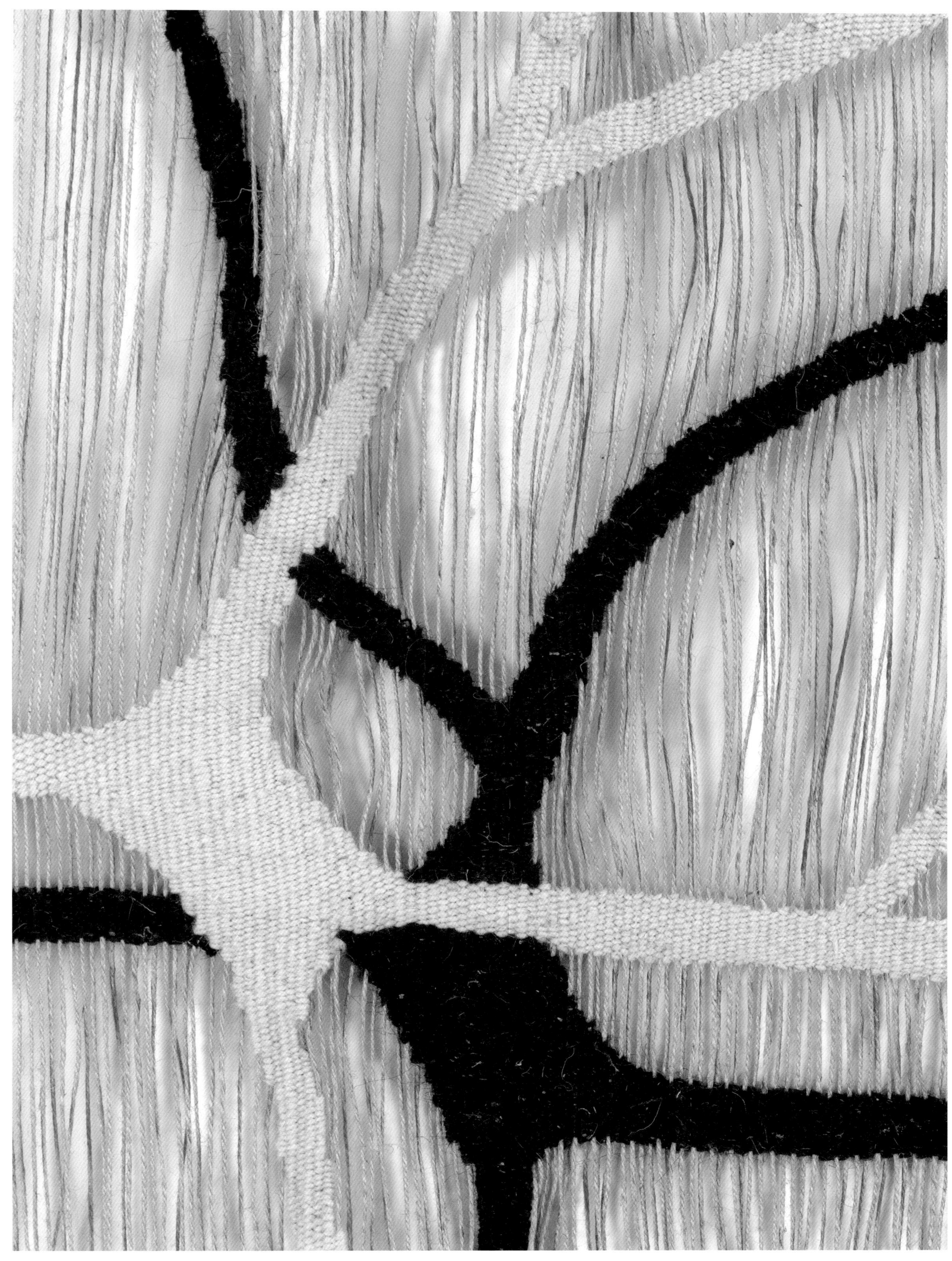

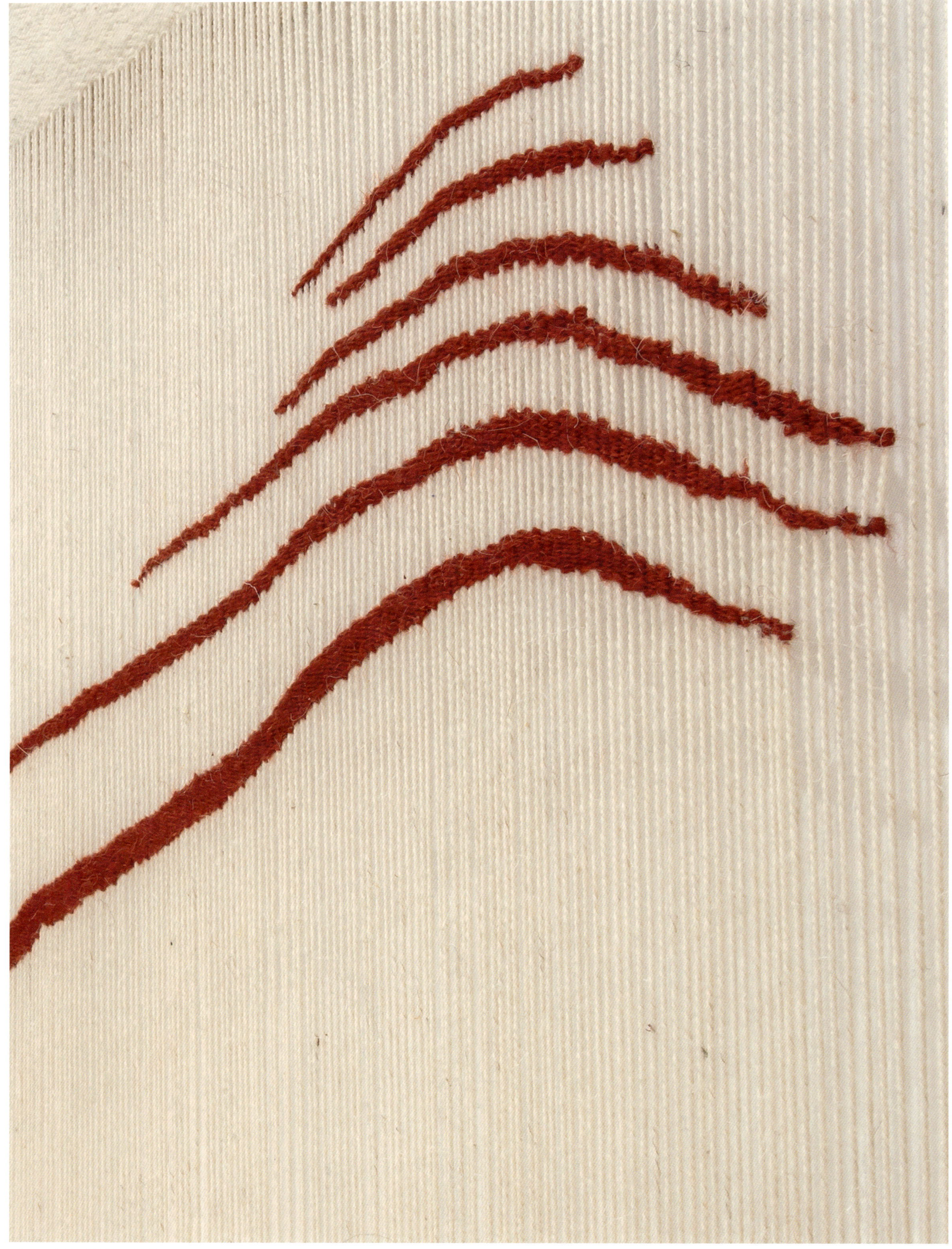

Flow-4, 2017, 75 x 120 cm,
private collection

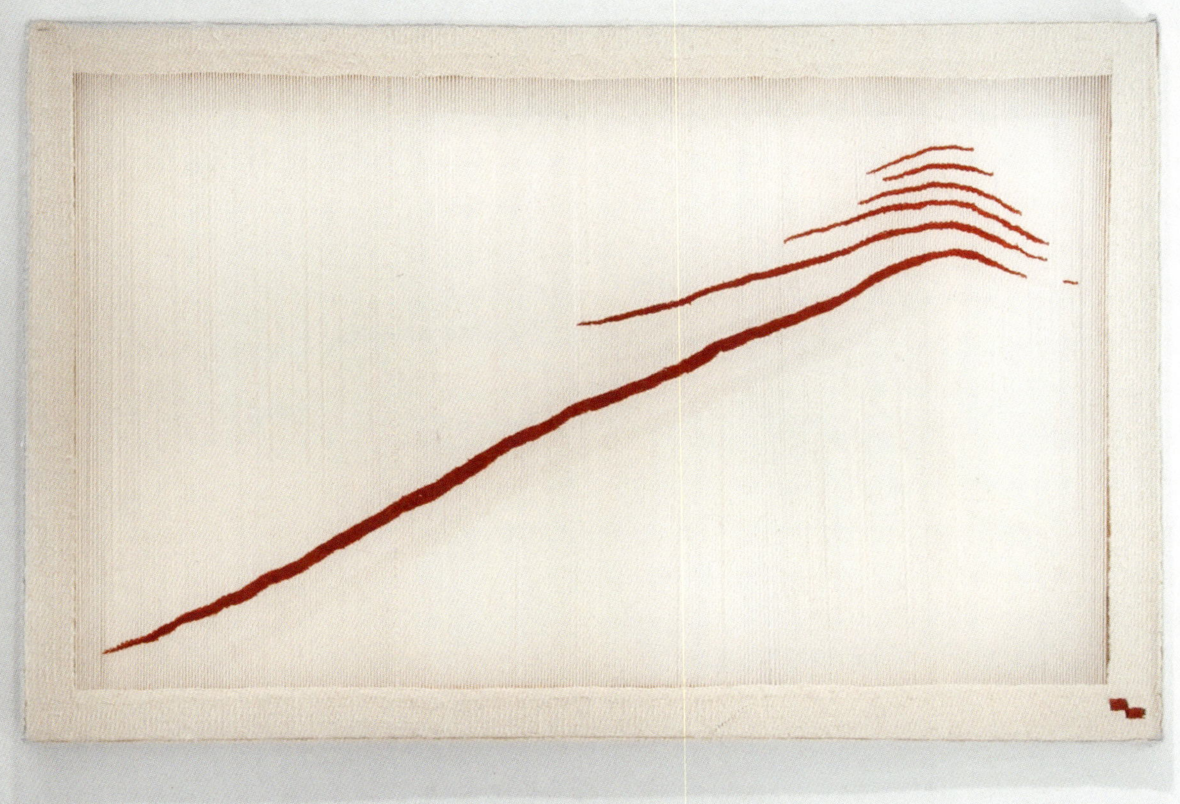

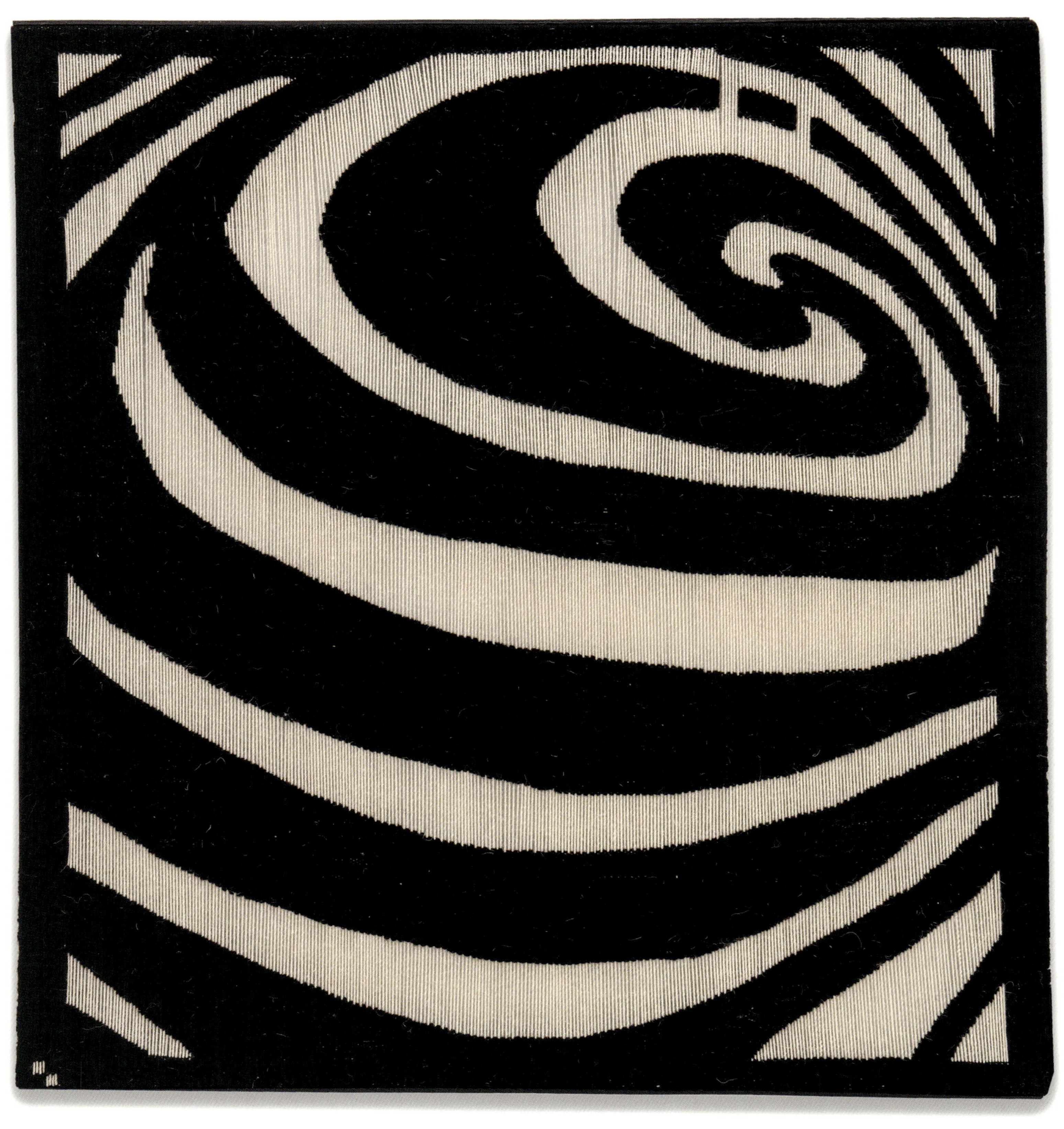

Eye-1 and 2, 2019, 130 x 130 cm,
private collection

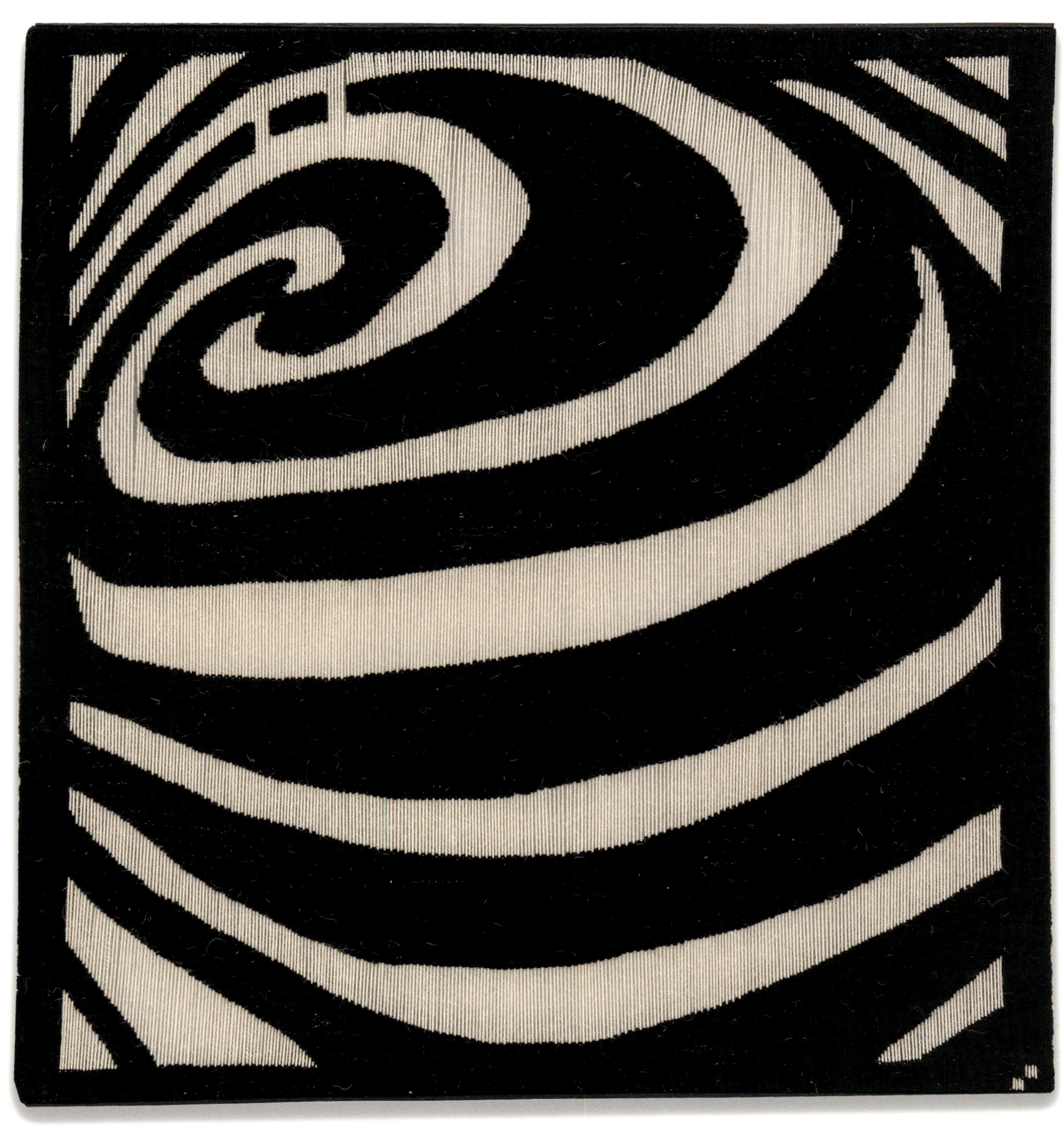

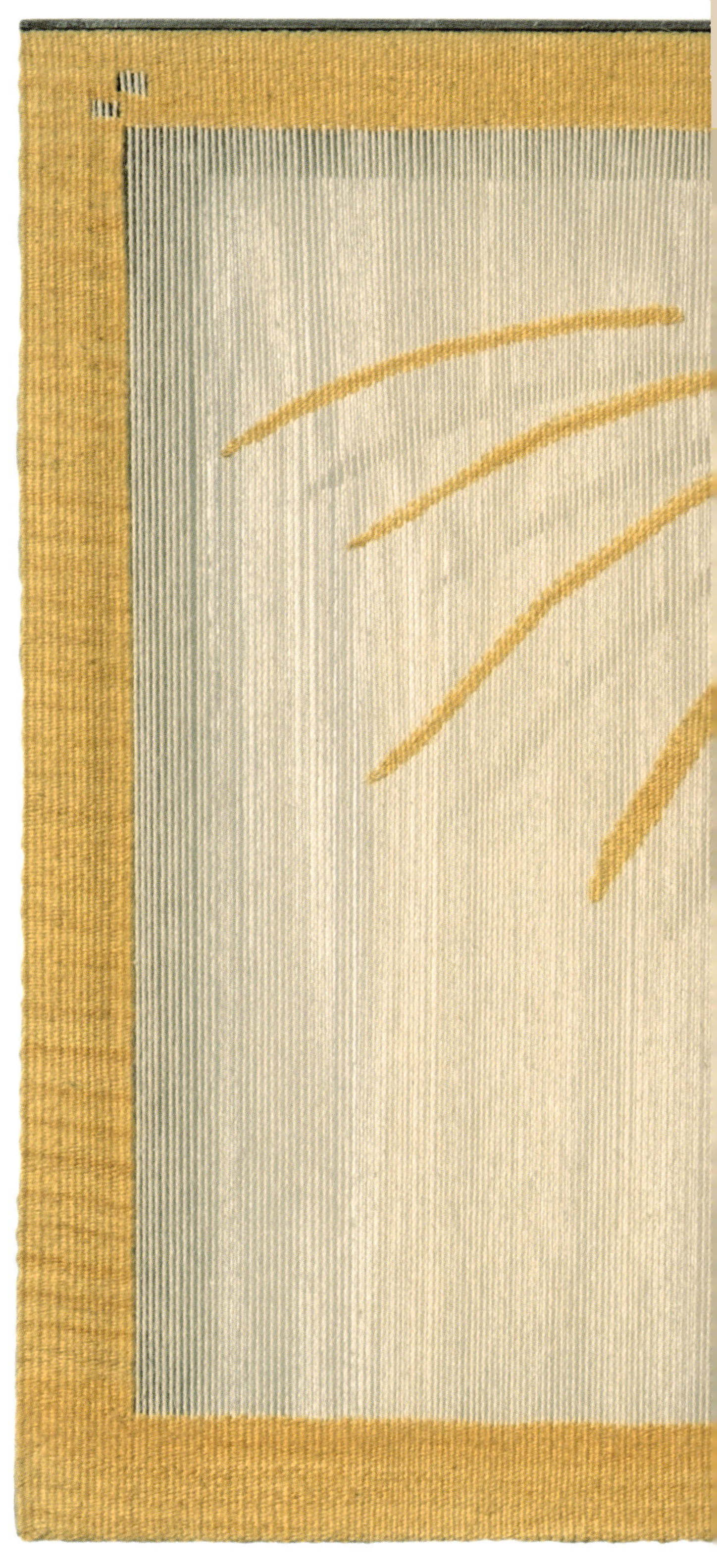

Whirling Sun, 2020, 135 x 85 cm,
private collection

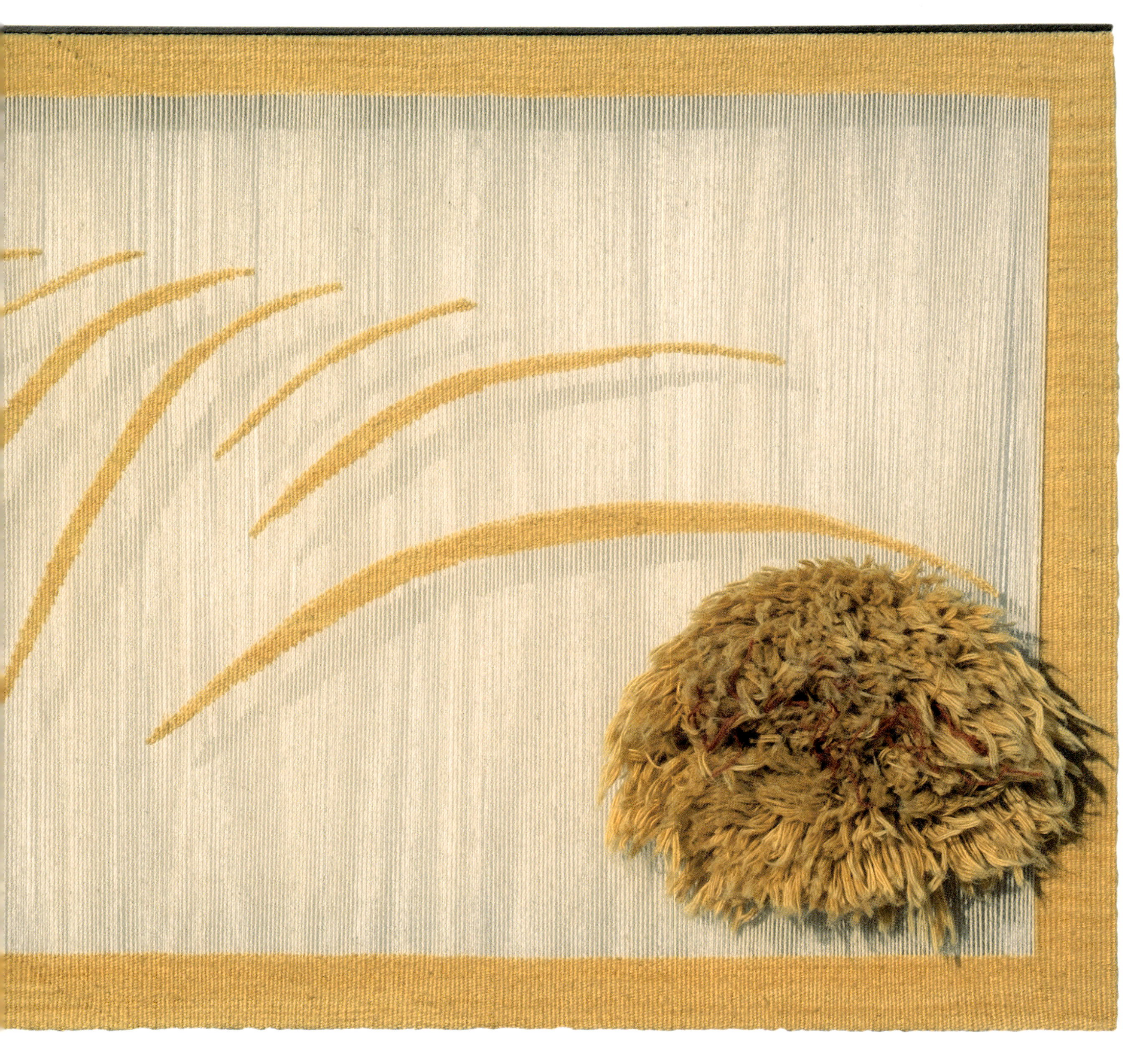

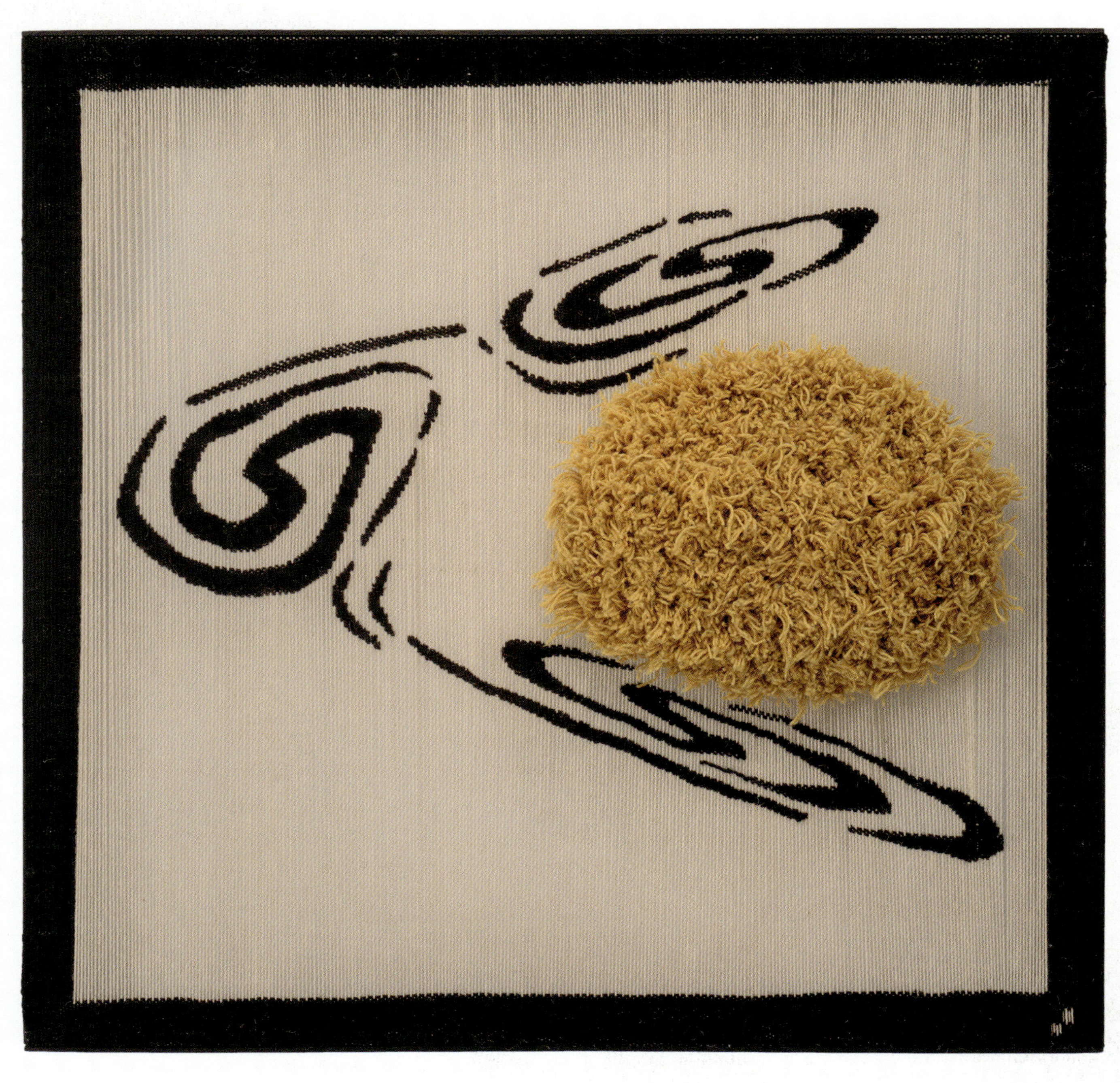

Galaxies and Sun, 2021, 114 x 120 cm,
private collection

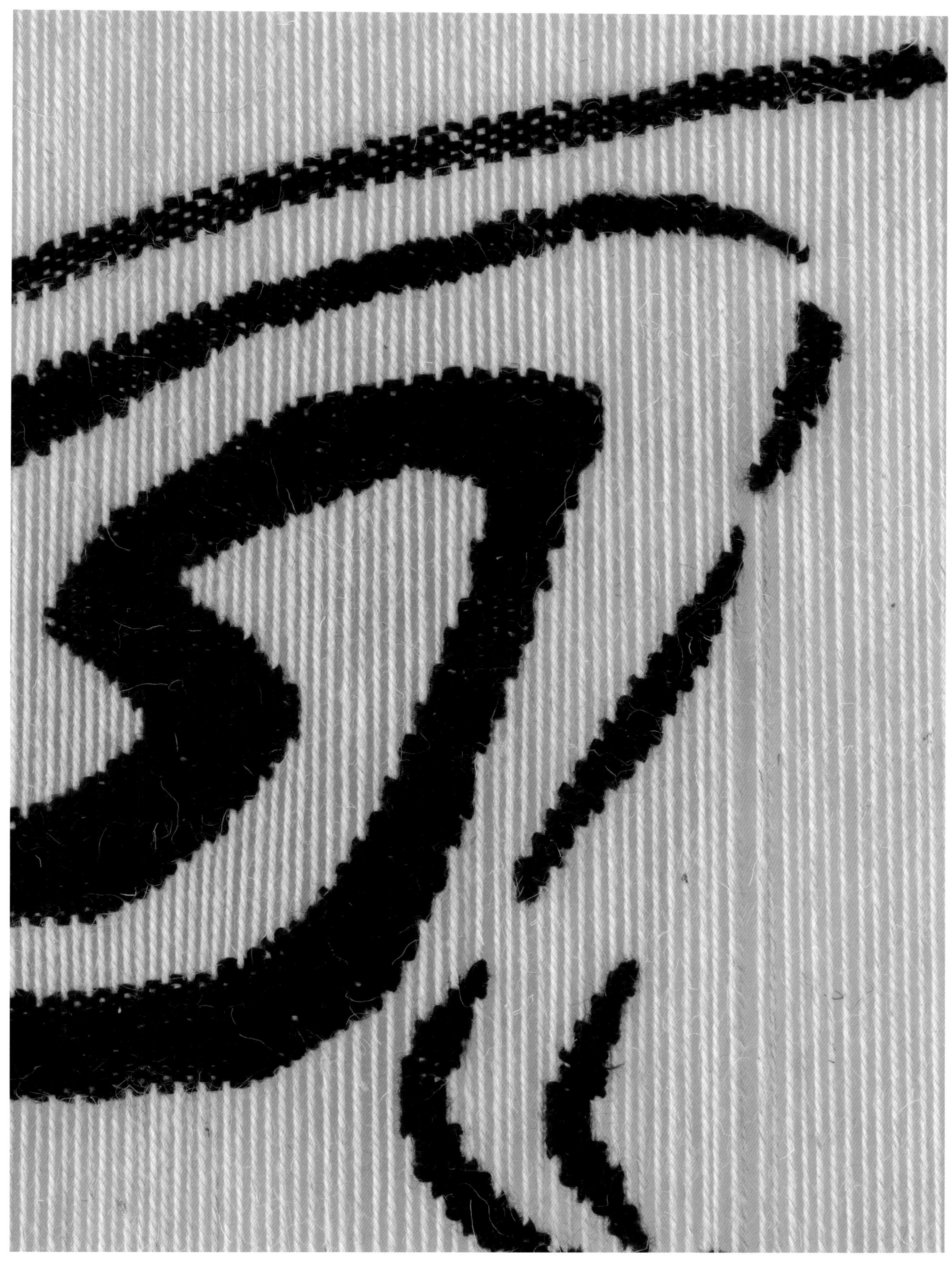

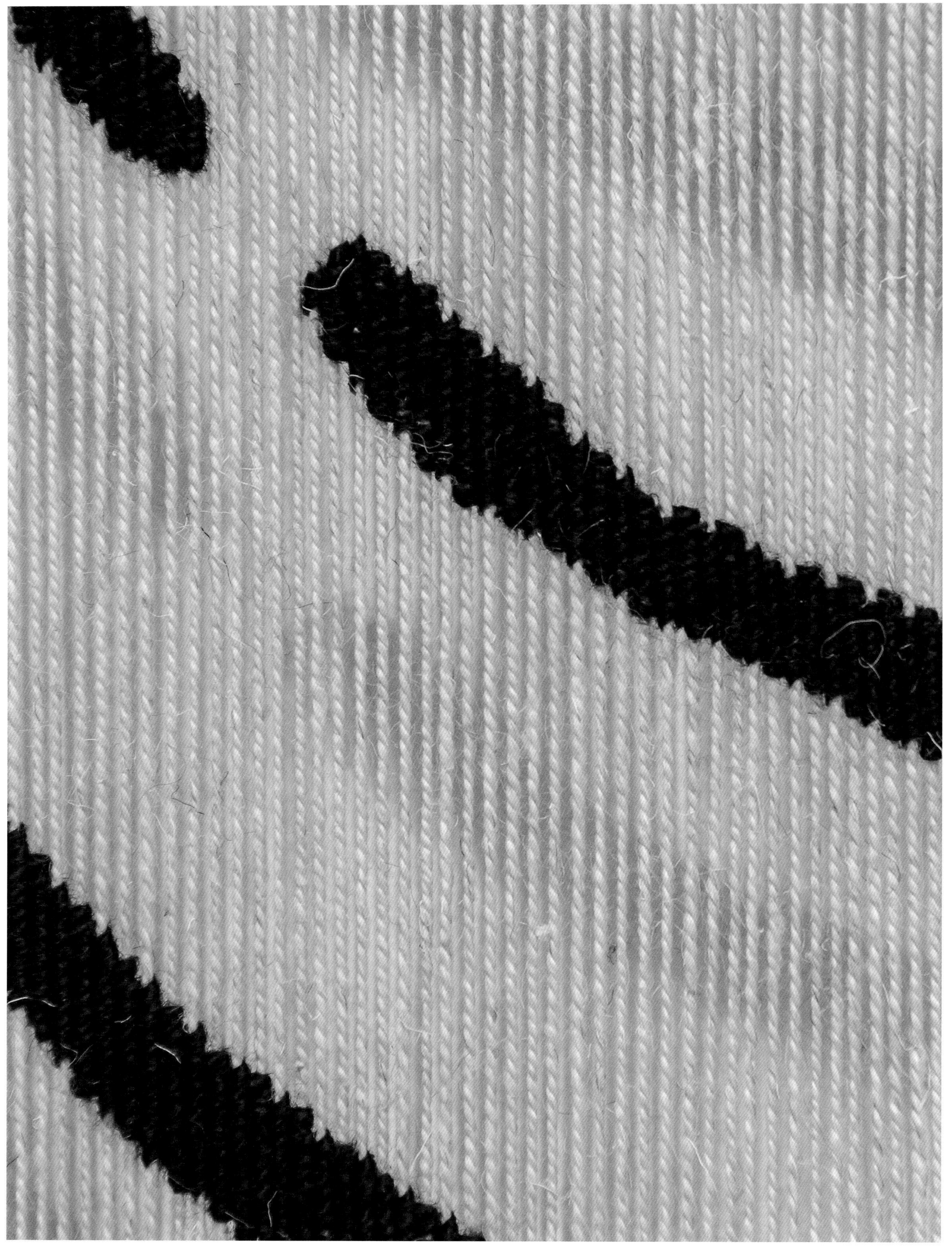

Archipelago

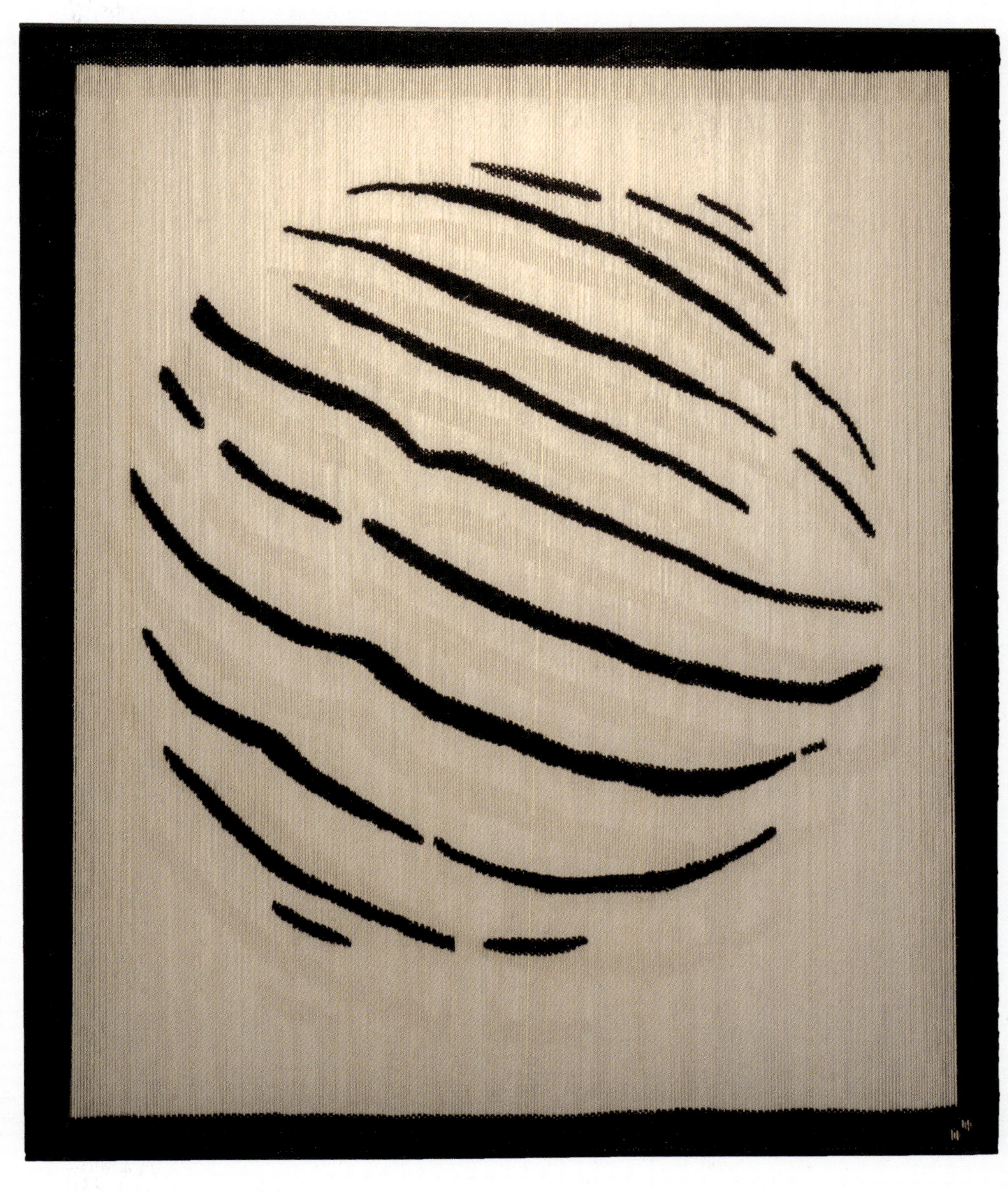

Planet-3, 2021, 138.5 x 120.5 cm,
Anna Laudel Gallery

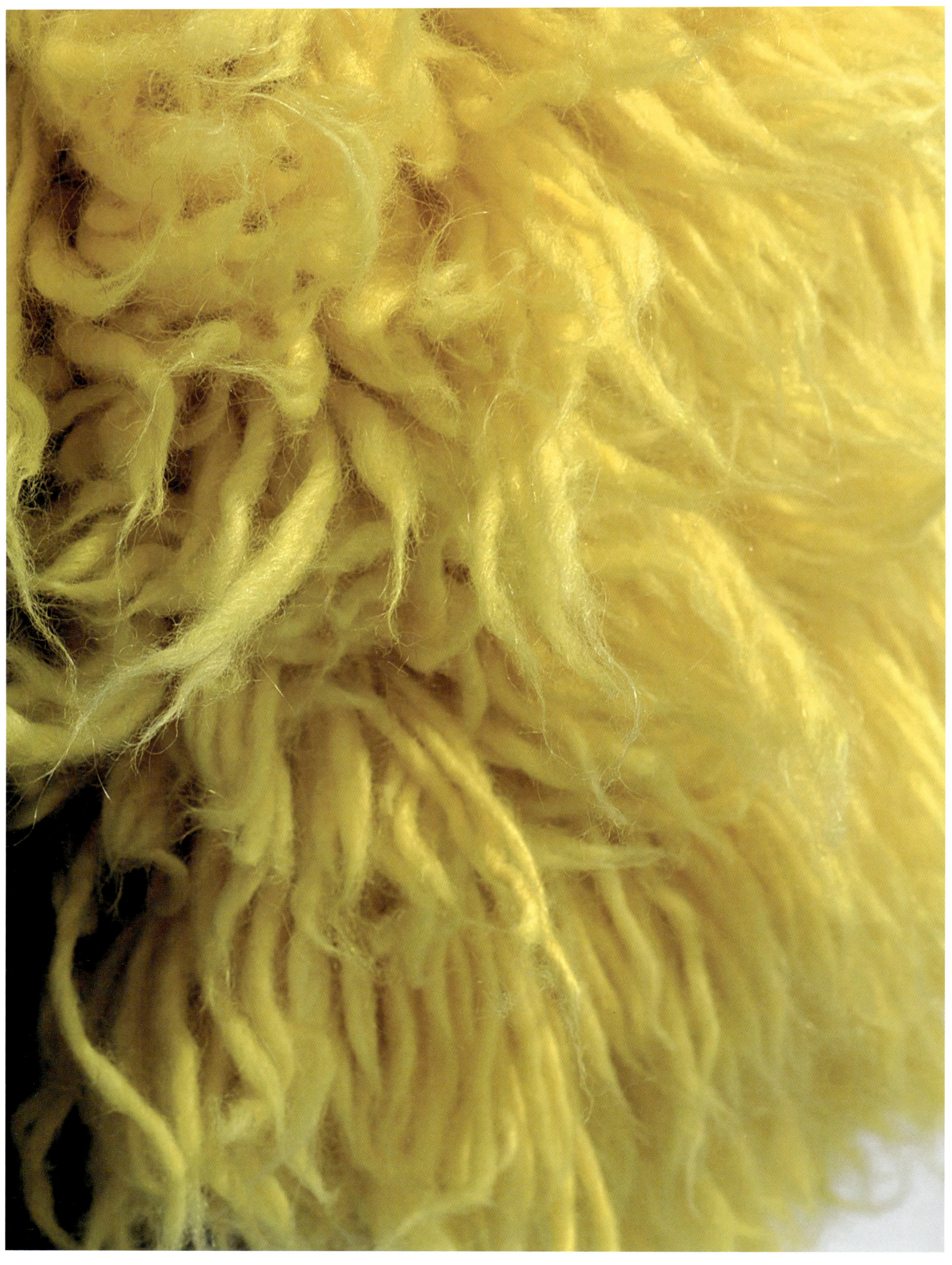

Archipelago

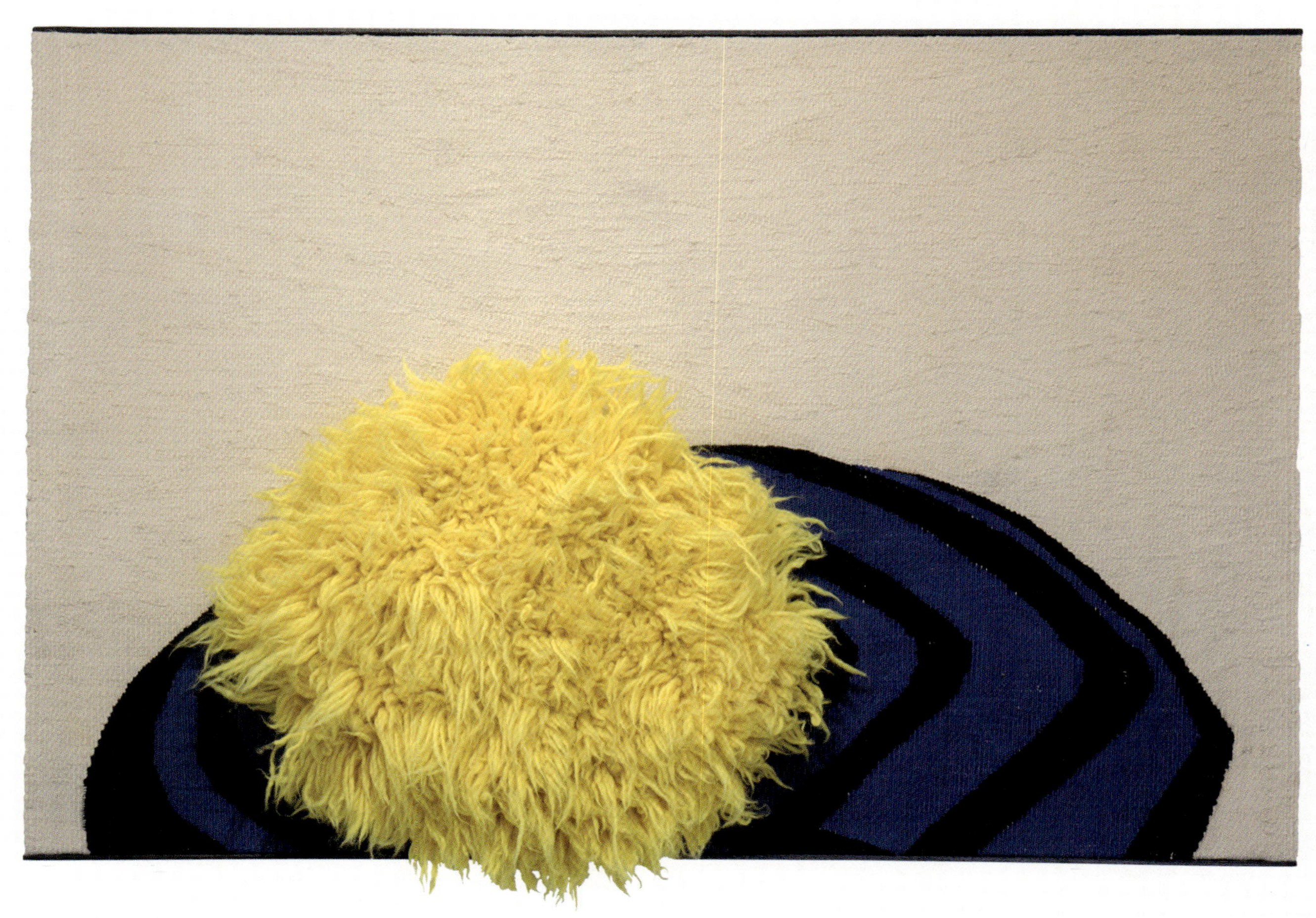

Sunrise, 2022, 80.5 x 125 cm,
Anna Laudel Gallery

Untitled, 2022, 250 x 110 cm,
Anna Laudel Gallery

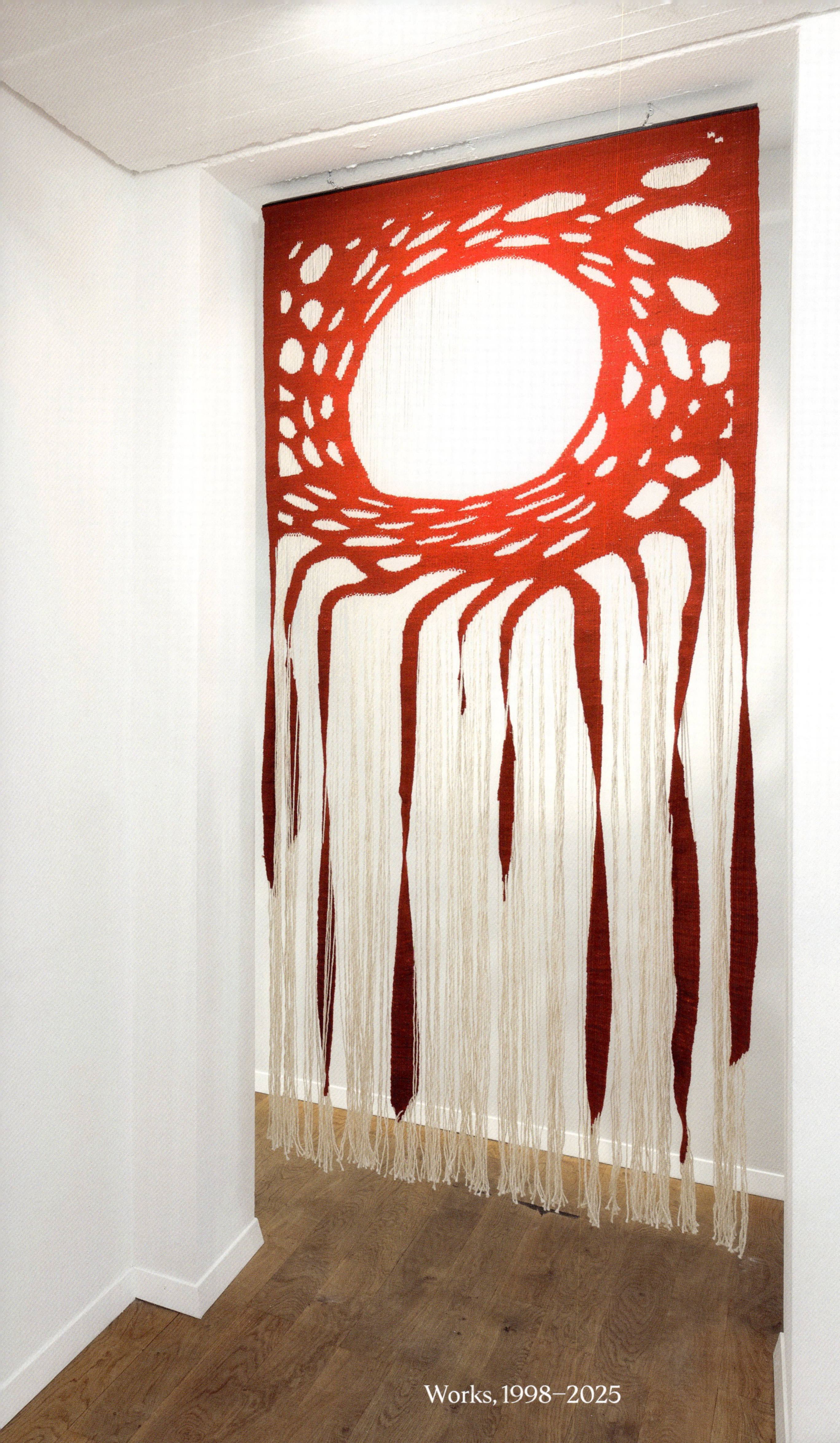

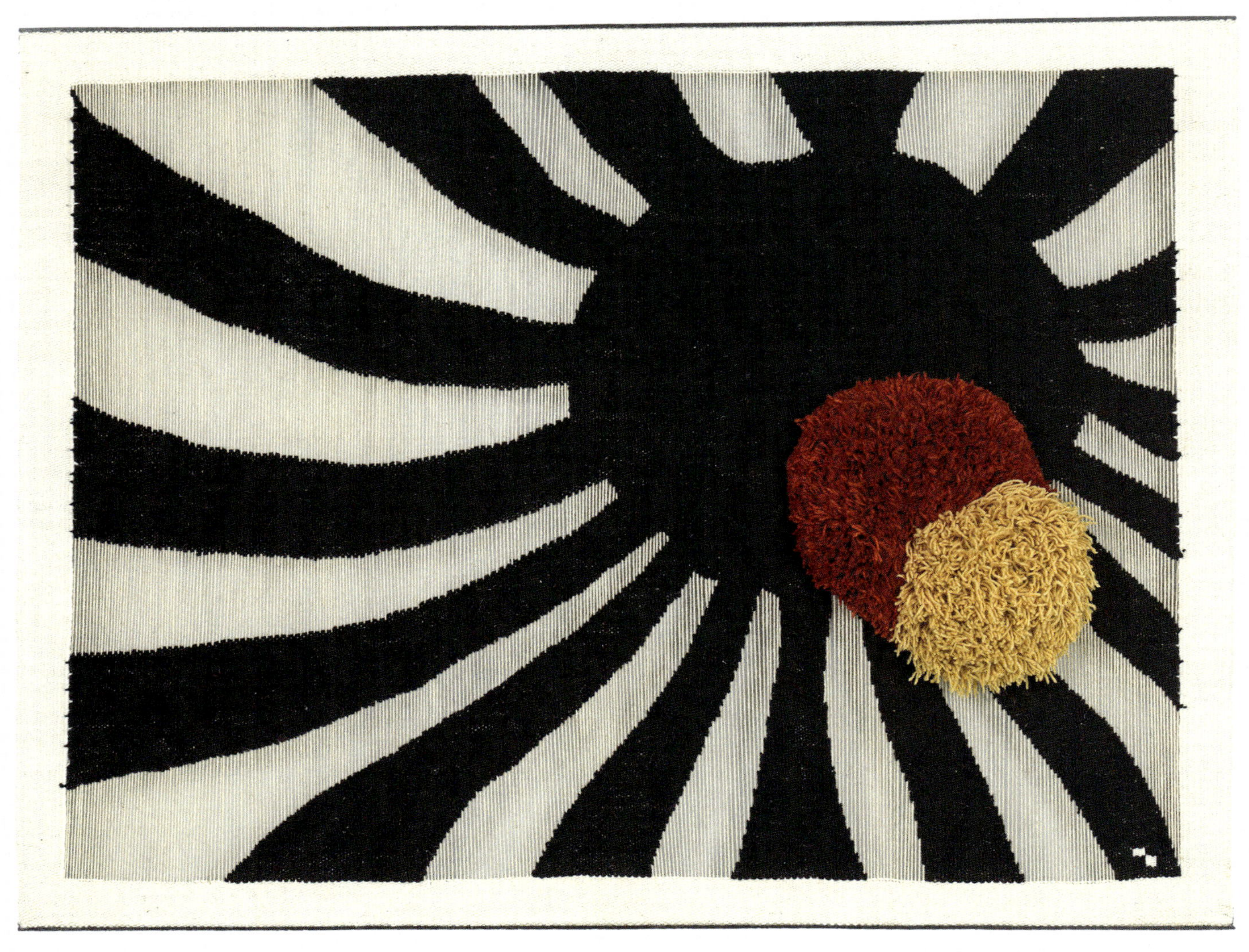

Escape from the Black Hole, 2022, 130 x 140 cm

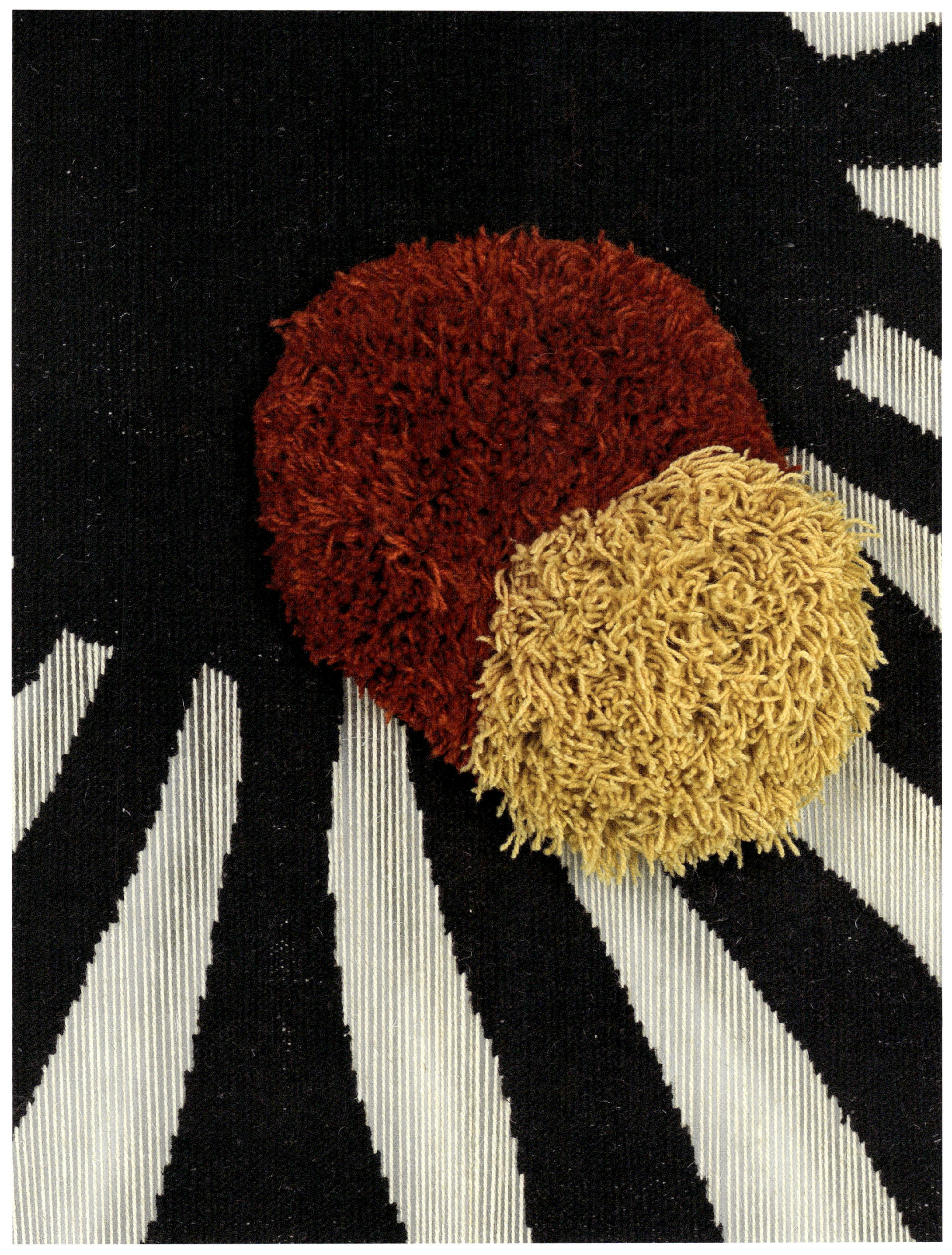

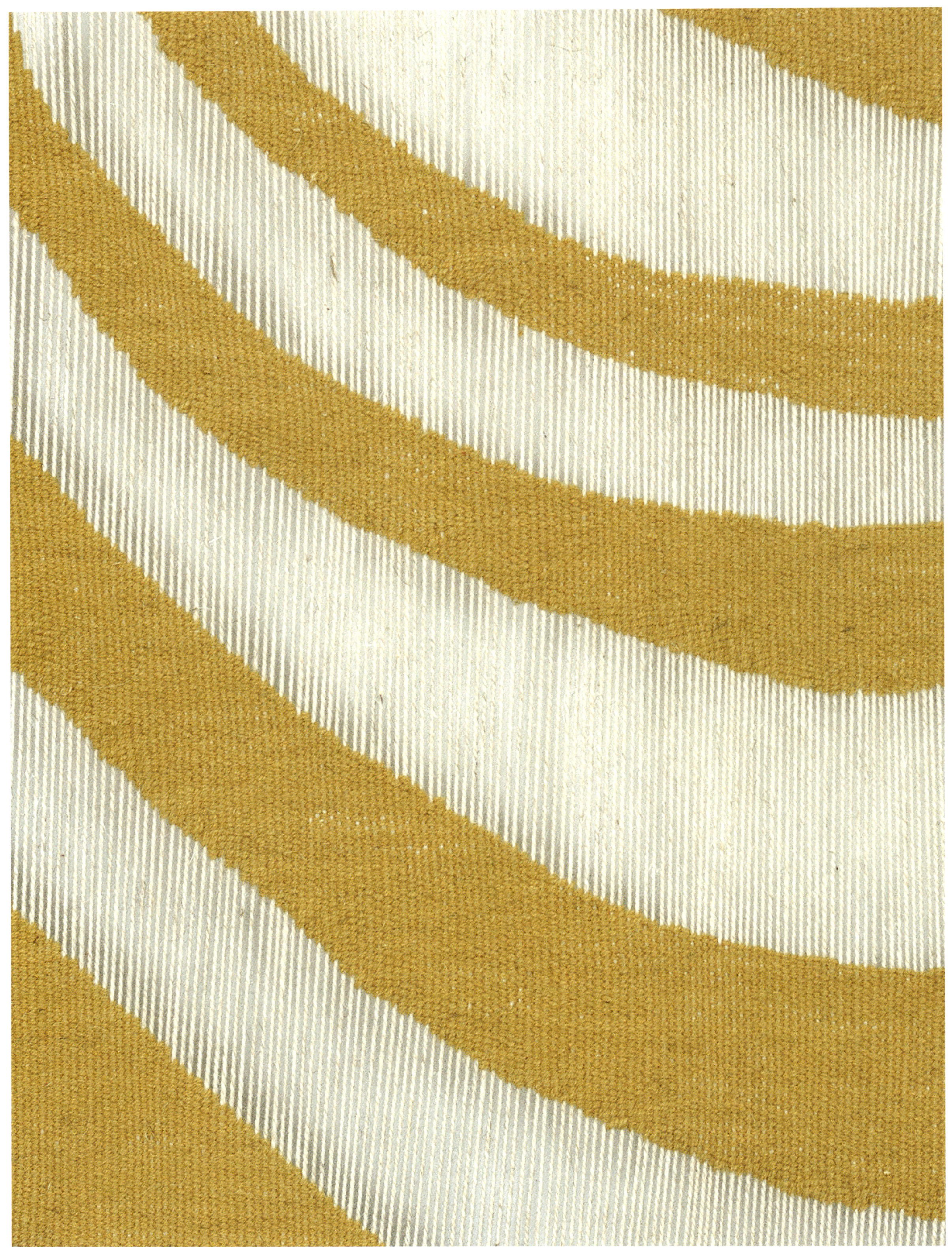

Archipelago

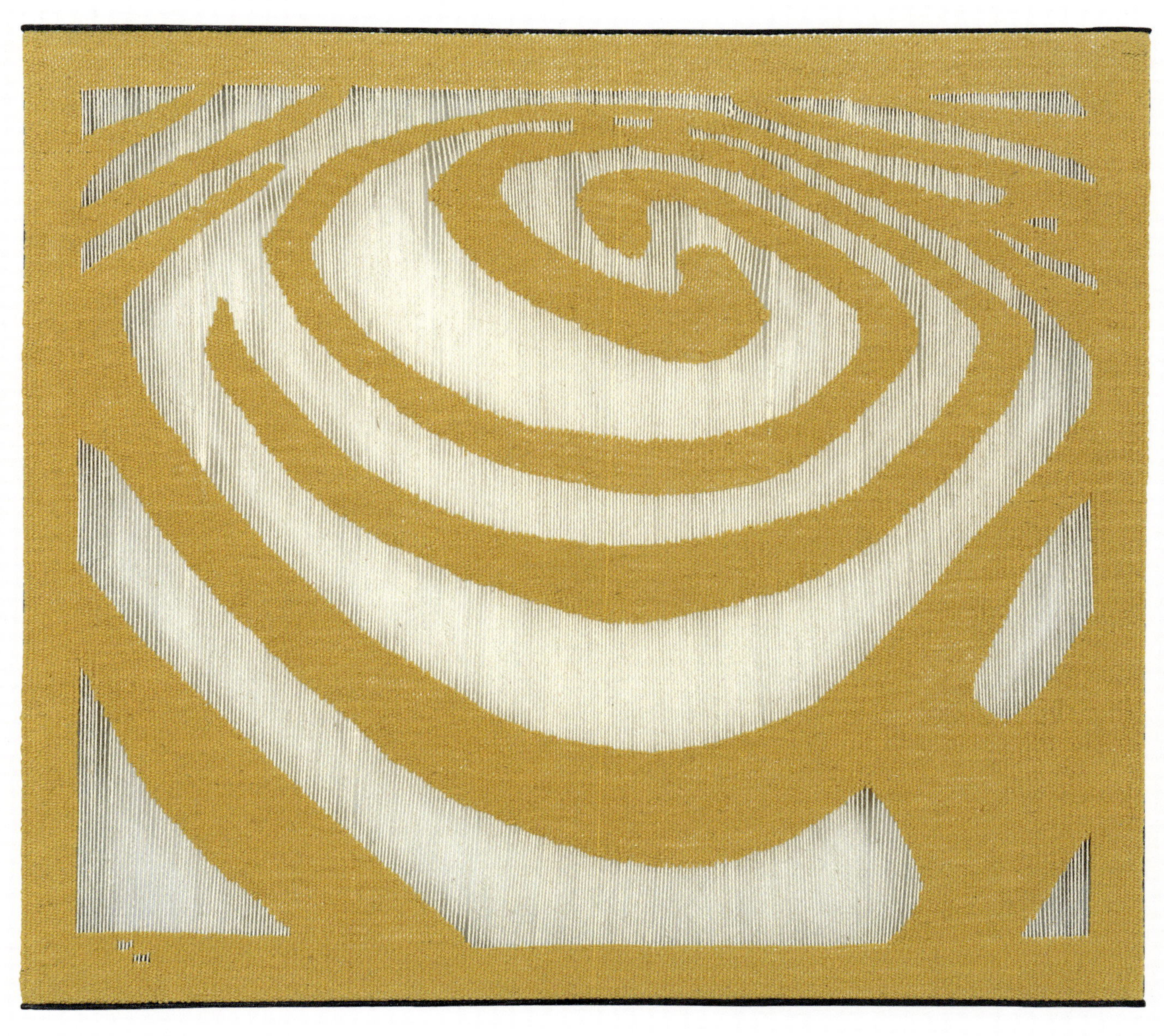

Melting-3, 2022, 92 x 111 cm,
Anna Laudel Gallery

Flowing Time, 2022, 240 x 140 cm,
Anna Laudel Gallery

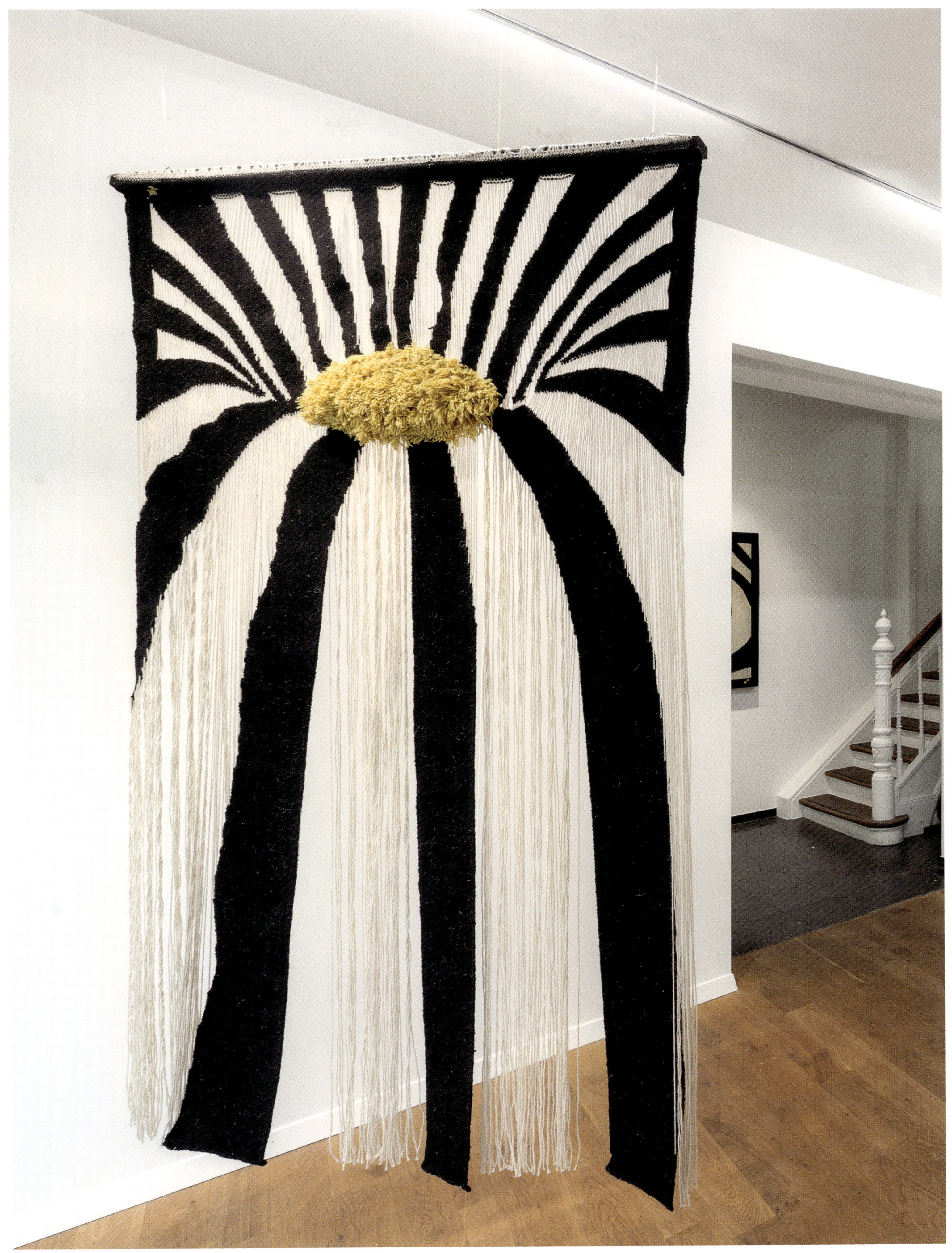

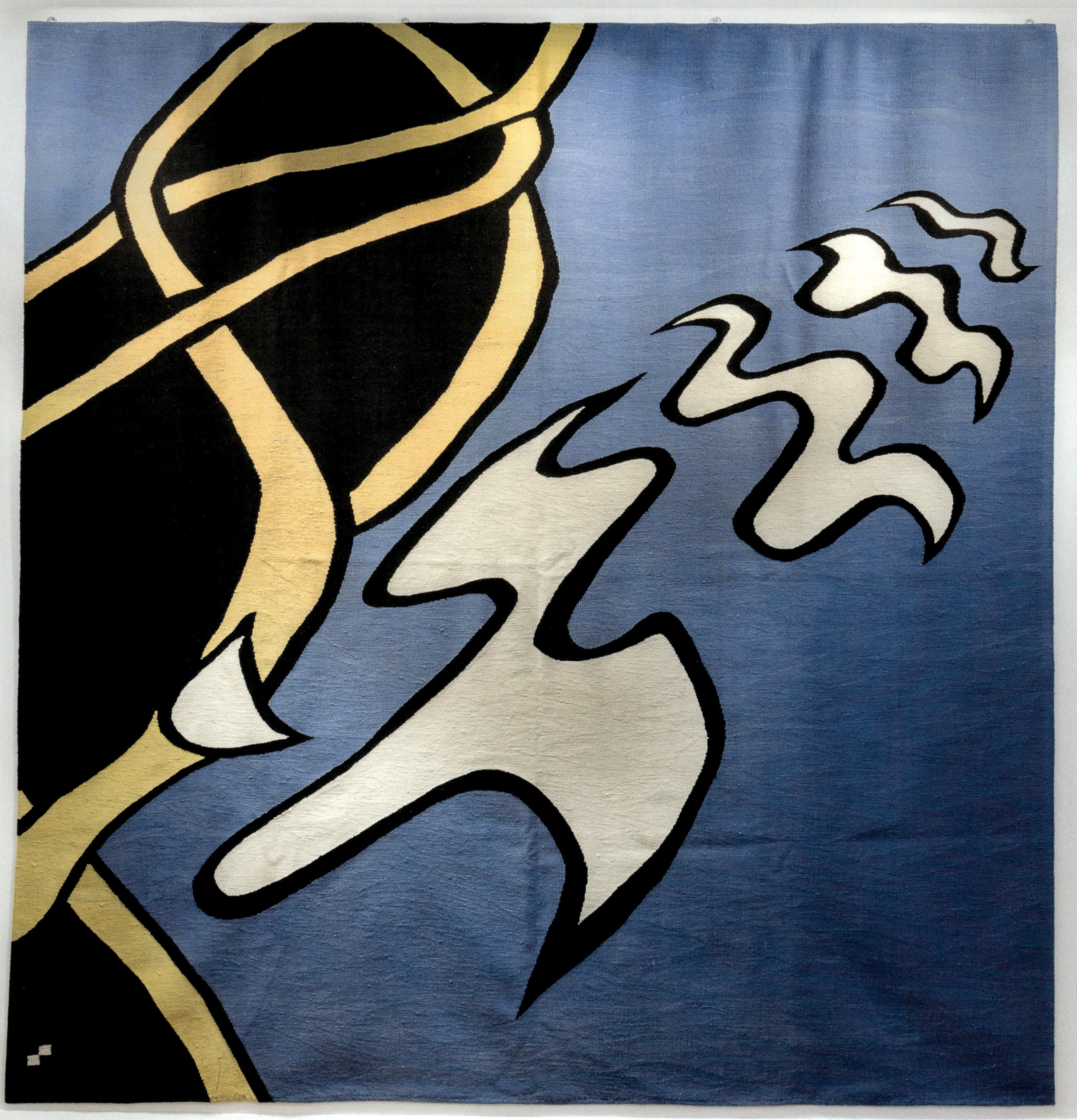

Dive, 2022, 308 x 304 cm,
Anna Laudel Gallery

Time Plane-2, 2022, 130 x 140 cm,
Anna Laudel Gallery

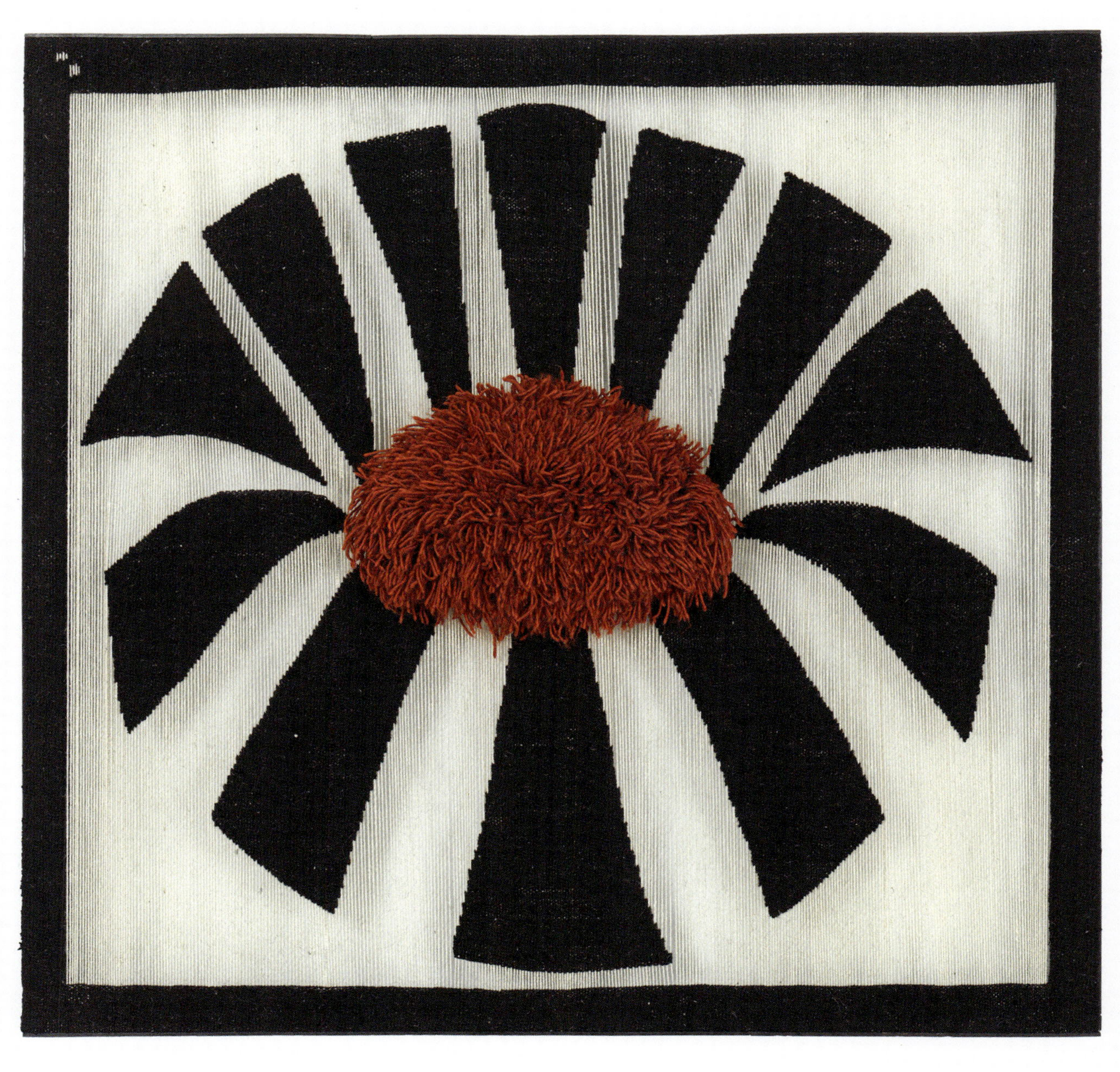

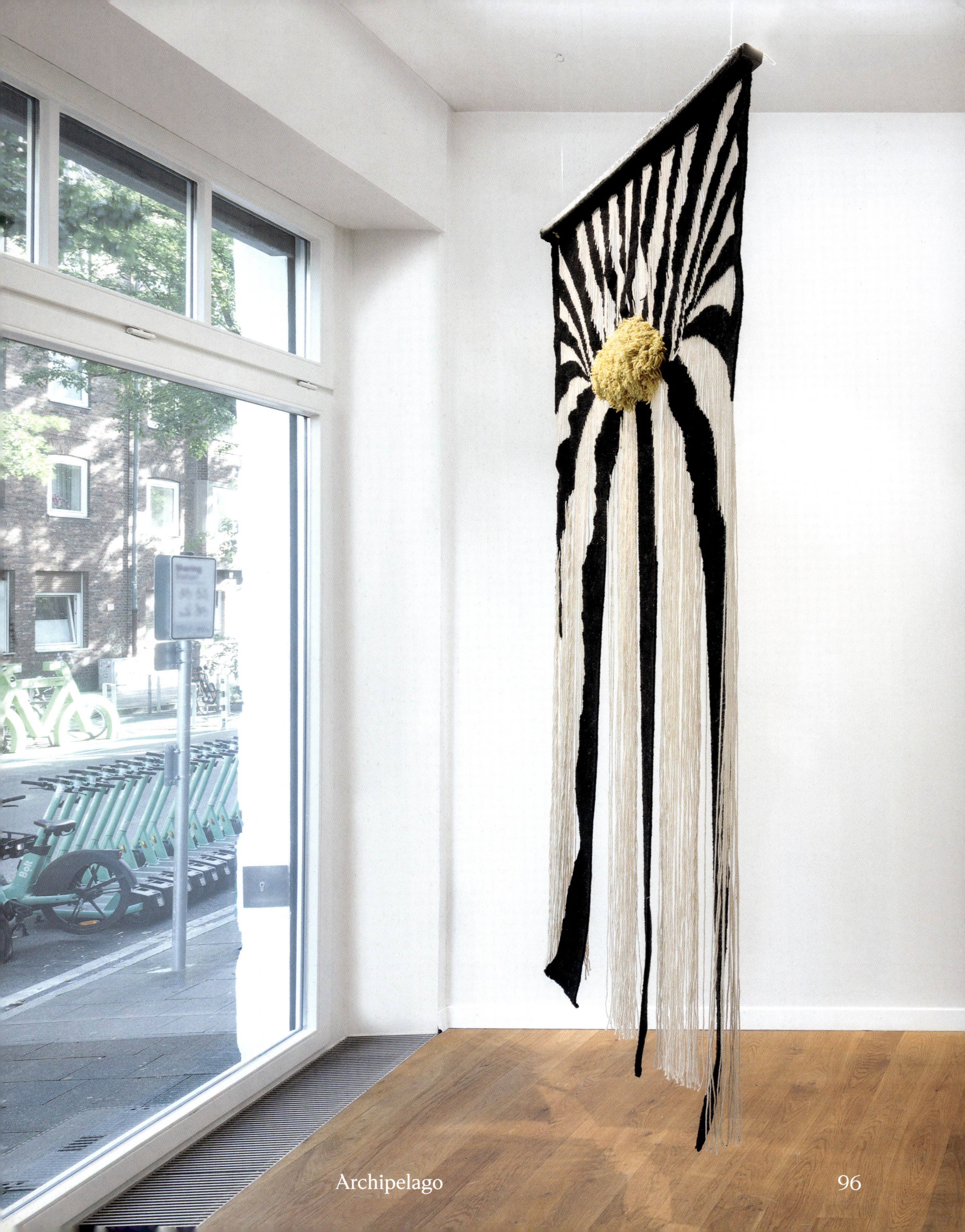

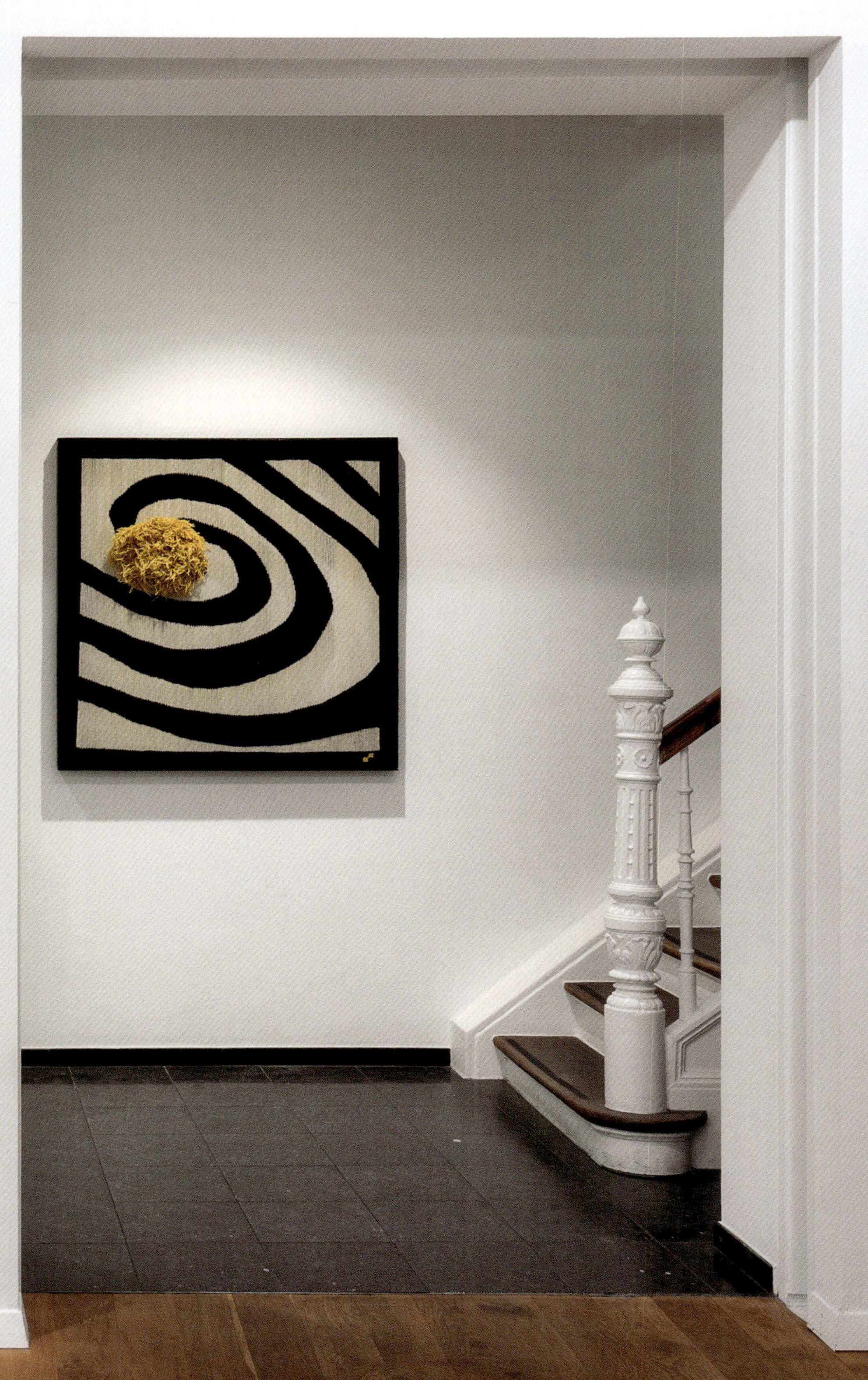

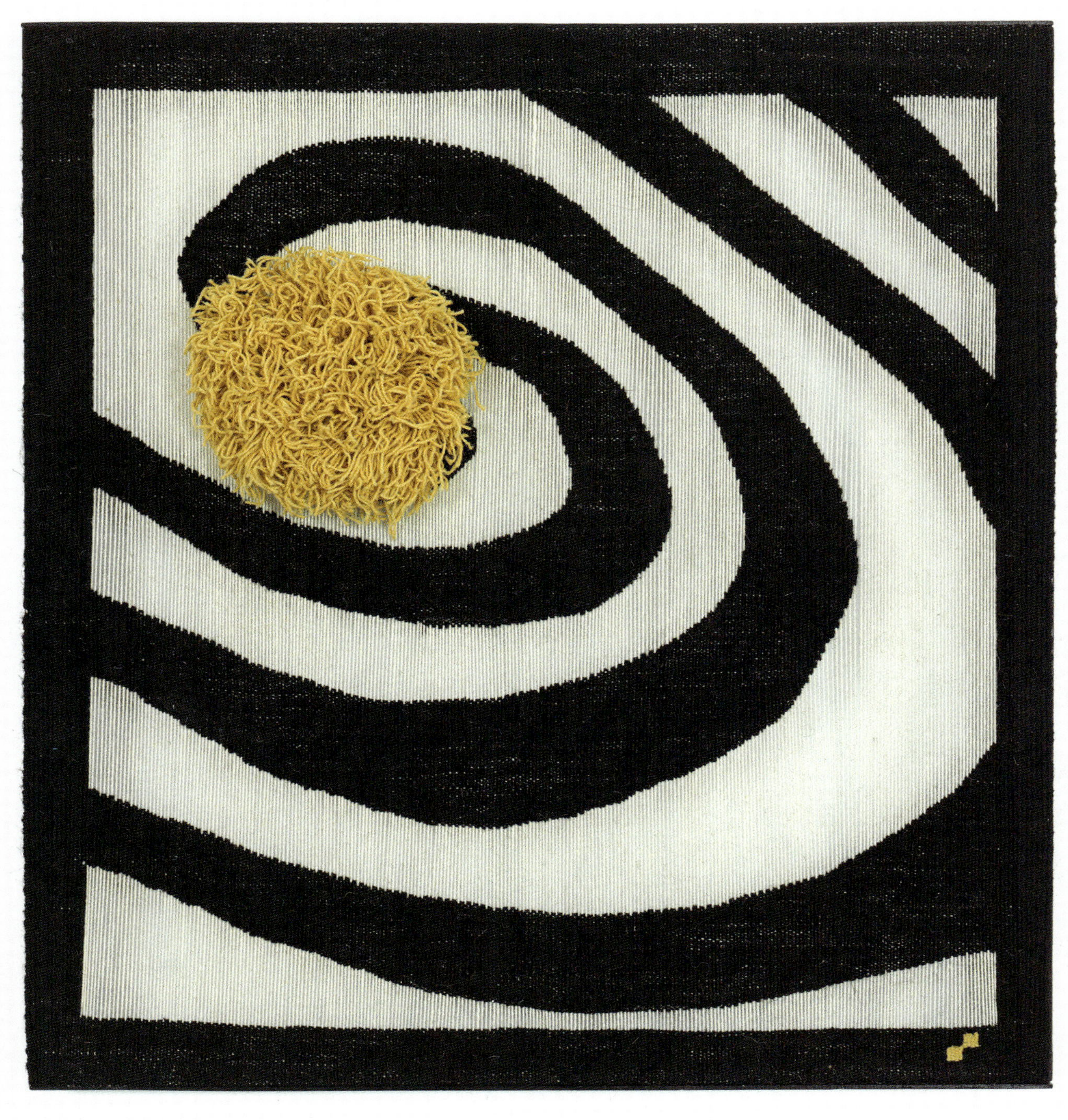

Archipelago

To the Sun, 2023, 111 x 107 cm,
Anna Laudel Gallery

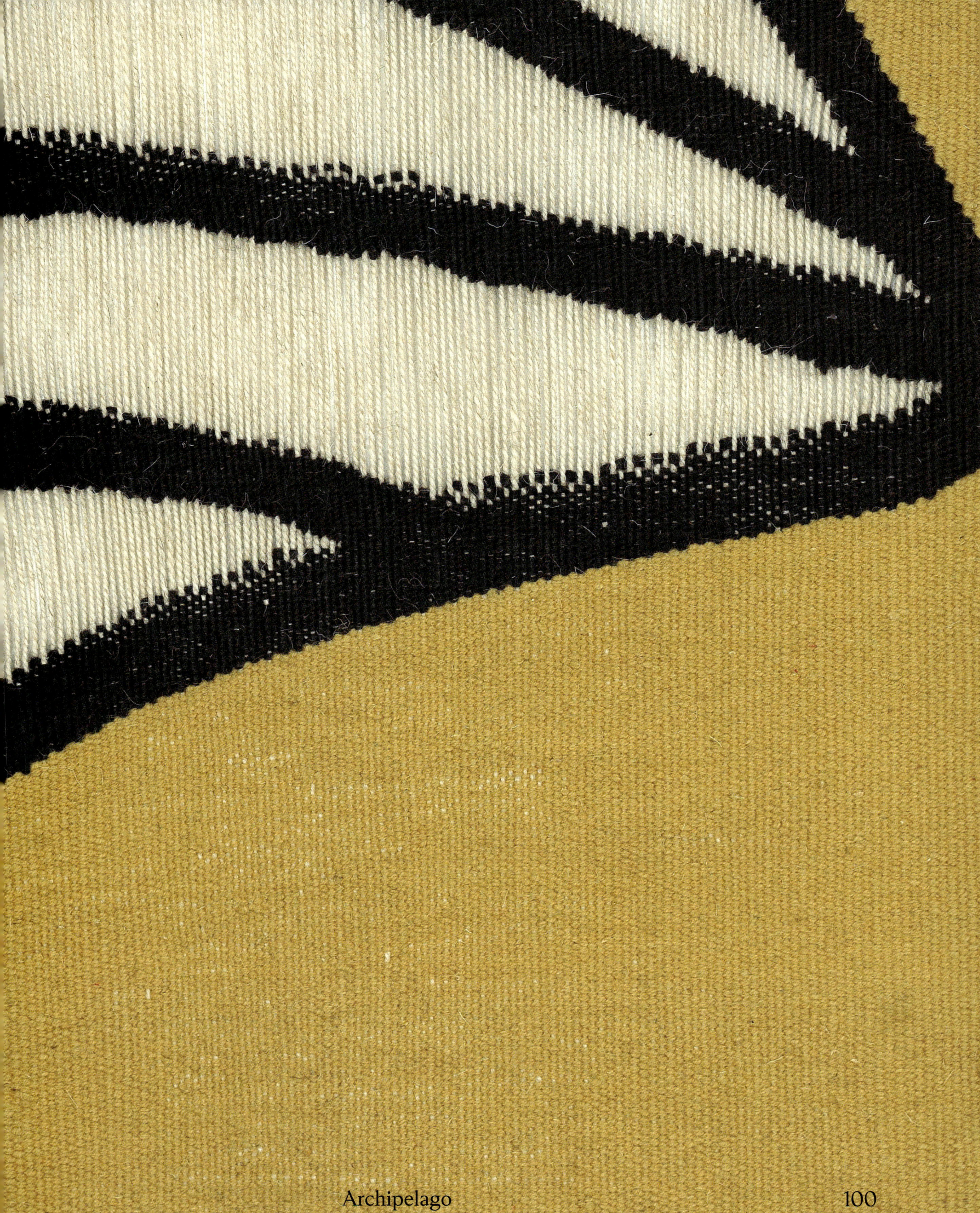

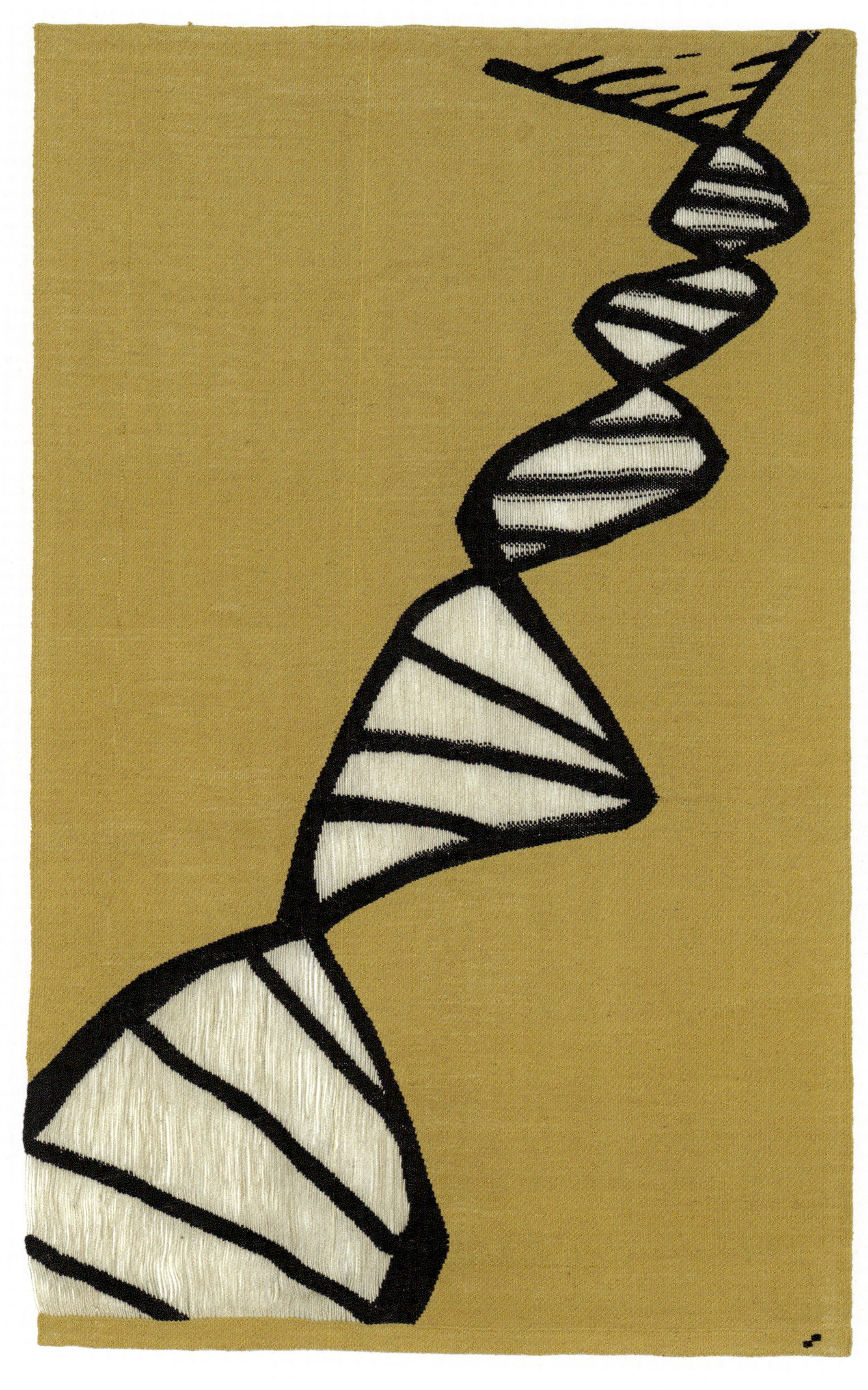

DNA-3, 2023, 226 x 136 cm,
Anna Laudel Gallery

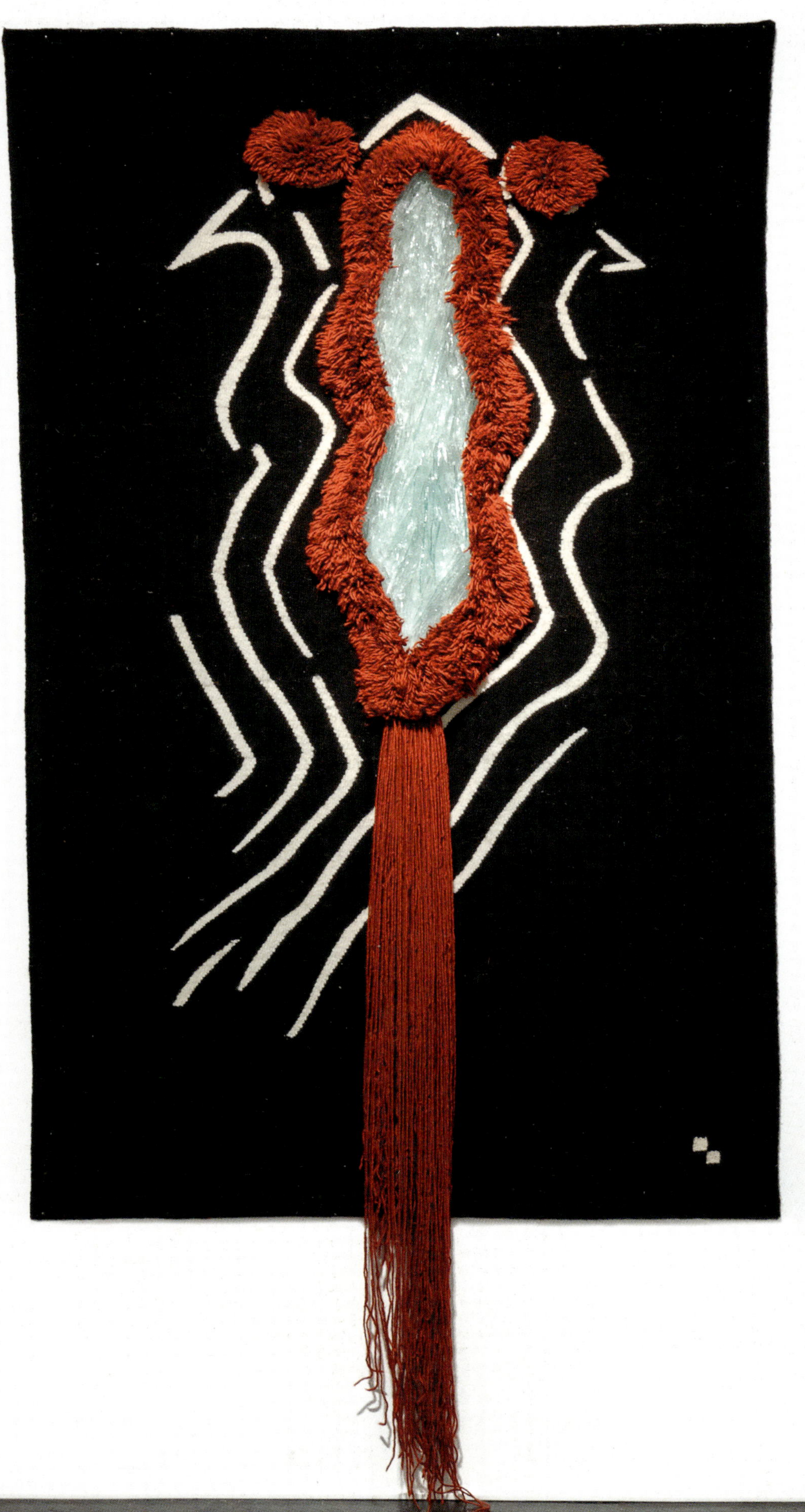

Female, 2024, 245 x 130 cm,
collaboration with Ardan Özmenoğlu,
Anna Laudel Gallery

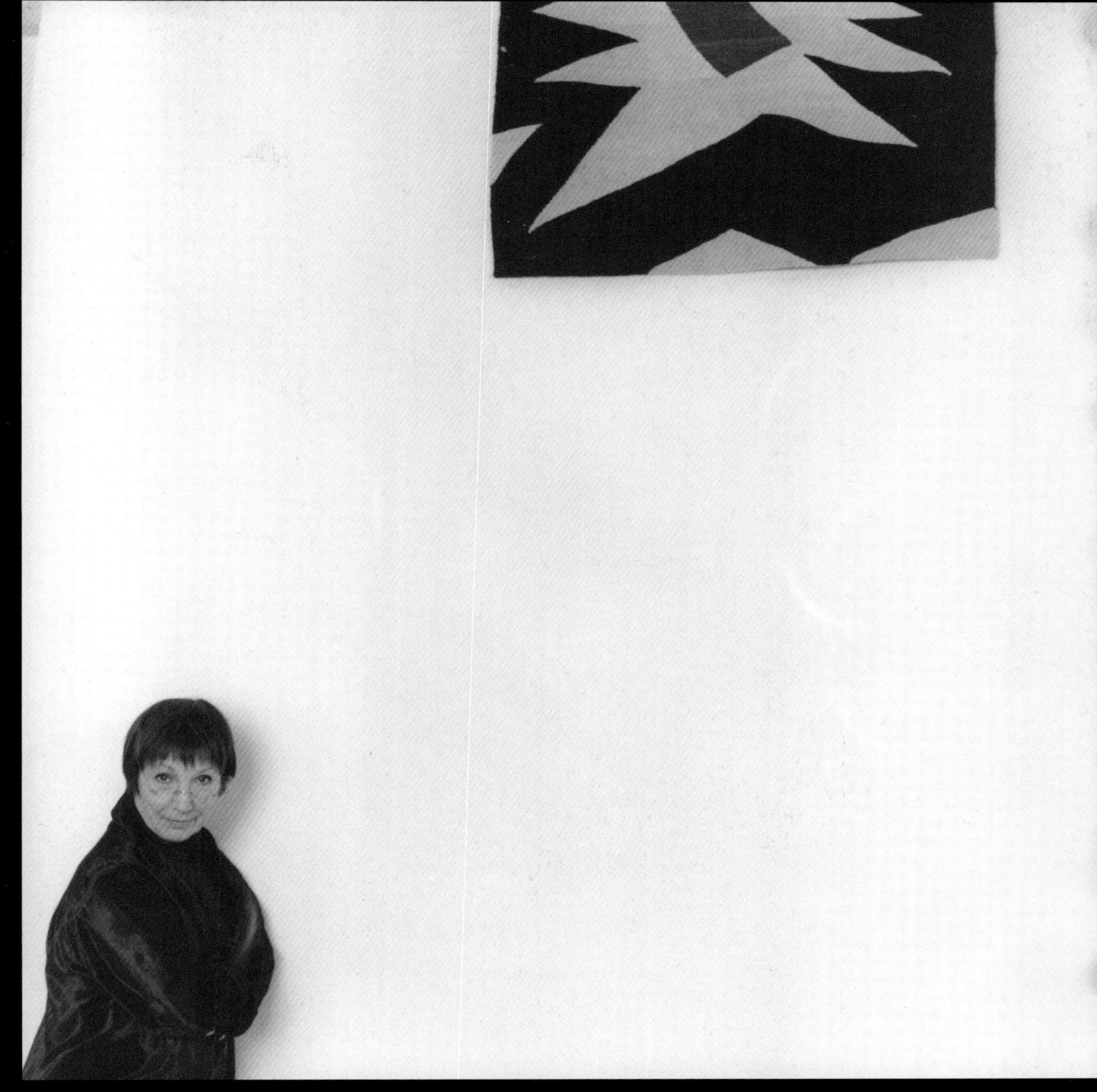

Belkıs Balpınar in her studio
in Demirciköy, Istanbul, 2001.
Photo Laila Pozzo

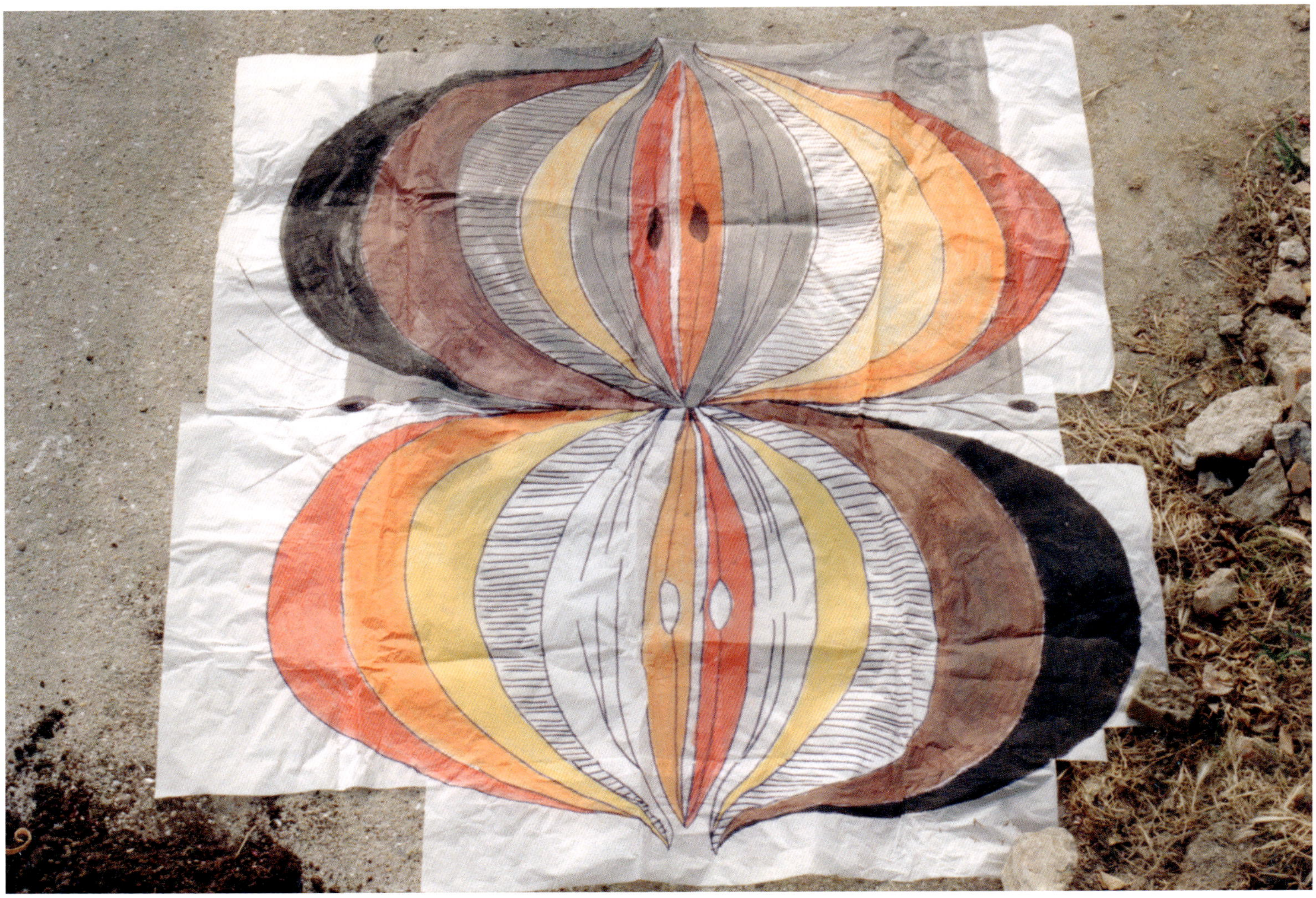

1979   1985

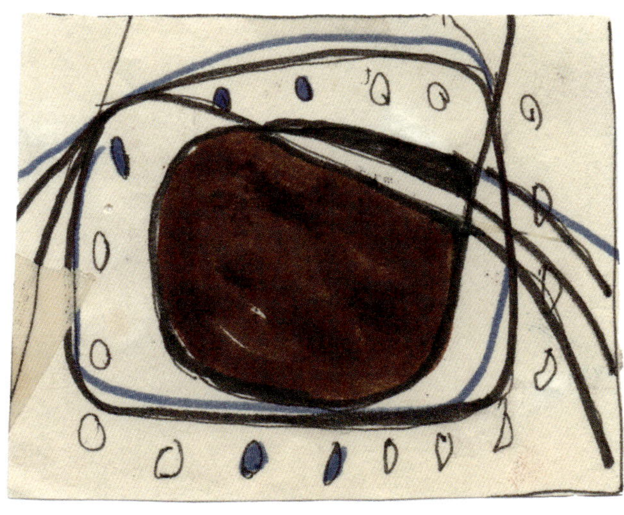

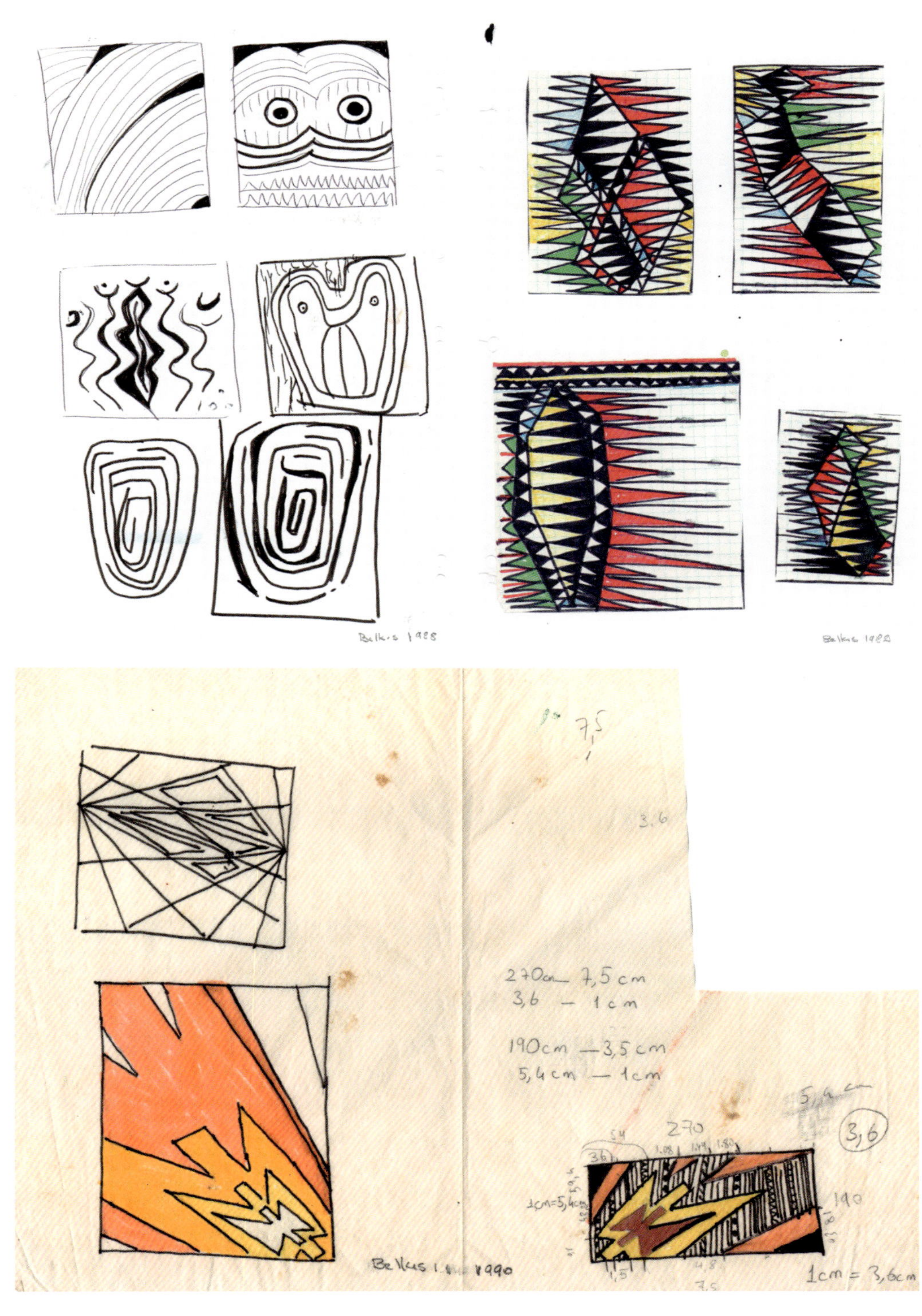

1988   1989
1990

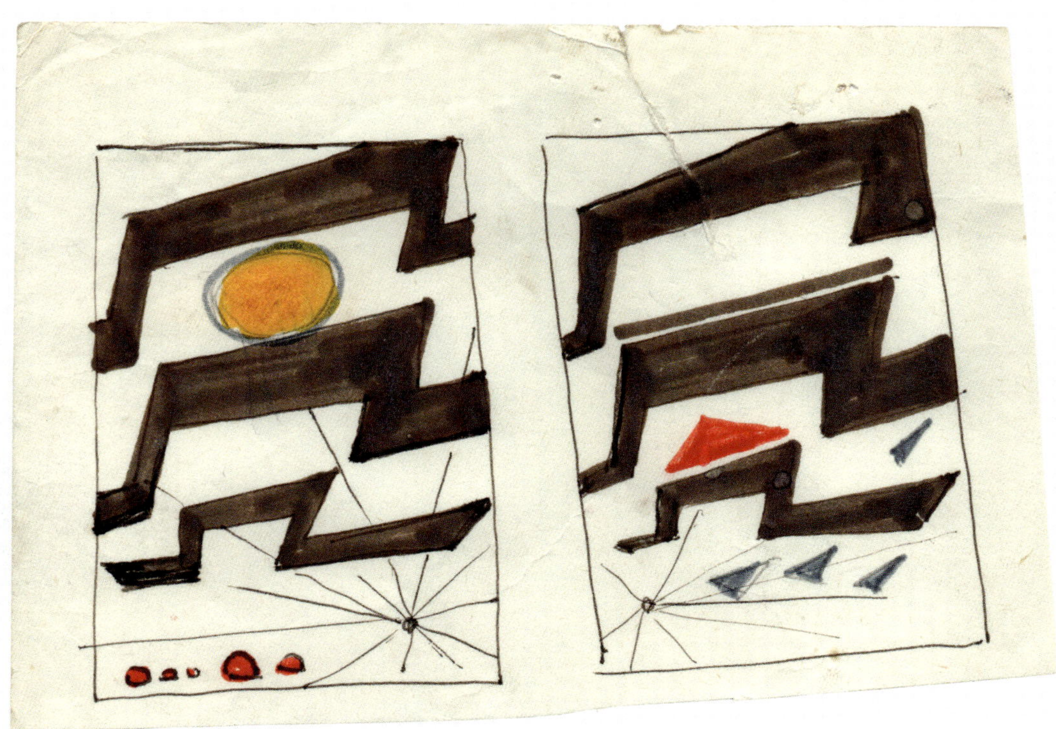

1990

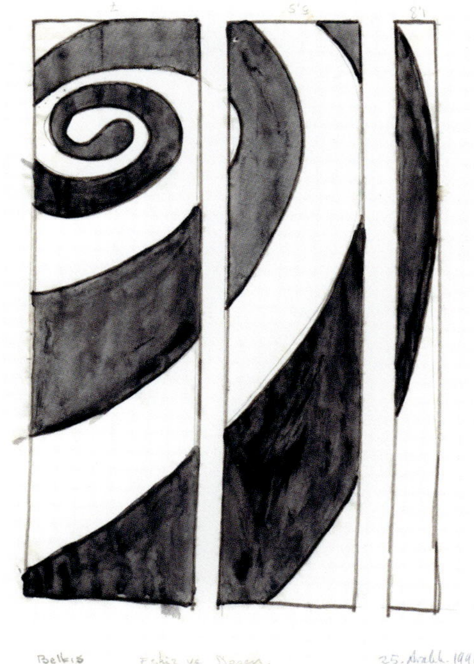

Belkis   Eclis ve Basan.   25. Aralık 1994

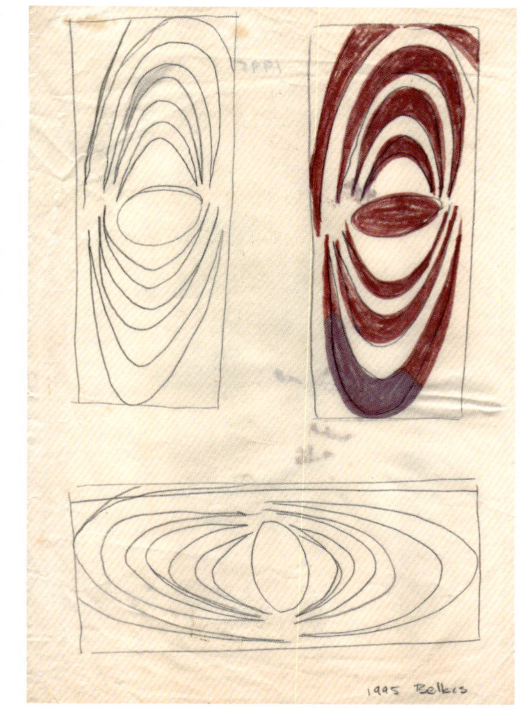

1995 Belkis

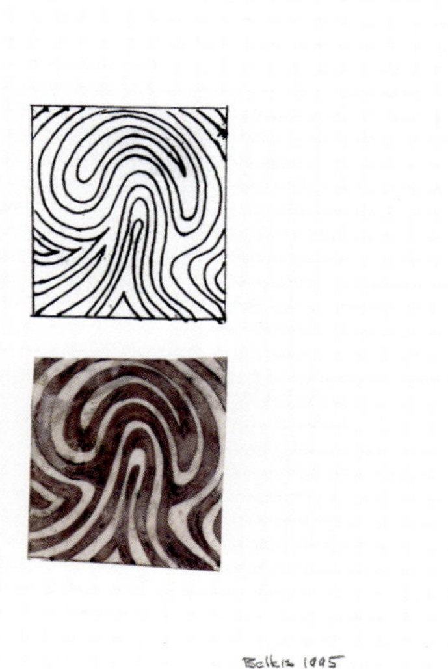

Belkis 1995

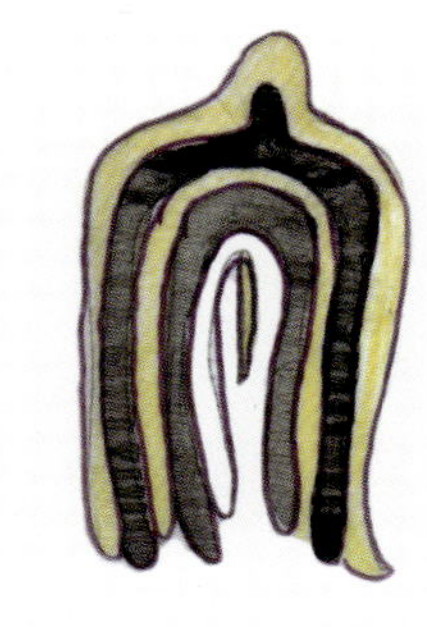
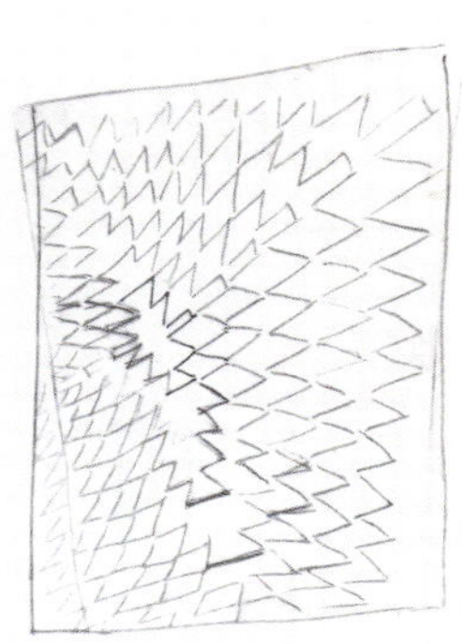

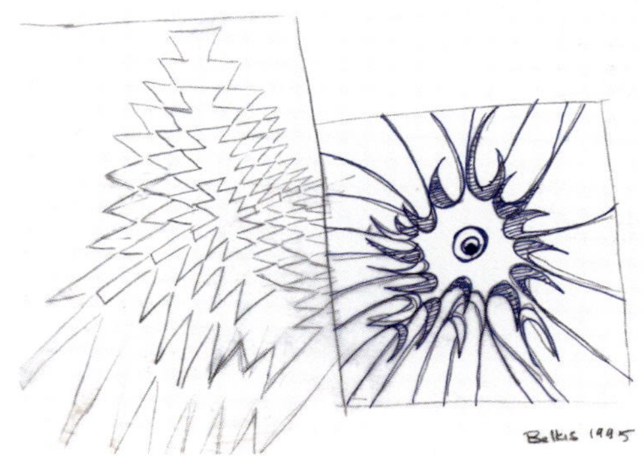

Belkis 1995

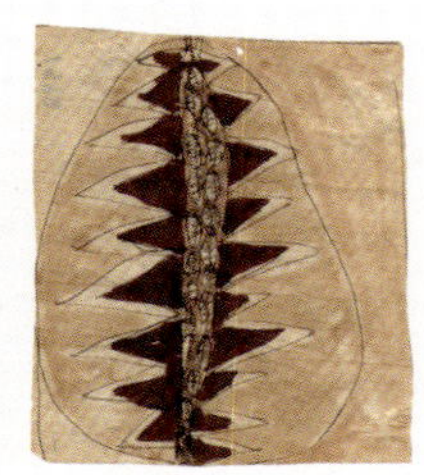

Belkis 1998

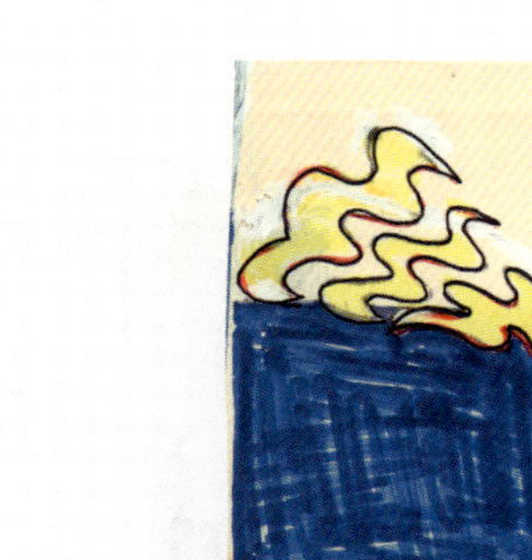

Belkis

↑ 1994   1995   1995
↓ 1995   1998   1999

Zeynep Eray

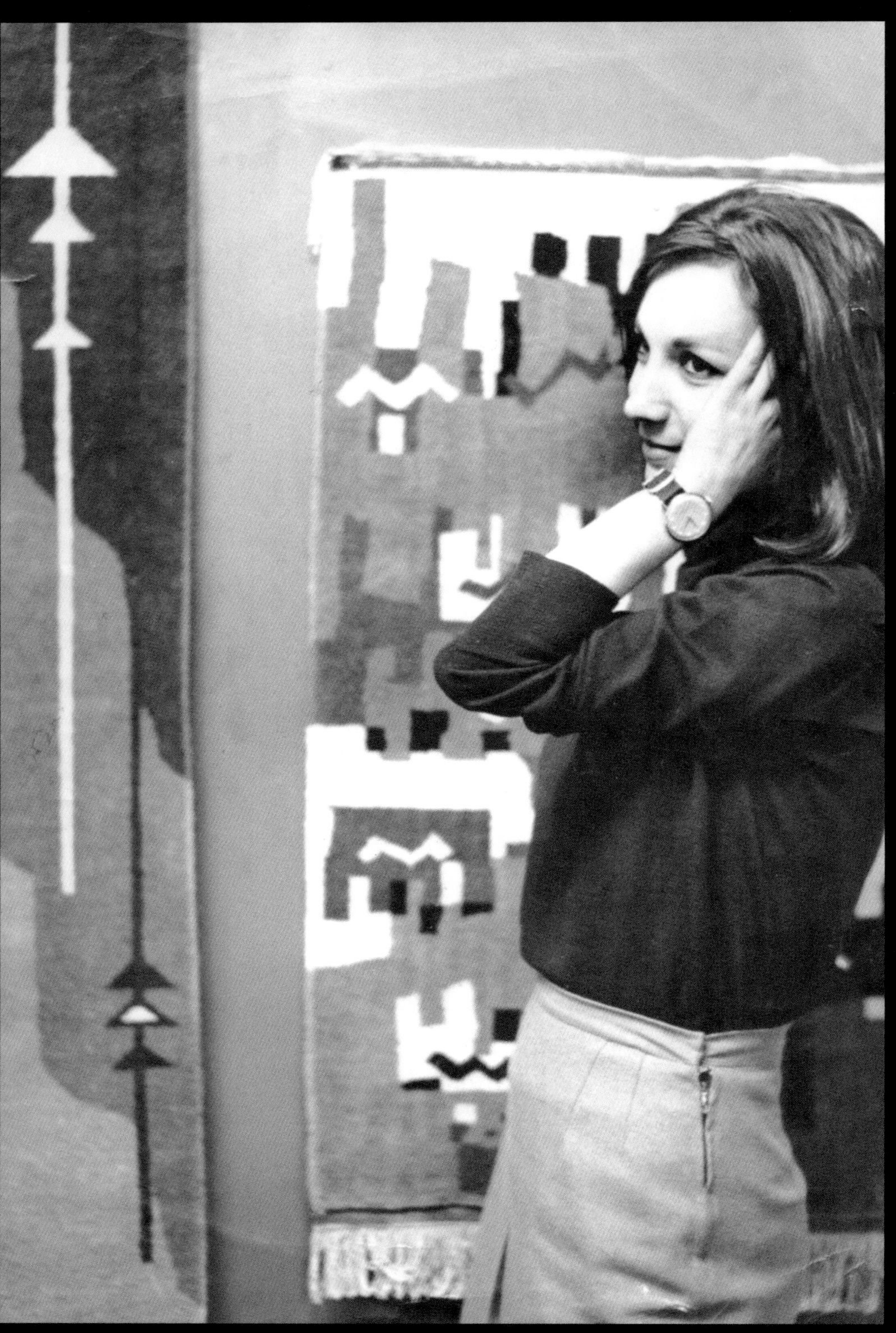

Belkıs Balpınar's first exhibition
at Beyoglu City Gallery, Istanbul, 1964.
Photo Baha Gelenbevi

Belkıs Balpınar

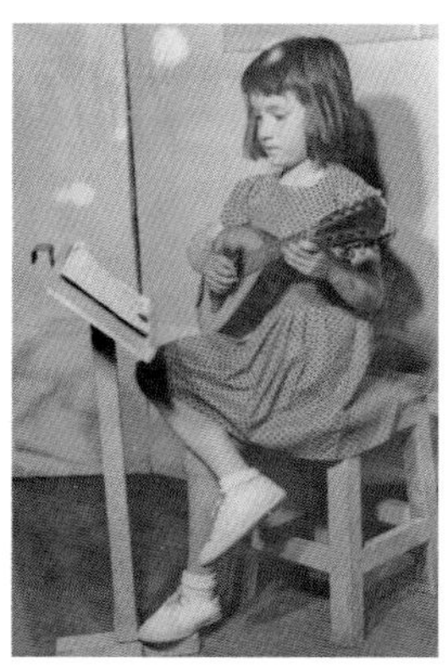

Belkıs Balpınar at Dumlupınar Elementary School in Eskişehir, 1949

1941

Belkıs Balpınar was born in Eskişehir as the first child of Mehmet Bey, a teacher, and Münevver Hanım.

1954

Belkıs graduated from Eskişehir High School alongside classmate Yılmaz Büyükerşen, who became Mayor of the Metropolitan Municipality and transformed the appearance of the city.

1955

She passed the entrance exam to enrol in the textile department at the Istanbul Academy of Fine Arts and completed her education. She later received a scholarship from Sümerbank to continue her studies.

1963

To fulfil one of the conditions for accepting the scholarship, she began her mandatory service at Sümerbank as a carpet designer, a position she held until 1968. This marked the beginning of her journey with carpets and later kilims.

1964

Beyoğlu City Gallery exhibited the modern carpets she wove while taking the Sümerbank carpet workshops. Displayed for the first time in Turkey, her modern carpet designs attracted attention, owing to the strong national tradition of rug-making.

1968–1973

After publishing her research on carpets and kilims in mosques, she was appointed head of the Carpet and Kilim Department at the Turkish and Islamic Arts Museum. During her tenure she initiated the collection of old carpets and kilims from mosques under the Directorate of Vakiflar, which led to the establishment of the Carpet and Kilim Museums.

1971

Her book *Göçmen Kuşlar* [*Migratory Birds*] was published by Redhouse Publishing House. Later, she published a guidebook titled *Kuşlarımız* [*Birds*].

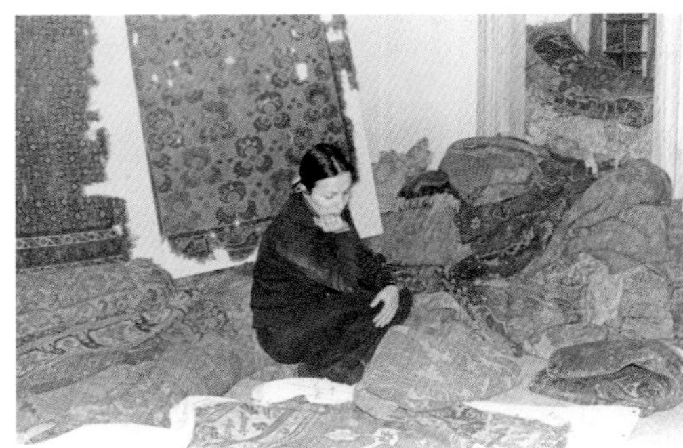

Establishment works of the Carpet Museum, 1979

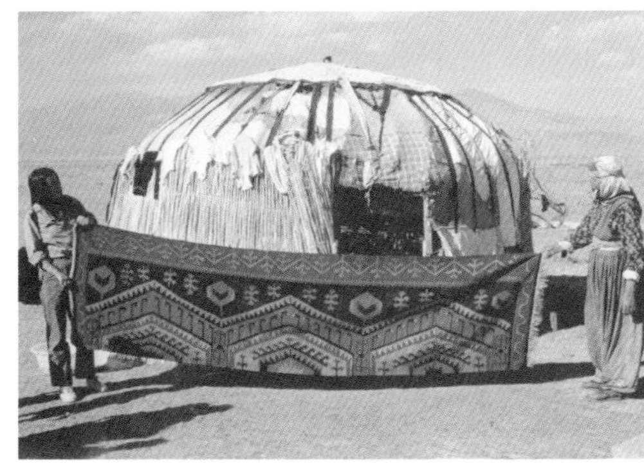

Research trip for the Carpet Museum, 1979. Photo Udo Hirsch

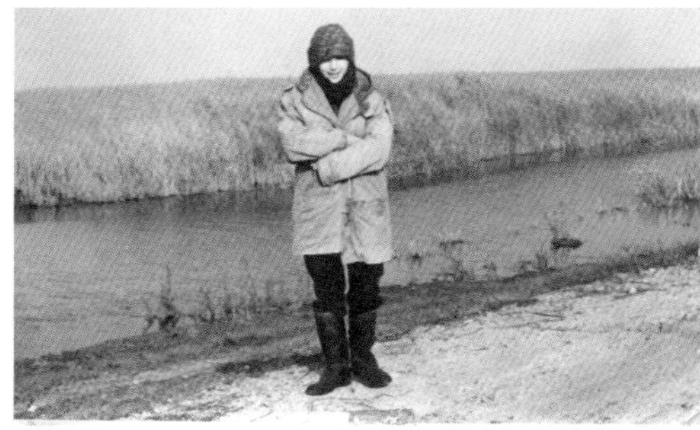

Manyas Lake, Field work for WWF Office, 1970–1980

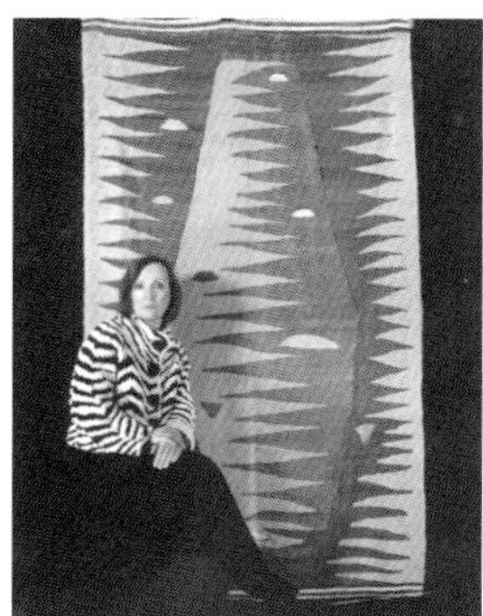

Belkıs Balpınar with *Cocoon*, one of her early works, 1989

1975

She co-founded Doğal Hayatı Koruma Derneği [Nature Conservation Society] with a group of friends. Through the international connections cultivated by this society, Turkey's lesser-known nature reserves, such as Manyas Bird Paradise National Park, were added to international conservation lists.

Kilim ve Düz Dokuma Yaygılar [*Kilims and Flat Weaves*], which explained weaving techniques for the first time through illustrations, was published by Akbank. It was the first comprehensive book containing detailed information about the origins and weaving techniques of Anatolian kilims. Renowned expert on Eastern textiles, May Hamilton Beattie, wrote the foreword for this book:

"Her enthusiasm for the flat-woven rugs of Anatolia is now well known and her studies should provide that first-hand information about techniques terms and provenance, which are very much in demand by the ever-increasing number of collectors."

1977

She became the secretary-general of Doğal Hayatı Koruma Derneği with the support of the Roche company.

1978-1979

She collected thirteenth- and nineteenth-century carpets and kilims from the Divriği Ulu Mosque in Sivas for the Directorate of Vakiflar and established the Carpet Museum at the Sultan Ahmed Mosque's Hünkar Pavilion. At the age of 32, she became the founding director and curator of the museum, responsible for arranging exhibits.

She delivered a lecture on "Istanbul Vakiflar Carpet Museum Collection" at the Second International Congress on Oriental Carpets in Munich.

During the Istanbul visit of Prince Philip, Duke of Edinburgh, and also Prince Bernhard of Lippe-Biesterfeld, she helped the organization of workshops on behalf of the Doğal Hayatı Koruma Derneği.

1980

She presented her paper, *A Study on a Group of Anatolian Weavings*, at the 3rd Oriental Rugs Congress in Washington, D.C.

1981

She had the stables behind Sultan Ahmed Mosque restored and opened the Vakiflar Kilim and Flatweaves Museum. This museum, which displayed Anatolian kilim, cicim, zili, sumak, and other flat-weave examples, accompanied by interpreta-

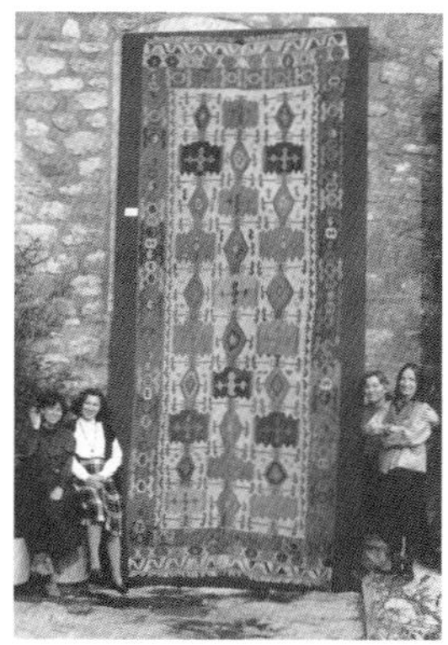
Nazan Ölçer, Şule Aksoy, and two unidentified women at the Turkish and Islamic Arts Museum, Istanbul, 1980s

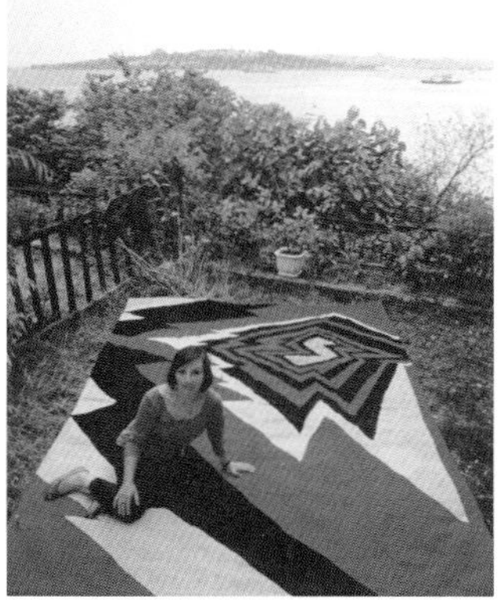
Belkıs Balpınar in Salacak, Istanbul, 1988. Photo Udo Hirsch

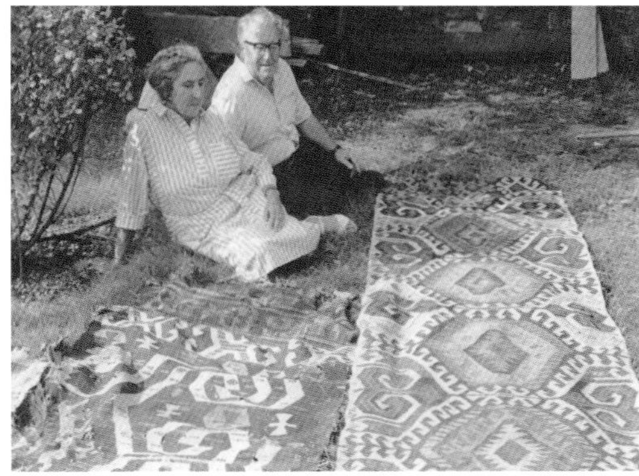
Arlette and James Mellaart in the garden of Balpınar's apartment, 1990. Photo Belkıs Balpınar

tions of their historical development, brought about a new, international awareness of the topic.

1982

The books *Vakiflar Museum Istanbul Carpets Teppiche* and *Vakiflar Museum Istanbul Flatweaves Flachgewebe* were published by Verlag Uta Hülsey in Wesel (photographs by Udo Hirsch). These publications, among the most comprehensive resources in their field, not only earned Belkıs Balpınar significant international recognition but also highlighted the importance of flat-weave kilims alongside pile carpets.

1983

She left her job at the Istanbul Vakiflar Carpet Museum and opened a rug restoration workshop in Üsküdar. During this period of rug restoration, her knowledge of the carpet and rug texture "structure" (are they both necessary?) increased. With this background, she started working on her own rug designs.

1986

She provided looms and wool to women in Istanbul who had migrated from Malatya and knew how to weave carpets and rugs, and began to collaborate with them to weave her own modern designs.

1989

Together with James Mellaart and Udo Hirsch, she co-authored *The Goddess from Anatolia*, published by Eskenazi (Milan). In this comprehensive four-volume work, she argued that Neolithic mother goddess symbols showed continuity in the "hands-on-hips" motif.

She rented apartments in the Soho district of New York and spent two–three months there every year for three years.

1990

Journalist Marianne Ellingworth published an extensive article about her work in *HALI: The International Magazine of Fine Carpets and Textiles* (Issue 51):

"Balpınar is fascinated by the 'ordered disorderliness of the universe'. Her work reflects its sense of coexisting chaos and harmony. There are paradoxes inherent in the balance between her work as an individual creative designer and the contribution of the weavers, in her attempt to strain and twist old designs and the individual creativity on which she draws. Her work raises some fundamental and fascinating questions about the nature of creativity, its sources, and our response to it. The tension between modernity and traditionalism,

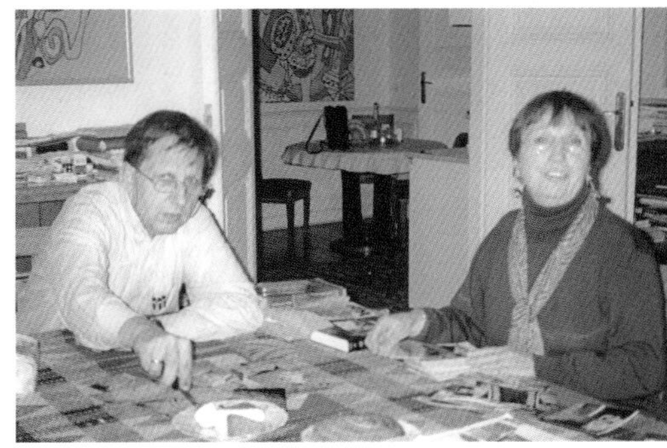

Belkıs Balpınar with Stefanos Yerasimos, 1990s. Photo Belkıs Taşkeser

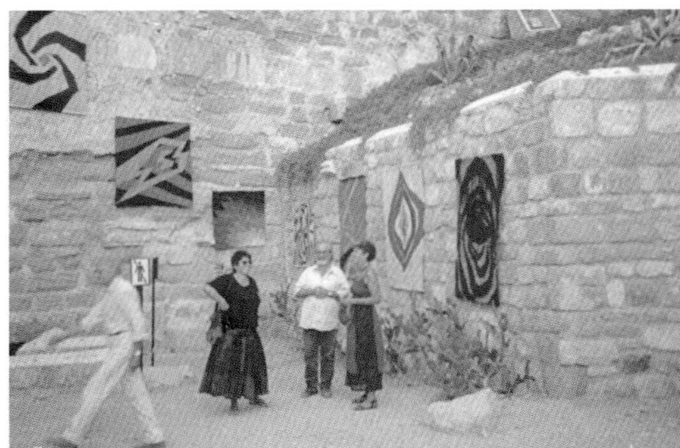

Belkıs Balpınar's solo exhibition at Bodrum Castle (the walking figure is İlhan Berk), 1995

individual expression and set formulae, is finely balanced in the work of this researcher-turned-designer."

Nancy Hoving published an article on her work in *Connoisseur* magazine:

"The newest rugs, with curves and subtleties of shading unknown in traditional kilims are Balpınar's best. She handles color — her 'brushstrokes', as she calls them — better than she did at first. As she watches her design emerge from the loom, she makes variations as it proceeds — a process she compares to musical improvisation. Nothing is unalterable. She likes manipulating forms, standing traditional motifs on their heads, distorting them, adding new ideas, sometimes mixing pile with kilim, breaking rules, though never the basic rules of the kilim structure."

1992

Her works were featured in the exhibition *Earth and Fiber,* curated by Nuran Terzioğlu at the Ankara Painting and Sculpture Museum. This was one of the first exhibitions to introduce international textile art comprehensively in Turkey.

1993_1996

She taught at Marmara University's Traditional Arts Department.

1995

Amelie Edgü curated her first comprehensive solo exhibition, titled *Modern Kilims*, at the Millî Reasürans Art Gallery.

Selçuk Erez conducted an interview with her to discuss the exhibition, which was published in *Cumhuriyet Dergi* (May 22, 1995). In it, he asks:

"So, do the women you work with, who weave these kilims, find your designs strange?"

"Especially at the beginning, they found them very strange. This is because, in our traditional kilim weaving tradition, a certain set of forms taught by the mother are repeated without deviation. By the time a girl reaches the age to weave kilims, she has already seen and absorbed these forms throughout her life. These forms are generally symmetrical. However, my designs largely feature asymmetrical shapes. Moreover, when I gave a woman one of these unfamiliar forms and said, 'Here, weave this', it was something she was seeing for the first time in her life. Initially, I leaned toward shapes reminiscent of Anatolian kilims out of a concern for making it easier for the weavers to adapt... But as the years went by, they became accustomed to the new designs, and I became more courageous."

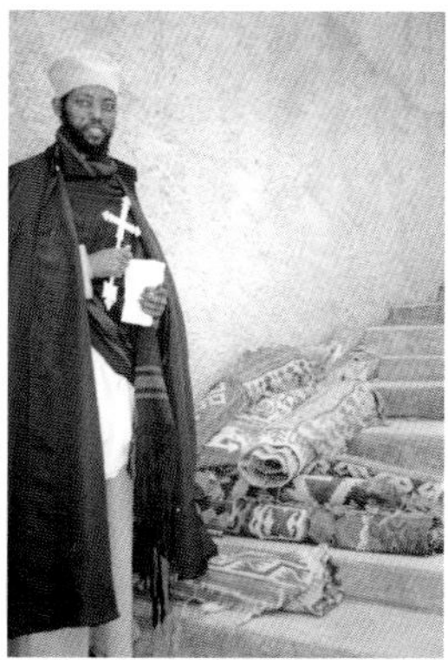

Priest of a Catholic church with Anatolian carpets, Ethiopia, 1998

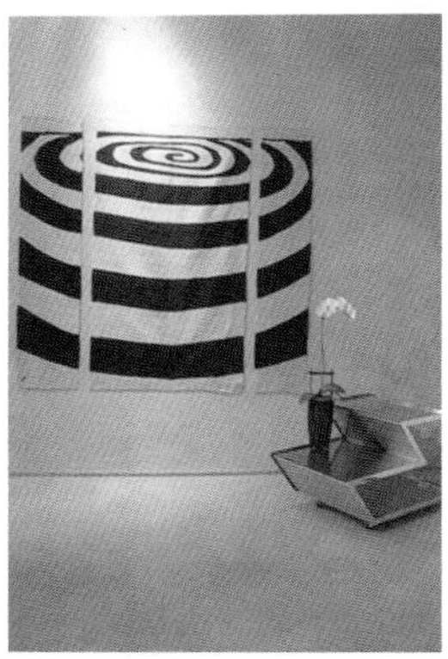

Belkıs Balpınar's solo exhibition at Nilufar Gallery, Milan, 2000. The photo features a chair by Ron Arad

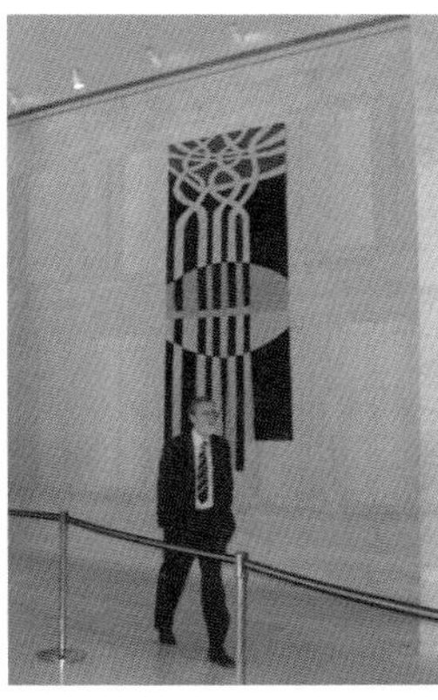

Presentation of the collection in the foyer of Building H, World Bank, Washington, D.C., 2001

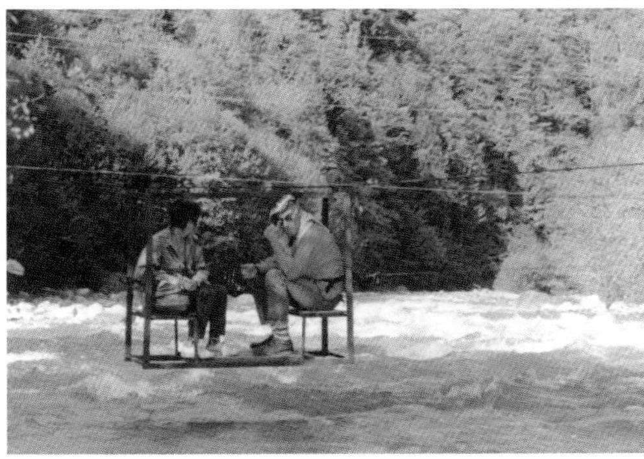

Belkıs Balpınar with Bob Rafelson during a Black Sea trip, 2003

1998

She conducted extensive research on the local weaving traditions and techniques found in Ethiopian churches. She observed that local weavers used wool directly from sheep without washing it, causing an intense odour and attracting moths that damaged the textiles. She taught them how to wash the wool, preventing both the odour and damage, thus extending the life of the textiles.

1999

Her modern kilims were exhibited in the *DOKU-N-MA* exhibition, curated by Susan Platt, at Yıldız Technical University.

2000

She held a comprehensive solo exhibition of her modern kilims at Galleria Nilufar in Milan.

2001

She took part in the restructuring of Doğal Hayatı Koruma Derneği as WWF-Turkey (World Wide Fund for Nature).

Photographer Laila Pozzo visited the artist, capturing her portraits and photographs of her works. Hugh Hawes wrote an article about her work. These were featured in the first issue of the *International Cartier Magazine*.

2001_2010

She gave lectures on Anatolian kilims in twelve American cities, including Washington, D.C., Los Angeles, San Francisco, Seattle, Boston, and Philadelphia.

2004

She held solo exhibitions at Aoyama Green Gallery and Fujiya Gallery in Tokyo. Additionally, she gave lectures on Anatolian kilims in Tokyo and Kyoto.

2005

Her work and life were extensively covered in the documentary film *Voices Unveiled: Turkish Women Who Dare*, directed by Binnur Karaevli.

2006

She moved from Istanbul to Bodrum and settled there.

2013

Her work was analysed in the master's thesis *Oriental Carpets: History, Techniques, and Designs*, written by Sabine Feil at the University of Applied Arts Vienna. Additionally, her work was featured in student theses at several Turkish universities.

2018

Her solo exhibition *Dokuma-ma / Un-weave* was held at Anna

Laudel Contemporary in Istanbul, which began representing her. In the exhibition catalogue, the artist linked her work to the studies of Richard Feynman:

"The world created by humans is very complicated. On the other hand, in the billion galaxies and billions of stars within them, we see a regularity and order regarding our perception of time. Many artists are trying to grasp and reflect on something from the chaos throughout the world. Yet, I try to capture images that imply spaces created by the movements of galaxies and planets in the macro-state or particles in the micro-state that seem more ordinate in regard to our understanding of time."

2019

Her solo exhibition, titled *Weave-Knot*, opened at the Ethan Cohen Gallery in New York.

2023

Her first solo exhibition in Germany, *Relative Points of View*, was held at Anna Laudel Düsseldorf. Discussing the exhibition, the magazine *unlimited* published a conversation between the artist and Necmi Sönmez in which she said:

"Like many people, I am under the constant bombardment of images and information as a 'global person' following what's happening in the world. Amid all these influences, I try to express my unique thoughts through weaving. In recent years, I've been following an increasing number of publications on modern physics and space research, such as quantum, chaos, coincidence, and string theories. Did I start creating such patterns because I began reading these publications, or did I start reading them because of my patterns? I can't remember. They must have started together."

Exhibitions

1964
Beyoğlu City Gallery,
Istanbul, 15 April – 1 May.
1990
Pera, Washington Design
Center. *Turkish Tapestries*,
W.P.A Gallery, Princeton,
New Jersey, 2–28 November.
1990–1991
Kilim Murals, Full Circle
Gallery, Virginia, 8 December 1990 – 8 January 1991.
1993
Turquoise Gallery,
New York, 15 October –
15 December.
1994
Kilim as Modern Art, Tarkett
Gallery, Stockholm, 25
November – 13 December.
1995
Bodrum Castle. *Modern
Kilim*, Milli Reasurans Sanat
Galerisi, Istanbul, 3–31 May.
2000
Art Contemporary Kilim,
Nilufar Gallery, Milan,
13 April – 25 May.
Kilim as Tapestry, Galleria
Morone, Milan, 16 September – 7 October.
2002
Modern Turkish Kilim,
Turkish Japanese Cultural
Center, Ankara, 18–23
March.

2003
Art Kilims, Port Art Gallery,
Göcek, 5–24 September.
2004
Relative Viewpoints, G-art
Gallery, Istanbul, 22 November – 22 December.
Tapestry Kilim, Aoyama
Green Gallery, Tokyo,
29 January – 21 February.
Moden Art – Kilim,
Fujiya Gallery, Ginza, Tokyo,
30 March – 4 April.
2005
Artkilims & Felts, Hadigari,
Bodrum, 8–9 July.
2007
Artkilim, Cankarjev Dom CD
Gallery, Ljubljana, 26 March
– 27 June.
2009
Artkilim: Probable Planes,
Ekavart Gallery, Istanbul,
8 September – 3 October.
3D Planes, 44A Art Gallery,
Istanbul, 28 May – 20 June.
2010
Artkilim, Wallhangings,
Krasniye Holmy Art Gallery,
Moscow, 22 April – 12 May.
2011
3D Planes, La Fontaine
Centre of Contemporary
Art, Manama, 27 January
– 27 February.
2012
ARTkilim, Çırağan Palace
Kempinski Art Gallery,
Istanbul, 5 April – 22 May.
2014
Perception Deception, Mine
Art Gallery, Yalıkavak,

Bodrum, 27 August –
15 September.
2015
Unseen Images, Kare Art
Gallery, Istanbul, 6 November – 12 December.
2017
Probable Weavings, Casa
dell'Arte Hotel of Arts &
Leisure, Bodrum,
7 July – 14 August.
Perception Deception,
Trafo Bodrum, November.
2018
Un-Weave, Anna Laudel
Gallery, Istanbul, 26 April
– 10 June.
2019
Red Sun, 50 Golborne
Gallery, London, 7 February
– 9 March.
Weave-Knot, Ethan Cohen
Gallery, New York, 17 January
– 20 February.
2021
An Open-Air Retrospective,
Istanbul '74, Maçakızı,
Bodrum, 30 July –
20 August.
2022
Post Gallery, Summer.
Micro – Macro, Anna Laudel
Gallery, Istanbul, 26 April –
10 June.
2023
Relative Points of View, Anna
Laudel Gallery, Düsseldorf,
19 August – 6 October.
2024
Shifting Perspectives,
Anna Laudel Gallery,
Istanbul, 6–9 June.

1991
Artexpo, New York,
25–29 April.
1992
Earth and Fiber (curator:
Nuran Terzioğlu), Ankara
Art and Sculpture Museum,
6–30 October.
1999–2000
Doku-n-ma (curator:
Susan Platt), Yıldız
Technical University,
Istanbul, 22 December 1999
– 4 January 2000.
2002
Crossings, Nilufar Galllery,
Milan.
2003
Sanatta Tarih (curator:
Tomur Atagök), Cemal
Reşit Rey Concert Hall
Gallery, Istanbul, 1– 14
March.
Art in Akmerkez, Akmerkez,
Istanbul, 3–28 September.
2005
Modernist New York, Nilufar
Gallery, Milan.
Basel Art Fair, Nilufar
Gallery, Miami, 1–4
December.
*Visions in Textiles: From
Tradition to Textile Art,
Design of Tomorrow*, İzmir
Art and Sculpture Museum,
10–17 September.

2006

Fesorient '06, Istanbul, 22–27 August.

2008

Domotex 2008, Hannover, 12–15 January.

2009

PLUS-Ist, Hayaka Artı, Istanbul, 9 September – 10 November.

2015

Contemporary Art 1985, Mine Art Gallery, Yalıkavak, Bodrum, 6 April – 3 May.

Contemporary Istanbul, 10th edition, Kare Art Gallery, 12–15 November.

2016–2017

25/25: From Past to Present, Ekav Art Gallery, Istanbul, 22 November 2016 – 10 January 2017.

2018

Op not Pop (curator: Marcus Graf), Plato Sanat, Istanbul, 11 January – 2 March.

4. Büyük Efes Sanat Günleri 2018, Swissôtel Büyük Efes, Izmir, 23–25 February.

Orphans of Painting II (curators: Raul Zamudio, Ethan Cohen), Ethan Cohen Gallery, New York, 18 May – 14 July.

Contemporary Istanbul, 13th edition, Anna Laudel Gallery, Istanbul, 20–23 September.

Art Miami 2018, Ethan Cohen Gallery, New York, 4–9 December.

2019

Art Karlsruhe 2019, Anna Laudel Gallery, Istanbul, 21–24 February.

The Event of a Thread: Global Narratives in Textiles (curators: Susanne Weiß, Inka Gressel [ifa], Öykü Özsoy), Istanbul Modern, 22 February – 7 July.

Collect 2019, 50 Golborne Gallery, London, 28 February – 3 March.

Tapestry, Woven Tales, Anna Laudel Gallery, Istanbul, 11 April – 24 May.

Housewarming, Anna Laudel Gallery, Düsseldorf, 16 May – 29 June.

Double X, Ethan Cohen Gallery, New York, 27 June – 22 August.

Bodrum Artists, Şevket Sabancı Culture and Art Center, Bodrum, 11 July – 14 August.

Contemporary Istanbul, 14th edition, Anna Laudel Gallery, Istanbul, 12–15 September.

2020

Art Karlsruhe 2020, Anna Laudel Gallery, Istanbul, 13–16 February.

2021

Contemporary Istanbul, 15th edition, Anna Laudel Gallery, Istanbul, 1–6 June.

CIF, Akrasia, Anna Laudel Gallery, Istanbul, 5–10 October.

Contemporary Istanbul, 16th edition, Istanbul '74, Istanbul, 7–10 October.

Contemporary Istanbul, 16th edition, Anna Laudel Gallery, Istanbul, 7–10 October.

2022

Artweeks, Akaretler, 6th edition, Anna Laudel Gallery, Istanbul, 30 March – 10 April.

CI Bloom 2022, Anna Laudel Gallery, Istanbul, 10–15 May.

Between Humankind and Nature, Istanbul '74, Maçakızı, Bodrum, 1 July – 10 September.

Nomad, Moment in Time, Istanbul '74, Certosa di San Giacomo, Capri, 6 – 10 July.

Contemporary Istanbul, 17th edition, Anna Laudel Gallery, Istanbul, 17–22 September.

On the Blue Track, Bodrum Art Melek & The Bodrum Cup, 13–22 October.

2022–2023

Walls and Beyond, Sakıp Sabancı Mardin City Museum, 9 December 2022 – 9 April 2023.

2023

CI Bloom 2023, Anna Laudel Gallery, Istanbul, 31 May – 4 June.

Contemporary Istanbul, 18th edition, Anna Laudel Gallery, Istanbul, 27 September – 2 October.

Artweeks, Akaretler, 8th edition, Anna Laudel Gallery, Istanbul, 3–16 November.

2023–2024

We Belong, Istanbul '74, Clubhouse Bebek, Istanbul, 29 October 2023 – 15 January 2024.

2024

Magic Mirror, Wilhelmina's Art Gallery & Istanbul '74, Hydra Island, 17 June – 21 July.

Contemporary Istanbul, 19th edition, Anna Laudel Gallery, Istanbul, 24–27 October.

Art Cologne 2024, Anna Laudel Gallery, 7–10 November.

Abu Dhabi Art, 16th edition, Anna Laudel Gallery, 20–24 November.